FEAR IN THE THERAPY ROOM

A survival guide for working with complex trauma

MICHAEL GUILDING

HH BOOKS

Hammersmith Health Books
London, UK

This first edition is published by Hammersmith Health Books
– an imprint of Hammersmith Books Limited
82 Wandsworth Bridge Road, London SW6 2TF, UK
www.hammersmithbooks.co.uk

Disclaimer: The information contained in this book is for educational purposes only. It is the result of the study and the experience of the author. Whilst the information and advice offered are believed to be true and accurate at the time of going to press, neither the author nor the publisher can accept any legal responsibility or liability for any errors or omissions that may have been made or for any adverse effects which may occur as a result of following the recommendations given herein. Always consult a qualified health practitioner if you have any concerns regarding your health.

British Library Cataloguing in Publication Data: A CIP record of this book is available from the British Library.

Print ISBN 978-1-78161-290-3
Ebook ISBN 978-1-78161-291-0

Commissioning editor: Georgina Bentliff
Page design and typesetting by: Julie Bennett of Bespoke Publishing Services
Cover design by: Oliver Pitt
Cover image: Oliver Pitt
Index: Dr Laurence Errington
Production: Anke Ueberberg
Printed and bound by: TJ Books, Cornwall, UK

Contents

Contents

Contents

Contents

Acknowledgements

I have received such a lot of support, encouragement and practical help from so many people over the evolution of this book. The first person I need to acknowledge is Dr Una McCluskey of the University of York, who introduced me to the concept of the fear-system and taught me so much about working with it. My own thoughts have evolved from years of working within her therapeutic approach.

When I first realised that the parasympathetic shutdown response of the fear-system was possibly the underlying mechanism behind depression, I was hugely supported by Dr Jonathan Egan, then of the University of Ireland in Galway, who affirmed and encouraged me and guided my reading. Without his help this project would never have got off the ground.

I owe a great deal also to Dzmitry Karpuk, the Director of the Complex Trauma Institute, who helped me to develop my ideas on depression, encouraged my writing and sent a constant flow of participants to my 'Fear and the Therapist' workshops out of which this book has gradually evolved.

I was only able to start writing once I had assembled a support group who agreed to read through my drafts and provide me with feedback. My wife, Fran, has always been my first editor (and has sent much back to be rewritten), and she was joined in this project by my sister, Anne Guilding, and dear friends and colleagues, Liz and Paul Arnesen, Christine Bailey, Jo Barnicle, Emily Burton, Martina Gaborova, Paul Griffiths, Tanya Jane-

Patmore, Adriana Lombari-Bonefeld, Amaia Mackle, Denise O'Connell, Hester Robinson and Jenny Turner. Their support, comments, suggestions, contributions and corrections, over a number of drafts, have guided me in the writing and have greatly improved the clarity and content of the book. I am deeply grateful for their generous help.

I am also grateful to my friend Richmond Heath, coordinator for TRE in Australia, for his helpful and supportive feedback and stimulating challenges.

Finally, many thanks to my gifted nephew Oliver Pitt for his splendid book cover which absolutely nailed the difficult brief I gave him.

Acknowledgements for copyright material

I would like to thank the following for permission to use their work:

For Figure 3: Meerkat in fear-alert. Indianapolis Zoo. https://www.indianapoliszoo.com/. Photo no longer available on website.

For Figure 4: Fox with marmot in fear-arousal. 'The Moment' by Yongqing-Bao; Winner of Wildlife photographer of the year 2019. Available at: https://www.nhm.ac.uk/wpy/gallery/2019-the-moment

For Figure 5: Leopard with antelope in fear-collapse. From You Tube video, 100100 Channel, available at: https://www.youtube.com/watch?v=lAtW7nJUcRA

For the quotation on p.40 from *Why Be Happy When You Could Be Normal?* by Jeanette Winterson published by Jonathan Cape. Copyright © Jeanette Winterson, 2011. Reprinted by permission of The Random House Group Limited.

Introduction – Don't panic!

This may come as a surprise, but as a therapist you will be constantly working with complex trauma, regardless of your level of training, therapeutic orientation or the context in which you work. You will be working with people whose fear responses are continuously activated, and this will trigger your own fear responses.

Our fear responses are powerful biological processes, stimulated by our nervous system, whenever it senses any sort of threat. Their purpose is to protect us from danger, but they also shut down both our capacity to think reflectively and our ability to relate to others and thus can render us far less effective as therapists.

When our own fear-system activates in the therapy room, we can experience tension, anxiety, fright, loss of our ability to concentrate or think clearly, anger, irritation, frustration, feelings of uselessness and hopelessness or extreme exhaustion.

So many therapists I have met have felt there was something wrong with them – that they were inadequate therapists because they felt these things. Nothing could be further from the truth. As one stringed instrument resonates when another is played, so our bodies pick up on the emotions our clients[1] are experiencing

[1] While in health service contexts those to whom we offer care are generally referred to as "patients", I will use the description "clients" throughout the book as being more appropriate to the relationally based therapies which avoid an expert stance. "Client" may carry associations of a commercial relationship, but it is the term I am used to, and it does carry implications of equality that match the reality that therapist and client are fellow-travellers.

and give us vital information about their distress, which enables us to be of real help.

However, this resonance, which involves the constant activation of our *own* fear-system responses, has a huge impact on our body and our mind, and without a good understanding of what is happening to us, of the complexities and difficulties we are up against in this work, and of the massive support that we are going to need, we can easily lose our self-confidence, become discouraged and overwhelmed and eventually burn out.

I am writing this book in the hope that it may help you avoid becoming fearful, confused or ground-down by this work. I will be arguing that complex trauma is everywhere. I see it as a normal condition of our traumatised species, though some are more severely affected than others. As therapists we need to understand its impact, on ourselves and on our clients, so I will be:

- Explaining the biology of the fear-system, so when it activates in you as you work, you will not become alarmed but can treat it as a source of information.
- Offering a clear theory of complex trauma so that you can understand how fear is activated in the therapy room and how you might work with it.
- Explaining the importance of working with the body in the context of complex trauma and illustrating various ways of doing this.
- Explaining the complexities, frustrations and setbacks of this work, and why there are no quick fixes. Without this understanding it is very easy to be daunted by the unrealistic societal expectations of therapy, which are often based on ignorance of our biological fear responses.
- Pointing out when it is possible to work in an exploratory way, and when you have to pause the work and focus on regulating fear responses, both in yourself and in your clients.
- Touching on the particular difficulty of working as a

therapist in fear-driven institutions, and the importance of finding or creating a professional support network within which you can feel genuinely safe, regardless of the context of your work.

This is not a comprehensive textbook on complex trauma. I am neither a scientist nor an expert in the many fields of human knowledge that I will be touching on. I am writing from my own experience as a therapist, clinical supervisor and service manager, and from what I have learned from running workshops on the human fear-system for counsellors, psychotherapists, clinical psychologists and other mental health professionals. This book has emerged from these workshops, and from my own journey through fear. This is a journey that each of us faces in our quest to live a fuller life, less restricted by human misery, and to help our clients to do the same.

Over the years I have worked and thought about this, many things have become clearer, but it has been a long journey.

> I still remember a client I saw in my training placement over 30 years ago who came for help with anxiety and depression. I remember sitting in the therapy room after the first session with this client, my sense of competence shattered, a feeling of dread in my gut and almost no recollection of what had happened in the previous hour. As a trainee I used to write detailed notes after each of my client sessions so that I was well prepared for my supervision, but this time I just stared at my notepad for about 20 minutes and eventually all I managed to write down were three disconnected words. At the time I had no clue what was going on but looking back I realised that this was my first encounter with severe complex trauma.

I wish I had known 30 years ago what I gradually learned over the subsequent years. There are many aspects of complex trauma I am still unclear about, and many perspectives and ways of working with it which I have not had the time or the energy to explore; this is a huge and evolving field of study.

Experienced therapists will recognise much in this book that you are already familiar with, but I hope you will find the particular perspective of approaching complex trauma through the dynamics of the fear-system of interest.

I hope that those of you starting out on your careers as therapists will not be too daunted by the sense of how much there is to learn. This is a lifetime's work, and it is a slow organic process – one step at a time with many random inputs and discoveries, and time needed to digest new knowledge.

There may be much in this book in terms of the ideas and the stories of clients that might trigger your own traumatic memories. Maybe set the book down if this happens and take time to look after yourself. Appendix 5 has some useful calming techniques, but nothing beats the company of good friends.

I found the perspective on the fear-system and its relationship to complex trauma which I describe in this book very helpful in my own work over the last few years of my practice. I hope that passing on my personal understandings and discoveries will contribute to your own exploration, and will help you too, to work with more ease and effectiveness, giving you a greater sense of competence and enjoyment in the invaluable work you do as a therapist.

Note on confidentiality of client material

I have used examples of my work with clients and supervisees throughout this book as a means of illustrating the points I am making, while still maintaining the confidentiality of our work together. In all cases I have used different names, and in many instances I have changed incidental details not relevant to the therapy to ensure people cannot be recognised. Where I have made few changes, I have been given written consent by my clients for the inclusion of their stories. I have at times ensured confidentiality by merging the work with two or more clients into one story. The resulting examples, which strictly speaking could be regarded as fiction, are nevertheless, in each detail, based on the real-life experience of myself and my clients.

Part 1

Understanding fear and complex trauma

Chapter 1

Defining the fear-system

The three oldest biological responses to threat –
Fear-alert, fear-arousal and fear-collapse

Understanding our fear-system is central to understanding trauma.

When we sense a threat, our body instantly, automatically and unconsciously reacts, making a number of physiological changes to help us to survive the threat. We experience three different types of reaction, depending on how close we sense the danger to be, and these different responses, taken together, are what I call the fear-system.

I describe these three responses as fear-collapse, fear-arousal and fear-alert.

Fear-collapse

This is the oldest response in evolutionary terms, emerging around 500 million years ago. It involves a metabolic shutdown – a sudden energy collapse – which allows a prey animal to appear dead to a predator. Fear-collapse is triggered when the danger is so close that there appears to be no chance of escape. Among animals in the wild we see it when a prey animal has been brought down by a predator after a chase. In humans it is most commonly activated when a sense of terror is combined with feeling trapped, so it is often experienced when a person is raped.[2]

For animals in the wild, bodily shutdown offers a chance of survival even in extreme danger as many predators will not eat an apparently dead animal, and the triggering of this collapse at the end of a chase affects the predator, switching off its instinctive attack. This can sometimes open up an opportunity for escape, especially where the predator may be distracted by competition from other predators.

Fear-collapse is commonly known as 'immobility' or 'tonic immobility'. It is often referred to as 'death-feigning', in other words, 'pretending to be dead', but this is a highly misleading term, implying some sort of conscious deception. When we look at the biology of this state in more detail in Chapter 5, it will become clear just how inappropriate this term is.

This same metabolic shutdown can also be triggered by a number of other threats to the body aside from physical attack, such as fluid loss, viral or bacterial infection, toxins or exhaustion,[3] so when using the term 'fear-collapse' I am purely referring to the shutdown response *when it is triggered by the activation of the fear-system,* whether this relates to a real physical threat, traumatic memories, disturbing attachment emotions or negative thoughts.

Fear-arousal

This response to threat, which evolved around 300 million years ago, is the exact opposite of fear-collapse. It involves a huge increase in metabolic activity which delivers a sudden burst of

[2] Many people feel extreme shame that they did not 'try harder to escape', but there is no conscious choice whatsoever in the body's reaction to this level of threat.
[3] Levine (2010).

energy to allow a prey animal to run from, or fight off, a predator. Fear-arousal is triggered when the threat is immediate and close, such as when the predator leaps into action, or a human realises they are under attack, but when there is still a good chance of escape.

This response has long been popularised under the term 'fight or flight', and it delivers the energy needed to escape the danger. However, it can also result in a 'freeze' when there is no clear escape pathway and muscles 'lock', like a rabbit in a car's headlights. Freeze can instantly switch back into fight-or-flight if an escape route opens up, or it can peak in 'fright', the highest point of fear-arousal, which is also a tipping point into fear-collapse. I use the term 'fear-arousal' to distinguish this threat response from other hyper-aroused states, such as in sports or exercise.

Fear-alert

Alongside the evolution of fear-collapse and fear-arousal, another response evolved which prepares the body for these powerful fear-reactions without triggering major biological changes or committing a huge amount of energy. Fear-alert is activated when the threat is still at a distance, or when a potential threat is sensed, but the level of danger is not yet clear.

Fear-alert helps us to scan the environment and makes changes to the body that would enable it to either switch immediately into the extreme action of fear-arousal, should that be necessary, or to quickly return to a calm state. It is also known as the 'orienting response', and it plays an important part in the biology of complex trauma.

The fear-system has its control centre in the brain, in the amygdala,[4] and is activated throughout the body by two

[4] Part of the limbic system – an evolutionarily older part of the brain that controls emotional responses.

different branches of the autonomic nervous system (the part of our nervous system that operates automatically whether we like it or not). In Figure 1 below,[5] image 1:1 represents the overall autonomic nervous system (ANS),[6] while 1:2 and 1:3 represent two of its three constituent parts. Image 1:2 shows the dorsal vagus nerve (going from the brainstem, directly to all the major organs of the body) which shuts down the body's energy production in fear-collapse. Image 1:3 shows the sympathetic nervous system (SNS – going from the brainstem via the spine to all the major organs of the body) which boosts the body's energy production in fear-alert and fear-arousal.

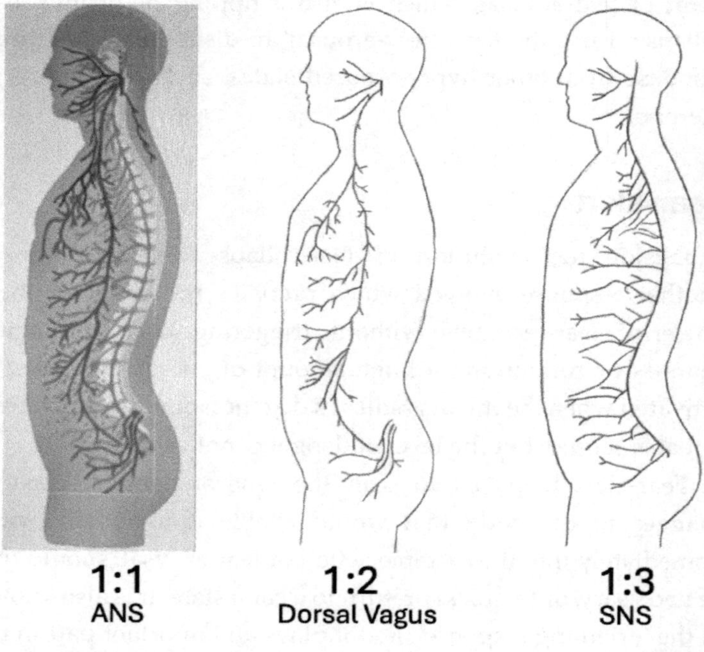

Figure 1: The autonomic nervous system – fear-system components

[5] Drawing of body in 1:1 © John and Anna Chitty (2013), Colorado School of Energy Studies, Boulder, Colorado, USA.
[6] This diagram can be seen more clearly in colour in my York Festival of Ideas talk, Guilding (2024) and on the publisher's website at www.hammersmithbooks.co.uk/product/fear-in-the-therapy-room

I should clarify that, when I talk about the fear-system,[7] I am not referring to just 'feeling fear'. As we will see when we look at this in more detail, the activation of the fear-system creates many different sensations in our body. We can, of course feel afraid, or even terrified, but our fear responses can also make us feel tense, angry, furious, numb, faint, frozen, nauseous, sweaty, dizzy, exhausted, blank, detached or unreal, while our most powerful fear-system response (a full fear-collapse) involves a complete absence of any feeling of fear.

I have used my own terms, fear-alert, fear-arousal and fear-collapse, to describe the human fear-system, because I found the existing literature examining our responses to threat to be a confusing mess. One problem is that the word 'freeze' is used by some authors to describe the orienting response[8] (fear-alert), while others use it to describe the 'locked' aspect of fear-arousal.[9] Other authors use 'freeze' to describe what they term 'death-feigning' (fear-collapse).[10]

We will see in Chapter 5 that fear-alert, arousal and collapse are quite separate biological states, so this imprecision in the use of language is hugely confusing.

[7] I was introduced to the concept of a 'fear-system' by Una McCluskey (Heard, Lake and McCluskey, 2012). This was based on the work of LeDoux (1998), and consisted of fight, flight and freeze responses (all of which belong to fear-arousal in my understanding). I have used the same term, but I also include the orienting response (fear-alert) and parasympathetic shutdown (fear-collapse) under this description. I note that LeDoux came to regret his use of the term 'fear-system' (LeDoux 2014), as it blurred the distinction between conscious feelings of fear and non-conscious processes. I decided, however, to retain this term, having found in my workshops that it clarified more than it confused once it is defined as covering our earliest biological responses to threat regardless of whether we feel afraid or not. I find the use of the term 'fear-system' particularly helpful as it categorises dominant, aggressive and bullying behaviours, as fear responses. This serves as a corrective to the mistaken but commonly held view that such behaviours, exhibited throughout the ages by those in positions of power, are signs of 'strength' deserving of admiration.

[8] e.g. Schauer and Elbert (2010).

[9] e.g. LeDoux (1998).

[10] e.g. Levine (2010); Van der Kolk (2014).

Another problem is that the phrase 'tonic immobility' is used to describe both the rigid muscle state of fear-arousal[11] and also the flaccid muscle state of fear-collapse.[12] This lack of a coherent vocabulary for understanding threat-responses is examined in more detail in Appendix 2.

Before moving on to look at how the fear-system is restrained, I want to look at a couple of examples of the fear-system in action in the wild as this can help to bring the theory to life.

[11] e.g. Schauer and Elbert (2010).
[12] e.g. Levine (2010).

Chapter 2

Two life-and-death escapes

Prey and predator: examples of fear responses in the wild

1. Seizing a window of opportunity

Under cover of bushes, a female cheetah stalks a group of antelope, trying to get as close as possible without being spotted. Sensing the best chance, she dashes forward but the antelopes take off at high speed. There is a fast chase, with many twists and turns among the bushes, but eventually the cheetah brings down one of the antelopes. It lies collapsed on the ground as if dead, its neck clamped in the cheetah's jaws, the cheetah panting, exhausted by the chase.

At this point a hyena arrives and makes a run at the cheetah and its prey. The cheetah no longer has the strength to fight and backs off. The hyena takes possession of the prey clamping its teeth into the antelope's stomach and tugging to rip the skin open. But the cheetah still hovers near, and the hyena is distracted. Leaving its meal for a moment it chases the cheetah further away. In those few seconds, the antelope suddenly rights itself and leaps up, dashing away at high speed before the hyena can get back to it.

In this example we see the survival value of fear-collapse. As the prey lies unmoving, to all appearances dead, the predator stops its attack, and things pause for a moment. Though most of the prey animal's body is shut down, it still has a residual sense of its surroundings, so if a window of opportunity for escape arises, it can be seized. The original predator, distracting the hyena just as it's about to rip open the antelope's stomach, provides just that opportunity, and there is a sudden switch in the antelope's body from complete collapse to a very powerful fight-flight response.

The antelope escapes both predators and, when it gets to a safe place, will rest and calm down, and its fear-system will deactivate. Despite the close brush with death, there will be no legacy of trauma,[13] and its fear-system will be ready to protect it as soon as it is next needed. Burning off the energy boost of fear-arousal in the escape, followed by calming, is the main way that the fear-system resets itself.

2. Rescued by baboons

We now come across a leopard which has already chased down and caught its prey – a large antelope which is lying on the ground with its nose clamped in the leopard's jaws. The leopard is recovering after the chase, while

[13] Levine (2010), p.24.

the antelope appears to be dead, though its eyes are still open. However, a successful hunt always attracts competition from other predators, and a hyena is spotted circling around. The leopard is distracted. It turns its head suddenly to watch the hyena, letting go its grip, and the antelope's head flops to the ground, showing the absence of any tension in the muscles in its state of collapse.

Having checked that the hyena is not going to pose a threat, the leopard turns back to the antelope, grabbing at its neck and then its head with its jaws, but there is another distraction, and the antelope is dropped again. The leopard has spotted two baboons emerging from the vegetation and heading in its direction. Baboons are not fond of leopards, and they are powerful animals. As the baboons approach, the leopard makes another grab at the antelope's throat, but its focus is now on the baboons, and as they get near, the leopard drops its prey and turns and runs. One of the baboons accelerates and chases the leopard away into the distance.

The antelope is now lying on its side, just as it was left by the leopard, completely still, its eyes open, but to all appearances dead. It lies still for some time, but eventually its abdomen moves, starting a series of huge deep breaths. After a time, it turns to lie upright, and it starts to shudder and shake all over. This lasts for a full minute, resolving then into more gentle trembling. Suddenly the antelope leaps up and bounds away. The leopard looks on from a distance – it has missed its chance.

In this second example we see another way that the fear-system can reset. The baboons have chased away the predator and they themselves are no threat to the antelope. The antelope is now in a safe place, and it can take its time to recover from the shutdown. It does this through deep spontaneous breathing, followed by shuddering or shaking, a form of neurogenic[14] tremoring, which discharges the energy of the previous fear-arousal. This physical mechanism deactivates the fear-response and, as with the previous escape, there is no aftermath of trauma.

Links to the videos of these examples

If you are able to at this point, you might find it helpful to view the videos of these two examples. The 'Window of Opportunity' example can be accessed by going into YouTube and searching for 'Gazelles escape' (manintoshsac channel), or by using the link: https://www.youtube.com/watch?v=IlwzPIUtRPcandt=1s

The 'Rescued by Baboons' example can be accessed by going into YouTube and searching for 'Baboons save impala from leopard and hyena' (100100 channel), or using the link: https://www.youtube.com/watch?v=lAtW7nJUcRA

I would recommend that you play the videos with the sound off, as I find the commentary gets in the way, and can be misleading.

[14] Arising directly from the nervous system. Herold (2015) gives a simple account of David Berceli's development of TRE as a means of helping people to recover this natural tremoring response in order to emerge from trauma.

Chapter 3

The social engagement system

The most recently evolved response to threat which makes social living possible

In Chapter 1 we saw three ways in which our fear-system reacts to threat: we check the environment and ready for action (fear-alert), there is a huge boost to our energy production enabling us to escape the danger (fear-arousal), or there is a collapse of energy production when escape seems impossible (fear-collapse).

There is, however, one further way that humans respond to threat, and that is by turning to others for help, support or care, which is known as our 'care-seeking system'.[15] This response is *not* included in my definition of the fear-system as it belongs to a set of biological processes which Stephen Porges[16] described as the 'social engagement system'. This system evolved most recently (220 million years ago) with the emergence of mammals and is of key importance to animals such as ourselves, whose survival depends on living together in social groups.

Porges points out that it is impossible to live socially without being able to restrain the 'kill or be killed' instincts of our body's fear responses, and this restraint is a key function of the social engagement system. Essentially, the social engagement system

[15] Heard and Lake (1997).
[16] Porges (2011).

connects us to others, and this gives us a sense of safety. This is the most effective way of switching off our fear-system.

However, when the social engagement system is not available, or we cannot trust it because it has failed us in the past, the fear-system takes over and shuts down our social engagement system. The fear-system is non-social. When it is active we are disconnected from others, and we feel isolated. We may survive the dangers that threaten us, but we survive without the wellbeing which comes from connectedness. If we can face a threat by seeking the support of others, we are no longer isolated and can survive with wellbeing.

The social engagement system, pictured below in Figure 2,[17] image 2:4, has its control centre in the cortex (the newest part of the brain in evolutionary terms) and it affects the body via the ventral vagus nerve, going from the brainstem to the heart and the lungs. When the environment is perceived as safe, an electro-chemical signal is sent to the heart via the ventral vagus nerve. This nerve connects directly to the heart's inbuilt pacemaker (the sino-atrial node). The default setting for this pacemaker is a fast heartbeat of around 90-100 beats per minute, which is right on the boundary between fear-alert and fear-arousal. However, when the social engagement system signals safety via the ventral vagus nerve, it overrides this default setting and slows the heart rate down to around 60 beats per minute,[18] calming us, and switching off our fear-system.

The ventral vagus nerve is connected at the brainstem to the nerves that control the muscles of the face, neck, larynx and inner ear. These are the muscles with which we communicate to each other whether we are safe or unsafe to be with. We communicate this by micromovements of the face and posture, and by tone

[17] Drawing of body in 2:1 © John and Anna Chitty (2013) Colorado School of Energy Studies, Boulder, Colorado, USA.

[18] This can vary a lot from person to person. Athletes tend to have much lower resting heart rates.

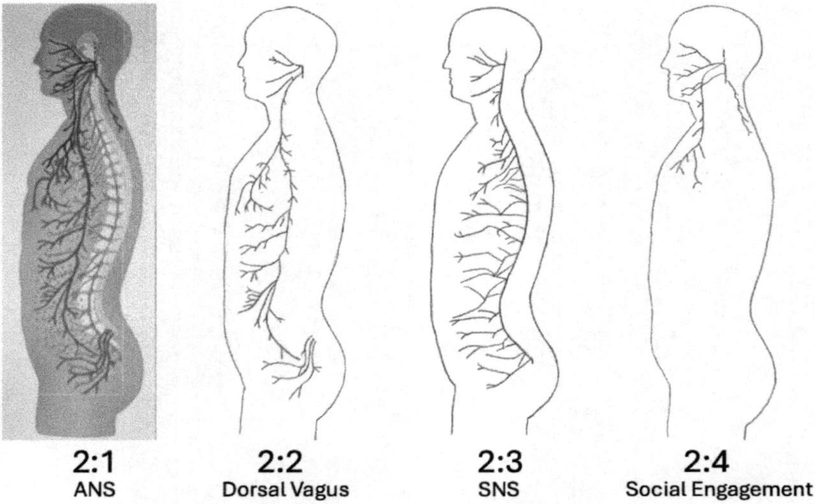

Figure 2: The autonomic nervous system – fear and social engagement systems

of voice, with our non-verbal signals being picked up and facial movements being replicated in the recipient via mirror neurons.[19]

If we see a clenched jaw, or a slight snarl and hear a raised voice, the signal on our ventral vagus nerve is switched off. So, the 'calming brake on the heart' is taken off. Our heart rate can now shoot up to allow our fear-system to meet the threat. However, if we see a smile and hear a calm tone of voice, we will probably smile back, the signal on our ventral vagus nerve will be activated (the brake is back on), our heart rate calms, and our fear responses reset.

[19] Rizzolatti and Sinigaglia (2008). Mirror neurons are brain cells which can activate in our body the same physiological changes we might observe in another person.

Chapter 4

What is complex trauma?

The underpinning theory – complex trauma seen as a 'fear-system dysfunction'

Trauma is a condition in which our biological fear-system (our body's defensive reactions to serious threats) has been unable to reset[20] when the threat that triggered its activation is no longer present and we are in a safe place. Those who suffer from trauma react to events, perceptions and thoughts in their present life *as if* they were still in danger from the shocking events of the past.

Simple trauma

Before defining complex trauma we need to first describe simple or 'non-complex' trauma. In simple trauma, our fear-system is activated by a threat, which is usually an isolated event, and cannot reset in the immediate aftermath. If help to process its impact is available in the months following this event, a recovery without further complications is possible and is often swift. Let me give an example:

[20] I use the terms 'reset' and 'deactivate' throughout the book to describe the 'goal-correction' of the fear-system, which means the way it activates when faced with a threat and then deactivates when the environment is safe. The fear-system never fully 'switches off' but goes into what has been described as 'vigilant quiescence' (Heard and Lake, 1997). It is this state of vigilant quiescence I am referring to when I refer to the fear-system as having 'reset'.

John, a young carpenter in a good relationship, was knocked off his motorbike by a car driver who didn't notice him at a junction. He recovered very quickly from his injuries but felt severe anxiety whenever he subsequently rode his motorbike, and he found himself avoiding the road where the accident happened. He was also unusually touchy and bad-tempered with his partner and had disturbed sleep which further worsened his mood.

Eventually his partner persuaded him to seek help and, realising that his symptoms were related to his accident, he found himself a trauma therapist offering eye movement desensitisation and reprocessing (EMDR) therapy.

After an introductory session, John had three 90-minute sessions of EMDR where he recounted the details of the accident he remembered, while the therapist moved her hand backwards and forwards in front of his eyes while asking him to follow her fingers. Each brief eye-movement segment was followed by a pause, with a reflection on what had happened during the eye movements. Sometimes John had felt heightened emotion and recalled details of the accident more clearly. Sometimes he felt very little, and his mind went off on other tangents, such as thinking about those who had helped him.

After just four sessions he was able to get back on his bike without anxiety. He stopped avoiding the road where the accident had happened, started sleeping better and was less short-tempered. His life quickly went back to the way it had been before the accident, though he remained a bit more wary when riding the motorbike, which was probably a good thing

Simple trauma can have a deeply disturbing effect on someone's life, but with timely treatment it can often be resolved in short-term work with few residual after-effects.

Complex trauma

Complex trauma looks very different from simple trauma. In complex trauma, the fear-system has been repeatedly activated by threats, or by a continuous state of threat, very often originating in childhood, and it continues active and unable to reset over long periods of time because of the absence of a place of safety. This affects the biological mechanisms that deactivate our fear-system, and these mechanisms become ineffective,[21] resulting in a fear-system that is unable to reset even when the environment is eventually safe.

This failure has devastating consequences for the highly complex and finely balanced organism of the human person. Over time the inability to reset in a safe environment results in emotional turbulence, problematic patterns of behaviour including addictions, restrictions to our ability to think and to learn, difficulties in relationships, and chronic physical conditions which either keep us trapped in unsafe environments, or which themselves contribute to the creation of unsafe environments. At a communal level, complex trauma results in a breakdown of our ability to function as a society with the subsequent loss of a safe environment for everyone.

The longer this state of constant fear-system activation continues, the harder it is for the fear-system to reset, which compounds the problems just noted, and increasingly complicates the chances of recovery. I would therefore define complex trauma as a 'fear-system dysfunction' – a chronic failure of the body's fear-system to deactivate in safe environments, and the detrimental impact of this failure over time on a complex

[21] See Chapter 7.

interconnected network of biological, behavioural, cognitive, relational and social systems.

The following is an example of a person suffering from complex trauma and the difficulties this presents for the therapist:

Laura's biological father left before she was born, and her mother was self-absorbed and neglectful. Laura felt there was no point trying to seek care, so she became self-reliant at a very young age. Dyslexic and emotionally troubled, she was dismissed by her schools as a failure despite being highly intelligent. Her stepfather sexually abused her, resulting in a traumatic abortion in her teens.

In adult life her partners were dominant and violent, and she found herself as a single mother of four children struggling to make ends meet. She suffered flashbacks that could leave her physically collapsed for hours, anxiety, panic attacks, depression, agoraphobia, chronic back pain and low energy. Many of the people she thought of as friends disappointed her – they relied on her support, but when she needed help, they weren't there for her, leading to friendship rifts.

For years she was unable to work because of the level of her anxiety, so she was trapped in a hostile benefits system that intermittently pulled the rug out from under her. She found herself having to live in substandard housing with bullying neighbours, which caused her great distress. She was very easily triggered by disappointment and would reject those who were in a position to help her at the first sign that they might let her down, leading to fallouts with police, advocates, support workers and doctors. Laura worked with me for over 10 years. Progress was very slow, sometimes just focused on getting by day to day as her external environment threw up so many disturbances for her.

By the end of the therapy, Laura had a good understanding of her body's defensive reactions and she was no longer scared of them. She had a stronger sense of self, and was in a long-term affectionate relationship, but she still faced many of her old difficulties, and while much better at regulating her fear responses, she still had to deal with much emotional turbulence day to day.

The slow and frustrating progress in therapy, with clients who have complex trauma, can often be attributed to the client's 'poor motivation', or 'failure to engage' in therapy. This way of thinking does a great disservice to our clients whose nervous systems have been 'hard-wired' to react to constant threat, during critical years of their development. The task of re-wiring the autonomic nervous system in these circumstances takes even more years, of repetitive 'safe enough' experiences in adulthood, and far more resources than are normally available to the individual therapist.

While Laura helped me to understand how complex trauma could turn every single aspect of life into a terrible struggle, it can affect us in a huge variety of ways, from Laura's constant high levels of distress, to a sort of frustration, general worry, and low-grade lack of motivation with an underlying sense of not feeling up to the challenges and opportunities of life, which affects many millions of us without our distress being in any way apparent to most of our acquaintances. My next example comes from somewhere in the middle of this continuum.

Adrian was a young man with a well-paid and responsible managerial post in a multinational banking firm, who came to see me suffering with low mood connected to constant high levels of generalised anxiety, fearful predicting of the future, not knowing what he wanted, and being unable to make decisions about work and relationships, which led to constant self-criticism.

He had vague memories of his mother getting really upset when he was 3 years old when her own mother died – he carried a sense that his mother's distress was his fault, and as a child constantly tried to make her happy but saw himself as a failure. As an adult he exhausted himself trying to please those around him and keep them entertained.

He was very fearful of intimate relationships. He was nearly 30 before he engaged in his first serious relationship. He felt trapped and overwhelmed by his sense of responsibility for his girlfriend, so the relationship did not last long.

He tended to be a perfectionist in most things but worked for an aggressive boss whom he felt treated him a bit like a slave. Until he came to see me he had shared his inner distress with no-one else. He couldn't respond to questions about how he was feeling. His sense was that all the pain and confusion was in his head, with his mind always overactive and his body 'numb from the neck down'.

I worked with Adrian for nearly five years. He didn't feel safe with any of my proposed ways of working with the body, so initially I worked more cognitively with him than I would usually do, with little success (he had previously found CBT unhelpful). I felt under huge pressure to alleviate his anxiety quickly, but our work was painfully slow.

It wasn't until some major events in my own life had helped me to better regulate my own fear-system that things started to shift in the therapy. I stopped reacting with anxiety and tension to his pressing need for a cure and stopped over-working and over-thinking. I think I became a calmer presence, and Adrian responded to this, eventually agreeing to work with breathing and becoming aware of his bodily sensations through focusing-oriented work.[22]

By the time he finished work, he had become far less of a people pleaser, had found himself a different boss and asserted himself more at work. He was in a relationship where he was gradually allowing himself to be more open about his feelings and learning that he could seek care as well as give it. He was starting to discover a sense of independence and freedom, which gave him a lot of satisfaction, and his generalised anxiety had greatly diminished.

I need to clarify at this stage that when I talk about complex trauma, I am not referring to 'complex PTSD' (CPTSD), although Laura in the earlier example would meet the criteria for this diagnosis. The World Health Organization's *International Classification of Diseases, 11th Revision* (ICD 11) gives a list of the experiences and symptoms which need to be met for someone to receive a CPTSD diagnosis (which can be found in Appendix 1). This is a very recently formulated diagnosis, and unfortunately it does not yet appear to cover childhood emotional abuse or neglect which may be even more harmful in the longer term than some physical or sexual abuse.[23]

[22] There is an example of this approach in Chapter 14.
[23] Strathearn et al. (2020).

In this book I am using 'complex trauma' as a more general and comprehensive description than CPTSD, referring to the consequences of our nervous system being chronically stuck in 'fear-mode'. I see these consequences as a broad continuum which at one end encompasses the diagnostic category of CPTSD, and at the other describes a high-functioning but restricted experience of life. The frequent activation of the fear-system limits our ability to live our life as fully as we might wish, whether we struggle with severe difficulties in all areas, or just limp through life under-energised and dissatisfied. I will touch on this idea again in Chapter 11.

Chapter 5

The biology of the fear-system and how it affects us

What happens in our body when fear responses activate

I want to look in more depth at the different biological processes involved in the three components of the fear-system, considering them now in the order in which they would normally activate, which is fear-alert, fear-arousal and then fear-collapse. After outlining the changes that happen once each state is triggered, I will note how we might experience these changes in our own bodies. The illustrations remind us of our evolutionary history as a prey animal and the fact that we share these same biological systems with the other mammals.[24]

Fear-alert: Orienting to threat

Fear-alert is the first response to a potential danger which has just been sensed, when there is a need to find out more about what and where the danger is. When this response is activated, the

[24] While there are undoubtedly huge differences within mammalian species in the development of a social engagement system, the older threat-response systems are common to all mammals, including humans. As Peter Levine notes (2010, p.27): '…since we share the same survival parts of the brain with other mammals, it only makes sense that we share their reactions to threat'.

body becomes tense and motionless, with a raised heart rate,[25] and hearing, eyesight and sense of smell become more acute. The startle response is heightened, which involves an increase in the signal in the nerves controlling the muscles of the arms and legs, so these muscles can activate quickly. Additionally, the signal in the ventral vagus nerve is switched off[26] so the restraining brake on heart rate is removed and the body is now in a volatile state where it is ready to go straight into the extreme actions of either fight or flight with nothing getting in the way.

Figure 3: Meerkat in fear-alert

When we experience fear-alert, the most obvious thing we notice is our tension as we hold ourselves still, and the fact that we often hold our breath. We do this as the noise of our breathing can interfere with hearing sounds of danger. We may not notice that we can see, hear and smell more acutely, but we are likely to be aware of our thoughts. These are entirely focused on the

[25] Schauer and Elbert (2010) note that the immediate reaction is a decrease in heart-rate (a throw-back to the oldest fear response?) followed quickly by cardiac acceleration.
[26] Kolacz and Porges (2018).

potential danger, with an inability to concentrate on anything else, and our general sense is of being wary and on-edge. On a day-to-day basis we might notice fear-alert going into a room full of strangers or standing up to speak in public. We could also experience it if we hear a strange noise when we're alone in the house at night. When this happens, we stop and listen carefully and try to work out what the noise was. Once we have worked this out and we know there's no threat, we can settle back into whatever we were doing previously.

The important thing about fear-alert is that it saves energy, in contrast to fear-arousal which uses up an enormous amount of energy. If prey animals such as antelope went into full fear-arousal every time there was the slightest hint of danger, they'd all be lying exhausted on the ground by the end of the day, and the predators would just need to stroll up to collect their food. So, fear-alert provides a 'checking-out' state, where the body is readied for extreme life-saving action, but there is no big commitment of energy, and we can very quickly revert to a calm state once we are sure the coast is clear.

Fear-arousal: 1. Active defence (fight or flight)

Once the danger is obvious and close, the brain's fear centre, the amygdala, triggers a huge number of changes in the body, via hormones and the sympathetic nervous system, to enable survival through fight or flight.[27]

An immediate release of adrenaline causes the heart rate to shoot up, and the chambers of the heart expand to increase the volume of blood pumped with each heartbeat. The interlinked systems of the hypothalamus, the pituitary gland and the adrenal glands (the HPA-axis) are activated to produce a series

[27] Sapolsky (2004). *Why Zebras don't get Ulcers.* Sapolsky uses the term 'stress' throughout the book, but he is describing the same biological processes which I am referring to as 'fear-system activation'.

of cortisol-based hormones which trigger the release of glucose and other nutrients into the bloodstream from storage cells throughout the body.

The bloodstream is now nutrient rich, and blood is being pumped at higher speed and greater volume to the muscles of the limbs, hugely boosting strength and speed. The blood supply to the gut and other areas non-essential in crisis is shut down by a narrowing of blood vessels, and sweating enables the body to prevent overheating. The small muscles at the base of hair follicles contract, so hair stands on end, making a prey animal look bigger, which might scare off a predator.

The hormone vasopressin is released to retain water in case of injury and blood loss, and non-opioid painkillers[28] are released so the pain of injury is numbed and does not detract from the effort to survive. In the brain, the amygdala also inhibits the activity of the cortex[29] eliminating all focus on anything apart from the danger at hand.

When fear-arousal is activated in humans, the onset may be experienced as a sudden upwards-moving wave of energy with the heart pounding in the chest. The increase in blood pressure can sometimes be seen in flushing in the face, neck and chest. You will recognise what this feels like if you can remember the last time you really lost your temper, or saw someone you loved in real danger, such as a child running towards a busy road. We may also experience nausea and other abdominal discomfort as the gut shuts down, sweating as the body's cooling system operates, dry mouth as vasopressin prevents water loss and goosebumps as muscles contract at the base of hair follicles.

If we are hurt or injured, we may not feel any pain in the moment. There are many accounts of soldiers in battle who

[28] Painkillers which don't cause drowsiness and therefore don't interfere with fight-or-flight actions.
[29] The most recently evolved part of the brain which, among many other functions, governs thinking, willed actions and much social behaviour, including language.

were shot or seriously wounded and didn't even notice it until afterwards – that's how powerful the numbing effect of fear-arousal can be.

Finally, as the amygdala highjacks the workings of the cortex, we might notice that our ability to think is hugely limited. All our thinking mind will do in these circumstances is focus on danger and how to avoid or eliminate it. There is no space for reflective thought or taking in anything new. Our ability to be sociable is also compromised and we tend to see others as a danger to us, rather than try to connect with them. We might notice this in behaviours such as avoidance and withdrawal, irritation, arguments, bickering, anger, and attempts to control which might involve bullying, violence, manipulation or appeasement.

Fear-arousal: 2. Locked defence and tipping point ('freeze' and 'fright'[30])

However, when we cannot run or fight, we go into 'freeze', like a 'rabbit in the headlights'. The fear-arousal response as described above is still fully active in the body, with pounding heart and stress hormones in the bloodstream,[31] but muscles lock and are held in rigid tension,[32] which can result in trembling. This is 'shaking with fear', and I think it is different from the antelope's tremoring[33] (Chapter 2, page 18), which is part of the fear-system switching off.

[30] My thanks to award-winning wildlife photographer Yongqing Bao for allowing me to use his photo 'The Moment' of a Himalayan marmot ambushed by a fox. Nothing else I have seen so graphically captures the state of 'freeze'/'fright'.

[31] LeDoux (1998), pp.141-2.

[32] Levine (2003) describes the muscles as 'frozen stiff in heightened contraction of agonist and antagonist muscle groups'.

[33] From this point on I am going to use the words 'shaking' or 'trembling' to describe the result of sustained muscle contraction (muscle fatigue) in 'freeze', while using the term 'tremoring' to describe the body's natural reset response after fear activation. This better aligns with the use of the term 'neurogenic tremoring' in TRE. (referred to in Chapter 14) – see Herold (2015).

Figure 4: Fox with marmot in fear-arousal (freeze/fright)

Freeze has been described as a state of 'flight or fight response put on hold,'[34] and it can switch back instantly to flight if an escape route presents itself. If there is no escape, it can switch to fight as a last resort, hence the expression 'fighting like a cornered rat'.

For humans, the state of 'freeze' is aptly described as being 'petrified', in other words, 'turned into stone'. Externally we are rigid, though we might shake with fear, as our tense muscles start trembling, but internally our heart is pounding.

In my experience, this state feels far worse than fight-flight because our alarm is not being channelled into action, and the pounding heart is such a powerful sensation that many people experiencing this turn up at A&E departments fearing that they're having a heart-attack. Alongside sweating, nausea and dry mouth, we might feel lightheaded or dizzy and our mind can blank. There is more confusion around the use of the word 'freeze' than any other term in the literature of the human threat-response. It would complicate matters too much to go into this

[34] Kozlowska et al. (2015), p.269.

here, so I have included my thoughts on how to resolve this confusion as Appendix 2.

While 'freeze' can quickly switch to flight-or-fight, it also easily slips into 'fright'. Fright is the peak of fear-arousal when there is no possible escape and no perceived chance of survival. This is the tipping point at which fear-arousal can switch into fear-collapse,[35] so the symptoms of hyper-arousal described above may be combined with a sense of our legs going from under us as we reach this tipping point. We normally describe our experiences of freeze and fright as 'panic'.[36]

Fear-collapse: Passive defence (tonic immobility)

When fear-arousal has failed to save us and death seems imminent, the body goes into metabolic shutdown. There are two mechanisms for this. In the first, and possibly the earliest,[37] form of shutdown, the brain releases opioid painkillers[38] into the

Figure 5: Leopard with antelope in fear-collapse

[35] Schauer and Elbert (2010).

[36] A state which can include 'feeling dizzy, unsteady, lightheaded or faint' (American Psychiatric Association, 2000).

[37] Kolacz and Porges (2018).

[38] Painkillers which induce drowsiness, unlike those released in fear-arousal.

bloodstream. In the second form, the dorsal vagus nerve triggers a sudden drop in heart rate and blood pressure by widening blood vessels as in a faint.[39]

This means that all the cells in our body are starved of oxygen and nutrients, and the cell respiration cycle that provides the energy driving each cell slows or stops. The functioning of our brain cells, major organ cells (controlling our immune system), muscle cells, skin cells, and much else, becomes ineffective or ceases. In the brain, the cortex shuts down first, followed by the limbic system.[40] This creates a collapse of energy production throughout the body which is described in more detail in Appendix 3.

The activation of fear-collapse means that a prey animal suddenly collapses, and appears to be dead, lying limp and unresponsive on the ground, often with eyes open and showing little sign of breathing. As I mentioned earlier, this metabolic collapse serves as a key survival strategy as it triggers a shutdown of the predator's attack instinct, and this can open up a window of opportunity for escape, as we saw in Chapter 2.

As humans we experience fear-collapse as a downward drop in energy, or a 'sinking feeling'. We feel faint, our posture slumps, and our muscles feel heavy as lead. We might feel nauseous as the gut shuts down and may lose control of our bladder or bowels. We can experience numbness which dampens our emotional responses along with a sense of unreality or being 'out of body'.

As we descend into fear-collapse, it becomes increasingly difficult to think; the phrase 'thinking through treacle' catches a sense of cognition slowing down, and eventually thinking ceases. Our ability to be sociable, with its control system in the cortex, is also gradually paralysed. We lose the ability to make

[39] Porges (2017).

[40] The limbic system is a part of the brain that is older in evolutionary terms than the cortex and controls our emotional responses and social instincts such as affectional bonds.

sense of social cues and can no longer even hear the human voice properly.[41] We notice this when we lose the desire to be with others, even our friends whose company we would seek out at other times. We would also notice this in an unequal relationship where it becomes too dangerous or exhausting to fight, and we go into a collapsed submission to a partner or some other person who has established dominance over us and is behaving in a violent or controlling manner.

Finally, as the limbic system is shut down, we lose all emotional responses, including our sense of fear,[42] so an employee who has been off work with moderate depression, but who anxiously ruminates about what his boss will think about him, will simply stop caring about this if he sinks into a severe depression.

Many victims of serious accidents, violent assault or rape experience a full fear-collapse, including physical prostration. I would argue, however, that most people are familiar with fear-collapse in less extreme forms, as I hope will be clarified in my comments on low mood, depression and dissociation in Chapter 8.

Fast moving fear responses

So far, I've described the three aspects of the fear-system as if they were separate static states. However, in real life the activation of each state can be very fast-moving with rapid switching from one state to another. We find a good example of this in Jeanette Winterson's autobiography *Why be happy when you could be normal?*[43] She is describing a real setback when trying to trace her biological parents. She received a letter containing a cursory bureaucratic response to her application – 'Applicant should fill

[41] As the eardrum loses the tension it needs to distinguish the human voice from background noise (Porges 2011).
[42] Levine (2010).
[43] Winterson (2012).

in the usual form and refer back'. This is what she writes:

> *'I sat on the back step looking at it over and over again like someone who can't read. My body was slight-shaking all over in the way that you do if you get caught in an electric fence. I went into the kitchen, picked up a plate and threw it at the wall ..."Applicant...usual form...refer back... It's not a fucking credit card referral, you asshole."*
>
> *'And what happened next makes me ashamed, but I will force myself to write it: I wet myself. I don't know why or how. I know that I lost bladder control and that I sat down on the step soiled and wet and I couldn't get up to clean myself and I cried in the way that you do when there is nothing but crying.'*

This passage vividly captures a fear-arousal response showing first as freeze (the mind-blank and shaking) switching to a fight reaction (throwing the plate and the verbal outburst) followed immediately by fear-collapse (a physical collapse, in this case with loss of bladder control).

It is important to note that fear-system responses do not always activate in the order in which I have presented them in this chapter, nor do we choose at any given moment which state will be activated, as these are automatic processes acting faster than thought. Fear-arousal can be triggered without being preceded by fear-alert, and, within fear-arousal, freeze may be triggered without fight-or-flight, and vice versa. Certain threats may activate fright immediately without any intermediate steps, and a sudden threat can trigger a fear-arousal that switches so quickly into fear-collapse that only the collapse is noticed.

Chapter 6

How the fear-system resets

The physical reactions of the body that deactivate our fear responses

Why is it that some experiences of major threat can be recovered from quickly, while others leave a long-lasting traumatic legacy? This happens because in some cases the fear-system is unable to reset after a threat and remains chronically activated, which can be seen as a problem of 'goal-correction'.[44]

Goal-correction

Many biological systems are goal-corrected. This means that they are triggered by a threat or a need – for example, hunger – and reset when their goal is met – for example, by eating until full. The fear-system is triggered by threat. It switches off when the goal of survival is met. If it fails to reset, it remains chronically active (unregulated) and we have a type of 'fear disorder', just as, when the biological systems that tell us we have eaten enough fail to work properly, we can have an eating disorder.

Why does the fear-system fail to reset? To answer this we need to look back at the context of the evolution of the fear-system – the struggle between prey and predator. If an animal is

[44] Heard and Lake (1997).

attacked by a predator but manages to escape by the activation of its fear-system in fight-or-flight, it then burns off the energy generated by the fight-flight response in its escape, reaches a place of safety and rests. The muscles relax, heart rate returns to calm, stress hormone production ceases, and the fear-system switches off until it is next needed.

If the fight-flight response does not result in escape, and the animal is caught by a predator and goes into fear-collapse, there are two further ways the fear-system can reset, both of which we have seen in Chapter 2. The first way is that a 'window of opportunity' for escape can arise, in which case fear-collapse suddenly switches back to fear-arousal, and the animal gets away, reaches a place of safety and rests.

The second way is when the immediate context becomes a safe place, as in the earlier example where the baboons chase off the predator (page 17). What happens then is that the animal comes out of fear-collapse with deep, spontaneous abdominal breathing, followed by a period of tremoring, which I believe to be different from the shaking of the freeze state. These mechanisms 'reset' the nervous system, effectively switching off the fear-system.[45]

The key factor is *safety*. If there is no place of safety in the aftermath of a serious threat, the fear-system cannot reset. In trying to understand what this means, let's start by looking at what happens when there is a place of safety and the fear-system *can* reset.

In Figure 6 we see a chart[46] illustrating metabolic arousal and collapse in the example from Chapter 2 (page 16) where the antelope seizes a window of opportunity and escapes. The

[45] Levine (2010).

[46] This and subsequent graphs can appear to indicate that only one branch of the autonomic nervous system is activated at any given time. They are in fact co-active most of the time, and the graphs merely represent which system is dominant.

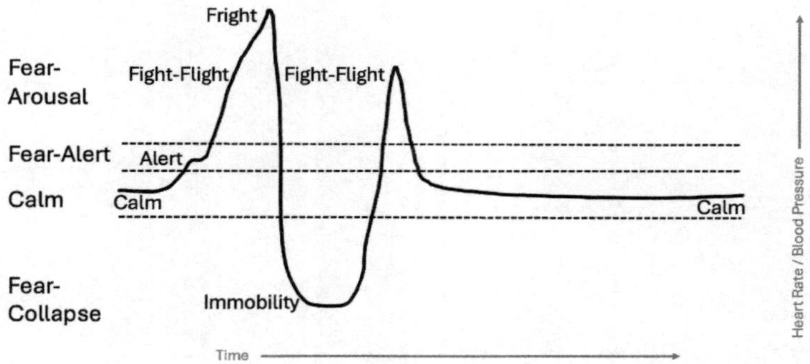

Figure 6: When the fear-system is able to reset

antelope started in a place of calm, went into fear-alert when danger was sensed, and then into fight-flight when the danger was imminent. At the moment of capture, the heart rate would have peaked in fright triggering an immobility collapse. Then, once an opportunity for escape presented, there was a sudden switch back into fight-flight and an escape to a place of safety, allowing a period of rest until a state of calm was reached. At this point the fear-system reset, switching off until it was required to meet the next threat.

Chapter 7

When the fear-system cannot reset

What causes us to get stuck in 'fear-mode'?

However, where there is no place of safety that can be reached after the original threat, the body cannot calm. This is illustrated in Figure 7.[47] The first part of this graph is identical to Figure 6, showing arousal, collapse and the switch back into arousal of the original threat. However, in humans, when we can't find a place of safety and calming, our nervous system remains stuck in fear-alert. This is a volatile state,[48] and less serious threats can trigger further states of arousal and collapse that again only resolve into fear-alert, rather than relaxing into calm. In this way, an ongoing cycle can be established which can repeat continuously at any indication of threat.

This ongoing cycle of fear activation, which I sometimes refer to as being 'stuck in fear-mode', is much more likely to affect humans than animals in the wild. Our modern surroundings, social organisation and lifestyle are now very different from the natural environments for which our fear-systems were adapted.

[47] I sometimes think of this graph as the 'polyvagal rollercoaster'. I prefer it to the widely used metaphors of the polyvagal ladder and the polyvagal curve, for reasons outlined in Appendix 4.
[48] See Chapter 5.

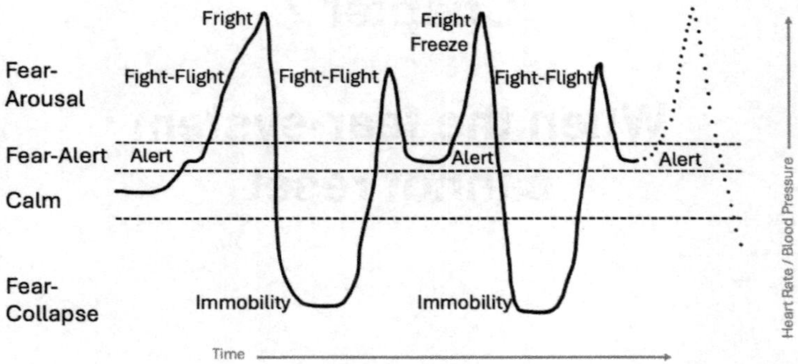

Figure 7: When the fear-system *cannot* reset

Phenomena such as socially isolated individuals and families, tedious pressured and exploitative work, huge inequality in the sharing of resources, or even just the dangers and frustrations of driving on our roads, create fear activation detached from the intense physical response that can contribute to resetting the fear-system.

As highly social beings, we experience social rejection as a major threat which triggers the physicality of the fear-system response. However, physically responding to social rejection may be inappropriate or impossible. For example, a neglected child may have the impulse to fight or run away, but cannot put these impulses into action, and may instead go into a chronic collapse, since the home, the only potential source of safety, is also the source of the threat.

The continuous cycle of fear activation is also kept going by our ability to predict the future, creating imagined threats that activate our fear responses as powerfully as real threats. However, while a real problem in the present can be responded to with action in the present that could resolve the issue, we cannot as easily resolve future imagined threats. We tend to ruminate on future scenarios such as potential problems at work, problems in relationships and financial difficulties, and this rumination continues to trigger our fear responses.

This brings us to the real crux of the problem of complex trauma. When the fear-system cannot reset and remains chronically active, the biological processes which normally enable it to reset start to become dysfunctional. This means that the longer the fear-system remains active, the harder it becomes to deactivate.

Let me give three examples of how this dysfunction can play out in our bodies.

At a physiological level, tension that is not released following a threat builds into a chronic state of tension in the body. Chronic tension tightens the diaphragm, which inhibits deep breathing, contributing to a habitual pattern of shallow breathing which supports the dominance of the sympathetic nervous system,[49] and thus the continuance of fear-system activation. I also think it is likely that being in a chronic state of tension inhibits the post-threat neurogenic tremoring that resets the fear-system.[50]

At the level of hormone production, if the state of fear-activation continues for too long the cortisol receptors in the brain, which shut down the activity of the HPA-axis[51] once a threat has been survived, become desensitised and unable to reset cortisol production.[52] This disables an important feedback loop, making it more difficult for the fear-system to deactivate.

At the level of the autonomic nervous system, chronic fear-activation disables what is perhaps the most important mechanism in switching off the fear response. This is the ventral vagus nerve, described by Porges as the 'calming brake' on the

[49] Tabor et al. (2019), p.2.

[50] This appears to be a view held in the TRE community. See for example Greenacre (No date): 'Complications occur if this tremoring process is thwarted as then the response that was activated becomes held, literally gets stuck in the body and discharge doesn't complete and the system is unable to return to normal afterwards'.

[51] The interlinked systems of the hypothalamus, the pituitary gland and the adrenal glands.

[52] Sapolsky (2004).

heart. The ventral vagus nerve connects directly to the heart's sino-atrial node, its inbuilt pacemaker. As noted previously, the sino-atrial node prompts the heart to beat at about 90-100 beats per minute, but when the ventral vagus nerve is activated, it overrides this default setting and slows the heart rate down to around 60 beats per minute, bringing us into a state of calm.

In the face of a threat, the activating signal in the ventral vagus nerve is withdrawn in order to enable the heart rate to rise in fear-alert and fear-arousal. However, Kolacz and Porges[53] note that when the fear-system is *chronically* active – in other words, when the ventral vagal signal is chronically withdrawn – this signal becomes 'dampened' or weakened. So, to use an analogy, just as a leg muscle will atrophy if not used for walking for a time, so the strength of signal on the ventral vagus will weaken if it is withdrawn for too long in fear-activation. The more constantly our fear-system is activated, the more difficult it becomes for us to restrain it.

It should be noted, however, that the 'calming brake' description given to the ventral vagus is only one half of the story. The ventral vagus nerve does not just slow down the fast heart rate of fear-arousal but also speeds up the slow heart rate of fear-collapse, acting as a regulator of the volatility of the autonomic nervous system under threat.[54]

Figure 8 is an attempt to illustrate the implications of a weakened (or dampened) ventral vagus signal. Image 8.1 represents the regulated fear-system with a strong signal in the ventral vagus. In the absence of a serious or life-threatening danger, this restrains both the rise of heart rate in fear-arousal and its fall in fear-collapse, so less serious or imagined threats have little impact. The fear-system is not activated and a state of calm is maintained.

[53] Kolacz and Porges (2018).
[54] Porges (2017).

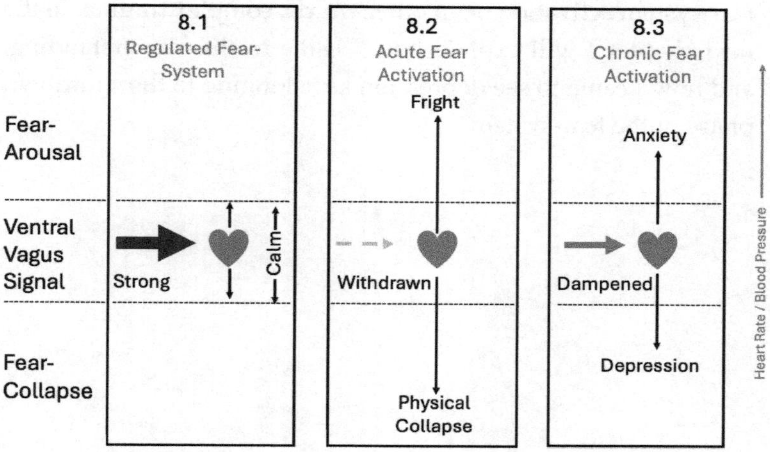

Figure 8: Fear regulation and the weakened (dampened) ventral vagus

In Image 8.2 we see acute fear-system activation where there *is* a serious threat, and the ventral vagus signal is withdrawn to allow the body to respond to the danger. Without the restraining force of the ventral vagus, the heart rate can rise, peaking in fright, or dropping to the point of physical collapse in order to best survive the threat.

In Image 8.3 we see the result of *chronic* fear-system activation. Here, since the signal on the ventral vagus has been withdrawn over long periods of time, it has become weakened, or 'dampened', so while there is still some restraining signal, this is insufficient to maintain a state of calm, and less serious or imagined threats can still activate the fear-system, resulting in intermediate, or partial, states of fear-arousal or fear-collapse.

I propose that these states represent anxiety (partial fear-arousal) and depression (partial fear-collapse),[55] and that anxiety and depression are the most common symptoms of chronic

[55] Levine (2010), p.52, notes that traumatised humans get lost in a 'chronic partial shutdown'.

fear-system activation or, in other words, complex trauma. In the next chapter I will explain how I came to this understanding, and how I came to see depression as belonging to the shutdown phase of the fear-system.

Chapter 8

Making sense of anxiety and depression

How I came to see anxiety and depression as aspects of fear-arousal and fear-collapse

In 2015, having come across Peter Levine's book, *In an Unspoken Voice*[56] which introduced me to the idea of physical collapse as a fear response, I started writing a conference paper updating the fear-system model that I and my colleagues had been using.

Experiencing shutdown

In the process of writing, I had an experience of exactly the same immobility response I was trying to write about. I had a bout of food poisoning, which involved an early morning rush to the toilet. Just afterwards, I felt faint and collapsed onto the bathroom floor. I lay there unable to move a muscle.

My eyes were open, and I could see the pedestal of the hand basin just in front of me, but my mind (normally constantly active), was a complete blank, with absolutely nothing

[56] Levine (2010).

happening. I had no sense of time. Parts of my bare legs that were on cold tiles didn't feel chilled. Then, suddenly, something shifted – I just got up and went back to bed; checking my alarm clock, I saw that I had been lying on the floor for around 30 minutes.

There was no fear trigger to this collapse, but Levine notes that the same shutdown mechanism is activated in the body not only by fear, but by many other factors posing a threat, such as bacterial or viral infection, poisons, exhaustion, blood loss or serious loss of liquids as in diarrhoea.

The link to depression

Having experienced shutdown in the context of learning about fear-collapse, I became sensitised to social interactions involving a similar though less severe drop in energy and I started to wonder whether depression might be connected to fear-collapse. When I suggested this to colleagues at the conference there was general agreement – in fact it seemed fairly obvious once it was stated.

Previously I had never been clear about what depression was, despite working with it for decades. I was not alone among my therapist colleagues in this uncertainty, and the medical profession was no clearer – some of the doctors at the GP practice I worked at saw depression as a 'chemical imbalance in the brain', but Johann Hari, in his excellent book on depression, *Lost Connections*, claims that this theory has no evidence base and was actually a successful fiction disseminated through drug company marketing.[57]

[57] Hari (2018), p.30. In quoting this I am not implying that there is no role for medication in the treatment of depression. I will pick up on this again in Parts 2 and 4 looking at antidepressant medication as a provider of safety and regulation without which therapeutic work can sometimes be impossible.

The *symptoms* of depression are clear – low mood, low energy, a slowing of thought and movement, and a loss of both the ability and desire to socialise with others. Other symptoms, such as loss of concentration, negative thinking and loss of pleasure and interest in activities, follow on from these. The symptoms, however, don't explain what depression *is*.

Table 1: Key markers of fear-collapse and depression

Fear-collapse	Depression
Slowing/shutdown of cell respiration	Drop in energy
Physical collapse	Muscle weakness/failure
Shutdown of cognitive processes in cortex	Slowing of thought/loss of concentration
Shutdown of social engagement system in cortex	Loss of desire and ability to socialise

However, as soon as you put the key biological markers of fear-collapse alongside those of depression (Table 1), you can see the parallels – the slowing down of cell respiration in fear-collapse mirrors the drop of energy in depression, with physical collapse showing in depression as muscle weakness.

The shutdown of cognition in the cortex in fear-collapse relates to the slowing of thought and loss of concentration of depression, while the shutdown of the control system for social engagement results in a loss of the desire and ability to socialise in depression.

With a growing conviction that depression was an experience of fear-collapse, but, lacking sufficient validation,[58] I thought I'd investigate my own mood changes. I got myself a Fitbit and a Polar chest heart-rate monitor and started to familiarise myself with my own heart rate patterns, focusing on lowered heart rate as

[58] Reading Porges (2011), a slow process for a non-scientist, I was heartened to find depression named as one of the aspects of immobilisation in a diagram on the influence of neuropeptides (p.292) but frustrated to find no elaboration on this.

an indicator of a shutdown triggered via the dorsal vagus nerve.

I had one minor result, which supported my hypothesis. I noted a moment of real despondency, when my heart rate had dropped to 47 beats per minute (my normal resting heart rate was in the mid 50s). However, on the whole, all I was able to notice were patches of mild low mood where I felt drained of energy, and normal daily tasks felt like hard work. On those occasions I noted that my heart rate was at least 10 beats per minute *higher* than it would normally have been for those same tasks.

These results, which conflicted with my focus on lowered heart rate as a marker of depression, led to me shelving my theory about depression and immobility for some time, but my interest was sparked again some months later.

> A client of mine, with whom I had discussed these ideas, noted his heart rate at the start of an episode of depression. This client had a history of early emotional neglect and depression. A family incident that reminded him of the way he had been treated as a child triggered the sudden onset of a depressed mood, and he had to sit down to avoid feeling faint. Our previous discussion prompted him to check his Fitbit, and he noted his heart rate had dropped to 48 beats per minute. He reported that his normal resting heart rate was around 55-60 beats per minute, and that even in sleep it never went below 50 beats per minute.

Perhaps there *was* a link between depression and fear-collapse? However, I was still stuck with the problem of my own low moods coinciding with a *raised* heart rate when other depressive episodes were associated with lowered heart rate. I got some clarification when I started reading Robert Sapolsky's book on stress, *Why Zebras don't get Ulcers*. Sapolsky discussed the complexity of depression and the contrasting symptoms of its various states, ranging from psychomotor impairment (where the person moves and speaks slowly, can't concentrate, and finds simple tasks exhausting), to a state where low mood and lack of energy go hand-in-hand with mental agitation, and high levels of stress hormones in the body.[59] This matched the differences I was noticing between raised and lowered heart rates in different stages of depressed mood, and made sense of the fact that many people experience anxiety *at the same time* as depression.

I had started to get interested in breathing and the way in which each in-breath prompts the sympathetic nervous system to raise the heart rate, and each out-breath prompts the parasympathetic nervous system to lower the heart rate. A continual balanced process of accelerator and brake is operating on the heart, governed by each breath we take. In this normal balance, the brake on the heart is provided by the evolutionarily newer ventral vagus.[60]

I wondered whether, in less severe depression, when this normal balance is disrupted by a triggering of the older dorsal vagus (fear-collapse), this puts a further brake on the heart which prompts a stronger opposing sympathetic nervous system reaction. In other words, the body raises the heart rate to counteract this additional brake. I imagined that this might be like trying to drive off in your car with the handbrake on, which would mean that you have to accelerate harder than normal to get anywhere. I wondered if this was what was happening when I noticed that my mood and energy were both low, but that my heart rate was raised? It would certainly explain why it was possible to experience anxiety and a certain level of depression at the same time.[61]

[59] Sapolsky (2004), pp. 275-6.

[60] Porges (2011).

[61] It would appear that this sympathetic nervous system co-activation with the dorsal vagus signal ceases in a full fear-collapse as the limbic system shuts down and our sense of fear disappears. The interrelation of these biological systems is complex and Figures 6 and 7 deliberately oversimplify, both in representing anxiety and depression purely as opposing states of arousal and collapse, and also in combining heart rate and blood pressure on the y-axis as if they always worked in tandem.

Gradual fear-collapse

While this made sense to me, I was still left with a question which puzzled me for a couple of years. Could fear-collapse be experienced as a gradual continuum as well as a sudden physical shutdown? If this was possible, it would explain the various stages of depression from mild to severe. I was heartened by coming across Schauer and Elbert's concept of 'flag' in their fear-cascade model.[62] In this model of fear activation, the shutdown response is divided into 'flag' and 'faint', which validated for me the idea that there could be gradual steps in a shutdown response, but I still could not understand what the mechanism for this might be.

I eventually found an answer to this question after writing to Stephen Porges. He sent me a pre-publication copy of an article[63] he wrote with Jacek Kolacz which referred to the fact that the signal on the ventral vagus nerve which shuts down the fear-system, is weakened if it is withdrawn for too long. So, when we get stuck in fear mode over long periods of time, the 'brake' becomes less effective at restraining our fear reactions.

The barn-door metaphor

The metaphor that then occurred to me, which made sense of this, was that our fear-system responding to threats was a bit like a barn-door flapping in a strong wind. If I superimpose this metaphor onto the rollercoaster of the fear-system (Figure 9),[64] we see it responding to threats by oscillating between fear-arousal (see 9.1) and fear-collapse (see 9.2) without any restraining signal from the ventral vagus nerve, in order that life-threatening dangers can be survived.

[62] Schauer and Elbert (2010).
[63] Kolacz and Porges (2018).
[64] A more detailed, animated version of this metaphor can be found in my York Festival of Ideas talk, Guilding (2024).

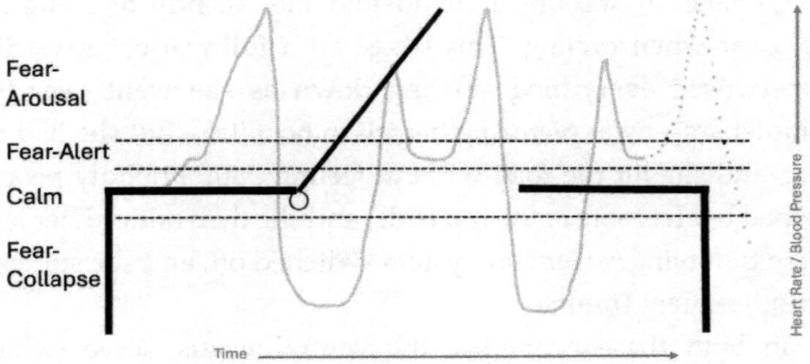

Figure 9:1 Full fear-arousal

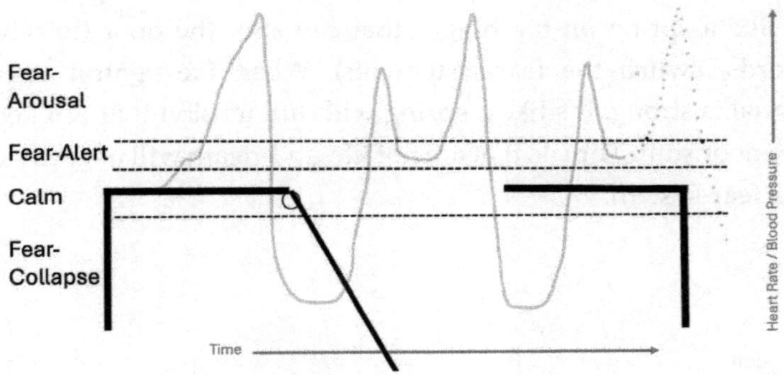

Figure 9:2 Full fear-collapse

Here are some examples of this. You're walking your dog through a field of cows, and they turn on you and chase you. This would trigger a full fear-arousal. You would let the dog go and run for your life and jump the fence like a gazelle. Once you'd reached safety, your heart would be pounding, but your fear-system would have done its job, and you would gradually calm down.

Or take an account a friend told me recently of being hit by a car when cycling. This triggered a full fear-collapse. She experienced everything slowing down as she went over the handlebars – even picturing herself in hospital – but she had no fear, and she hit the road without feeling pain. Friendly people helped her feel safe at the roadside, and she then noticed her legs were trembling.[65] Her fear-system switched off, and she suffered no subsequent trauma.

In both these examples, the ventral vagus nerve (which needed to be deactivated so that the fear-system could save the protagonist's life) now comes back into play. When we are once again safe, it activates and shuts down the fear-system.

In the barn-door metaphor (see 9.3), the ventral vagus nerve is like a spring on the hinges that can shut the door (in other words, switch the fear-system off). When the ventral vagus signal is strong, it's like a spring with full tension that can keep the door shut. Threats that are not life-and-death will not activate the fear-system.

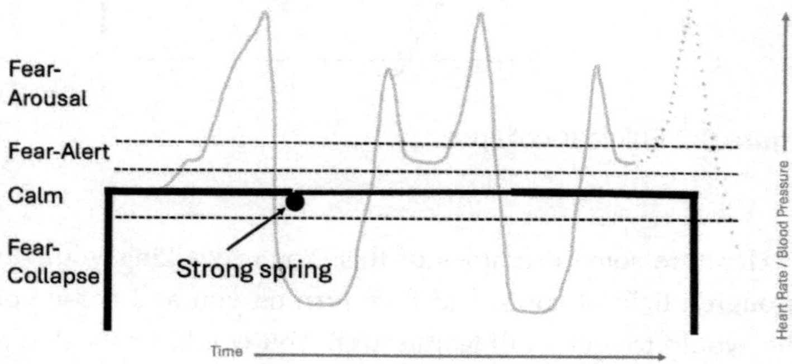

Figure 9:3 Regulated fear-system – strong ventral vagal signal

[65] My friend's word – I would interpret this as neurogenic tremoring as her fear-system was clearly able to reset.

For example, if someone says, 'The boss wants to see you right now', your heart might do a little jump. There might be a few upward wobbles, but you wouldn't get too agitated. You might just take a breath and think, 'I wonder what that's about – let's go and find out'.

Or if you'd applied for a promotion, but have just been told you're not short-listed, that would have an impact, but it would be limited. There might be a few downward wobbles, but you wouldn't collapse. You might just think, 'It wasn't my day; I'll have another go next time'.

However, when the ventral vagus signal has weakened, because we've been stuck too long in fear-mode, we could imagine it acting like a spring that has lost some of its tension, so it can't properly keep the door shut (see 9.4), and less serious threats (like moderate winds) keep swinging it into fear-arousal or fear-collapse. However, as the spring does still retain some tension (there is still some signal in the ventral vagus nerve), we don't see the extremes of fear activation as we did with the cows and the bike accident, but partial states of arousal and collapse.

With a weakened ventral vagus signal when we've been stuck

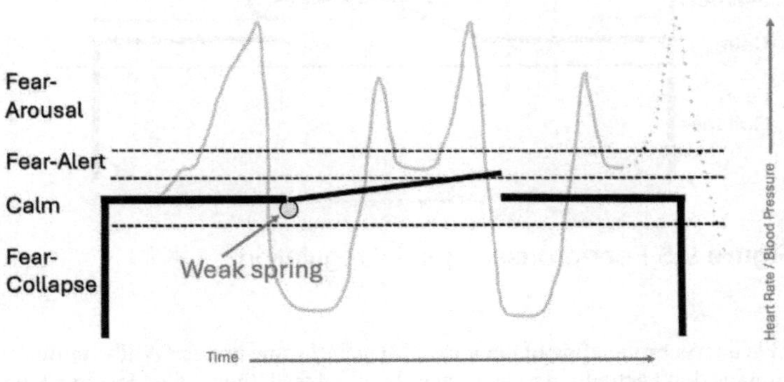

Figure 9:4 Partially regulated fear system – weak ventral vagal signal

in fear-mode, if we're told the boss wants to see us immediately, our heart might start beating faster and we might start frantically thinking we have done something wrong and imagine we're going to get the sack, so we go into the boss's office in a state of anxiety.

Similarly, if we heard we hadn't been shortlisted for promotion, our mood could really drop. We might lose confidence and think we're not good enough and that we'll never get promoted, and we might end up going through a patch of depression.

So, as I understand it, anxiety is an intermediate state of fear-arousal (see 9.5), and depression is an intermediate state of fear-collapse (see 9.6), both *partially* regulated[66] by a sub-optimal ventral vagus nerve. I therefore see anxiety and depression as the most common expressions of a fear-system that has become stuck in fear mode and can't reset.[67]

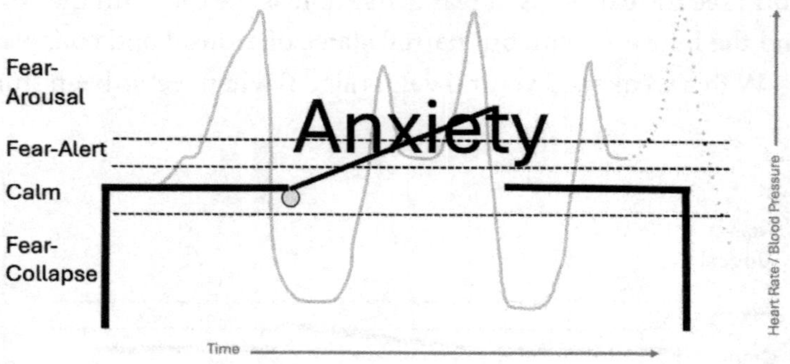

Figure 9:5 Fear-arousal – partial regulation

[66] On a recent re-reading of Levine (2010), p.53, I came across: 'While traumatised humans don't actually remain physically paralysed, they do get lost in a kind of anxious fog, a chronic partial shutdown, dissociation, lingering depression and numbness.' What I had considered my own thinking may owe more to Levine than I first assumed.

[67] Though depression is a more severe state of fear activation – a point which the polyvagal ladder and polyvagal curve illustrations (Appendix 4) clearly convey.

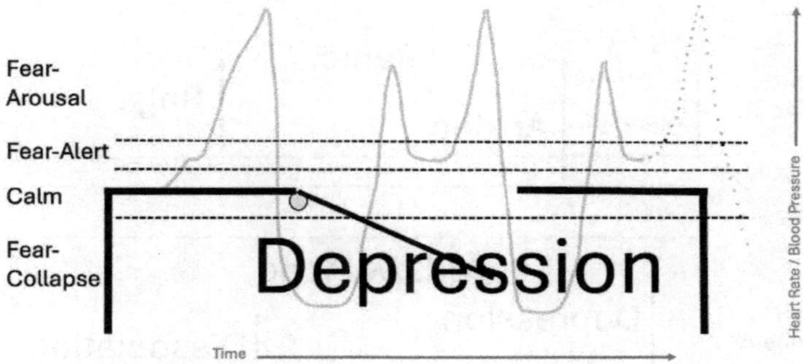

Figure 9:6 Fear-collapse – partial regulation

Mapping symptoms to fear-system responses

We could extend this hypothesis to map the common terms we use to describe our experience of fear-system activation alongside the biological responses of fear-alert, fear-arousal and fear-collapse (Figure 10). Anxiety, as noted above, is a persistent state of fear-activation varying from fear-alert to fight-flight, while rage (or uncontrolled anger) corresponds to the fight stage of fear-arousal. The symptoms of panic place it at the higher end of fear-arousal, covering 'freeze' and 'fright', which may involve the initial sensations of tipping into fear-collapse – for example, 'feeling dizzy, unsteady, lightheaded or faint'.[68]

I see low mood as a state where the immobility system has been triggered but there is still reasonably good ventral vagal regulation. Where there is less effective regulation I am suggesting that the shutdown response can be experienced as varying degrees of depression on a continuum from low mood through to severe depression and ultimately physical collapse.

[68] American Psychiatric Association (2000).

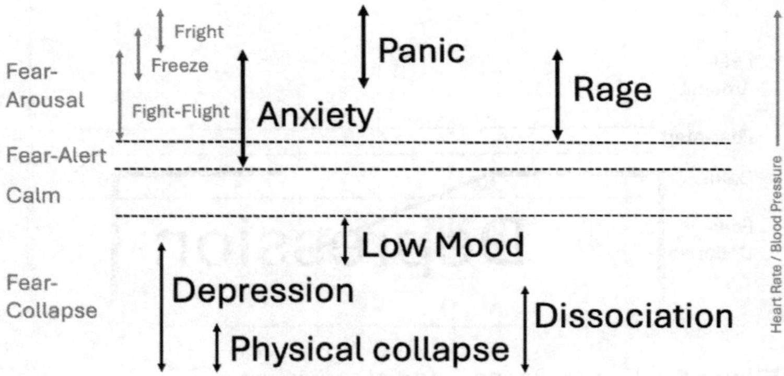

Figure 10: Conditions associated with chronic fear-activation

Dissociation

Alongside depression is the phenomenon of dissociation.[69] This is a poorly defined concept, but if we look for the biological changes that might explain the sense of unreality and being 'out of body' that it describes, it would seem reasonable to suggest that these sensations may be caused by the numbing opiates released by the brain in fear-collapse, or by our experience of perceptual parts of the cortex being disabled by oxygen starvation as a result of the metabolic shutdown, or perhaps both.

This view of dissociation as belonging to fear-collapse has been challenged by colleagues who use the term more broadly to also encompass the 'dizzy brain' and disconnect from reality experienced in the 'freeze' and 'fright' stages of fear-arousal. It makes sense to me that the way we perceive our own body could be profoundly affected by the non-opioid painkillers released in fear-arousal

[69] Porges (2017, p.12) speculates on the basis of polyvagal theory that: 'There may be gradations in reactions to life threat from total shutdown and collapse mimicking the death-feigning responses of small mammals to an immobilisation of the body during which the muscles lose tension and the mind dissociates from the physical event.'

which are powerful enough for soldiers not to notice major injury in battle. The narrow focus on danger and survival in fear-arousal clearly also affects our perception of our surrounding reality. I do think, however, that these interior and exterior perceptions generated by fear-arousal are different from those experienced in fear-collapse, and I wonder if we need a separate word for the sensations generated by fear-arousal ('detachment' perhaps?).

I am aware, however, that there is real difficulty involved in observing and describing fear reactions which are not static phenomena but switch rapidly between different biological responses. I wonder whether some experiences of what is termed dissociation, in the context of panic, may be generated by the sudden tipping into fear-collapse that can follow the 'fright' response.

Bereavement

A word on bereavement might be useful in this context. *The Diagnostic and Statistical Manual of Mental Illnesses* (DSM) has puzzled over the relationship between bereavement and depression for many years,[70] unsure whether bereavement is simply a form of depression or a special case. However, I think a fear-system perspective may help to clarify this issue. It seems to me that bereavement is just one of a number of major blows to the self (such as divorce or redundancy) that can trigger fear-collapse. Such major blows invariably involve a significant drop in mood and energy, but whether they result in longer-term depression seems to depend on a number of other factors, including the level of support available and any previous history of trauma.

While the underlying causes of depression are often not clear to those in contact with the sufferer, the loss of a partner, or someone to whom we are closely attached, is often a very

[70] Pies (2014).

public event, and for thousands of years many societies have known how to respond to such a loss. For example, communities would often move in to support the bereaved person, taking over practical tasks and offering companionship which allowed space for collapse and gradual readjustment to a new sense of self without the presence of the person we have lost.

In other words, bereavement is a natural depressive response to loss which resolves over time with community support. In contrast, many similar depressive responses where the cause is not clear to see, do not resolve and result in chronic depression in the *absence* of adequate support. This hypothesis would also explain ongoing complex bereavement and grief when a person does not have a supportive community or (due to past trauma) is unable to receive the care that may be on offer.

Chapter 9

The long-term impact of complex trauma

Impact on our emotional state, behaviour, learning, relationships, physical health, and ability to function as a society

At this stage I want to go back to my opening definition of complex trauma as a chronic failure of the body's fear-system to deactivate in safe environments (pages 25–26), and the detrimental impact of this failure over time on a complex interconnected network of biological, behavioural, cognitive, relational and social systems. We have just looked at the impact of this failure on the autonomic nervous system, leaving it over-responsive to threat, stuck in hypervigilant fear-alert, and cycling between fear-arousal and fear-collapse.

This continuing nervous system volatility affects multiple systems, which become dysfunctional and create feedback loops in which this dysfunction becomes more and more entrenched. This is particularly the case when threats were suffered in infancy and childhood, and even more so when the parent or parents who were meant to be the child's fundamental source of safety, were themselves the threat.

When faced with childhood trauma, the task of training the autonomic nervous system out of hypervigilance and hyper-reactivity into calm becomes highly complex, no simple short-term intervention is effective, and painfully-won progress in one area can easily be wiped out by a threat in another area.

I have already noted the emotional impact of an unregulated fear-system in terms of anxiety, rage, panic, low mood, depression and dissociation, but will now look at the other areas or systems that become dysfunctional as a result of complex trauma, and, in their turn, contribute to the chronic triggering of fear responses.

Impact on thinking and education

In their different ways, both fear-arousal and fear-collapse can profoundly affect our ability to think. In fear-arousal, the amygdala inhibits the cortex and focuses our thinking purely on detecting and surviving danger. Any other information may be heard, but it cannot be processed at the time. A chronic state of fear-arousal may result, over time, as this focus on danger becomes habitual, negatively affecting the way we think about others and the world we are living in. Such a habitual outlook can keep re-triggering our fear-system responses and closing down any openness to potential help.

In fear-collapse, oxygen starvation disables the cells of the cortex. As the body is de-energised, what thinking remains tends to become hopeless in nature. At a certain stage of collapse we can become unable to process anything we may hear, and we may also lose the ability to hear clearly what is said to us.[71] The de-energising of brain cells can then cause the mechanisms for memory encoding and recall to fail.

Chronic fear activation can thus have a highly detrimental effect on learning and education. A child from a home where there has been no emotional regulation, cycling between fear-arousal and fear-collapse, may not be able to take in and process

[71] As the muscles of the inner ear, that control the tension of the eardrum which enables us to distinguish the human voice from background noises, start to fail (Porges 2017).

information and may be unable to cope with schoolwork. At the time this will be a severe blow to the child's self-esteem, and these children are then also likely to be labelled as 'bad' or 'disruptive', further undermining their confidence and limiting educational opportunities. In the longer term, this can severely limit opportunities for work and income potential and make it far more difficult for people to escape from fear-dominated environments.

Impact on patterns of behaviour

Our fear responses are essentially physical reactions to threat, so they show themselves most clearly in our behaviours. We are born with our fear-system fully developed but without the ability to regulate it. This regulation has to be provided at first by our parents responding in an attuned way to our needs and soothing our fears. Our biological systems for regulating fear reactions develop in response to this good early nurture.[72] However, if our parents are unable to regulate their own fear responses, and as a result are anxious, depressed, angry or preoccupied, we don't fully develop these systems that regulate our fear responses, and we can potentially live our whole lives with a fear-system that cannot properly deactivate.

In more serious cases where the parents not only fail to create a context of safety for the child, but are themselves the source of danger, as in the case of physical, sexual or emotional abuse and neglect, the child lives in a permanent state of fear-system activation. These fear responses are powerful, and with limited ability to regulate them these develop into behaviours in adult life such as self-neglect, self-harm, avoidance, addiction or violence. Each of these brings practical consequences that make breaking out of the cycle of fear more and more difficult.

[72] Hart (2011).

Self-neglect repeats patterns of early mistreatment and can perpetuate fear-system activation. Self-harm can be a risky attempt at self-regulation, activating internal opioid painkillers to dampen emotional distress, but the shame aroused by self-harm can compound isolation and inhibit careseeking. Avoidant behaviours, driven by chronic states of either fear-arousal in flight mode, or of fear-collapse, progressively shut down opportunities for careseeking and self-development and can lead to an intensification of anxieties.

Aggressive and violent behaviours, driven by chronic states of fear-arousal in fight mode, generate hostile reactions and continual conflict with others, making it impossible for the fear-system to deactivate. Where aggression leads to offending behaviours there can often be further traumatisation within the prison system.

Addictions, such as the use of drugs, alcohol or gambling, which are an attempt to self-soothe or self-vitalise in the context of the emotional turbulence of an unregulated fear-system,[73] can destructively alter neurological functioning, put an end to supportive relationships and impair the ability to work.

Impact on relationships

Fear-system activation affects our social engagement system in two key ways. In fear-arousal, where we focus only on danger, we automatically start seeing those around us as a source of danger. In fear-collapse, our entire social engagement system is disabled as the cortex and then the limbic brain shut down, and we lose both the desire and the ability to relate to others.

Chronic fear-system activation can therefore have a disastrous impact on our ability to make and sustain relationships.[74] As the

[73] Maté (2012).

[74] Porges (2011), p.17. 'a neuroception of safety is necessary before social engagement behaviours can occur.'

social engagement system is our primary means of responding to threat and enabling 'survival with wellbeing'[75] by maintaining connectedness with others, this locks us into a feedback loop of reliance purely on the isolating responses of the fear-system.

As our relationships with our primary caregivers form a template for future relationships, those with a history of good early nurture, and thus of good fear regulation, are able to trust others and maintain relationships of equality which are supportive and companionable, and which then contribute hugely to the ongoing regulation of fear responses. However, children who have been unable to seek care from parents often struggle to be able to trust or seek care from others in later life, and trauma suffered in infancy and early childhood in relational contexts can create deeply defensive patterns of relating to others, such as are seen in personality disorders,[76] and many other relationship difficulties.

Where the fear-system is chronically active, relationships tend to be unequal. The relationship pattern can become 'one-up, one-down', with one party dominant and the other submissive, [77] either fixed in these roles, or switching between them in highly volatile exchanges. Where the 'other' is viewed as a threat, the fear response is to control them, either directly through force, or intimidation, or indirectly through various forms of manipulation. Such relationships cannot be safe places, though they may be familiar places, and so they contribute to the ongoing failure of the fear-system to deactivate.

Impact on our social context

I have focused up to this point on the impact on individuals of an unregulated fear-system, but individuals are part of societies, and fear-driven reactions of individuals and groups over time

[75] Heard, Lake and McCluskey (2012).
[76] Zhang et al. (2012).
[77] Heard and Lake (1997).

profoundly affect the culture and workings of human societies and can turn them into unsafe contexts for many, creating feedback loops which further dysregulate the fear-systems of individuals. In fear-arousal, both individually and as societies, we focus on danger, and we then find danger in any sort of *difference*, be it race, nationality, tribe, class, gender, religion or sexuality.[78] When societies react to difference with fear responses, the process of 'othering'[79] can result in oppression, persecution, war and genocide. In this way, complex trauma begets behaviours in groups, nations and cultures which inflict profound harm, endlessly perpetuating the problem of complex trauma throughout the generations.

Impact on physical health, pain regulation and energy production

We have so far covered a broad range of ways in which complex trauma affects our mental health, emotional wellbeing, relational support and life opportunities, but the unregulated fear-system also has a huge impact on our physical health. In this way, complex trauma has a profound impact on the lives of many millions of people. Our fear responses, as they oscillate between extreme metabolic activity and metabolic shutdown, hugely stress the whole organism and, over time, they can cause cardiovascular disease and chronic gastrointestinal disorders. They can also impair our immune system by over-stimulating it and causing autoimmune illnesses, such as rheumatoid arthritis when fear-activation is intermittent. Sapolsky notes that when fear-activation is continuous it lowers immune function, opening the body up to a whole range of viral or bacterial infections.[80]

[78] See Nussbaum (2018), for a contemporary account of fear-system activation in society.
[79] Brons (2015).
[80] Sapolsky (2004).

Unregulated fear-activation can also cause dysfunction in our pain-signalling systems. The ventral vagus nerve that is the key factor in regulating our fear-system responses also has an important role in inhibiting pain signalling throughout the nervous system. When the signal on the ventral vagus is weakened through chronic fear-activation, its ability to inhibit pain signals can fail, resulting in chronic pain conditions.[81]

Additionally, unregulated fear-activation can cause dysfunction in our systems of energy production. Sapolsky writes very clearly about the huge energy drain involved in repeated activations of fear-arousal. This is not just the considerable amount of energy required to fight or run for your life, but also the amount of energy taken up in the process of continually releasing nutrients into the bloodstream from storage-cells and then putting them back into storage if they are not burnt up in fight-or-flight, resulting in an ongoing energy deficit.

Fear-collapse also creates an energy deficit in the body as the metabolic shutdown disables aerobic (oxygen-based) energy production. This can leave us dependent on anaerobic energy production involving the production of lactic acid and then its subsequent reprocessing – a reprocessing which uses up more energy than is actually produced.[82] The energy-drain of the constant switch between fear-arousal and fear-collapse which is created when the fear-system cannot deactivate is likely to be a key contributor to energy disorders such as chronic fatigue syndrome.[83]

[81] Kolacz and Porges (2018).

[82] Myhill (2014).

[83] Gupta (2002). The other main contributor to chronic fatigue is viral illness, which also triggers metabolic shutdown (to enable the body to devote all its energy to fighting the illness), but when this continues for too long it creates the same ongoing energy-deficit as we have seen above. In many cases the chronic fatigue may have started with a viral illness but is then compounded by an overactive fear response experienced as stress. Similarly, an energy-deficit created by chronic fear activation will be compounded by viral illness.

So, the unregulated fear-system disrupts the normal functioning of many other biological systems. It can even affect cells at a genetic level by shortening the telomeres[84] which protect DNA during cell reproduction.[85] It can create chronic conditions of physical illness, pain and fatigue. These in their turn negatively impact a person's mood, mindset, ability to relate to others, to work and to earn a living, and thus their sense of personal autonomy and their ability to make changes to, or move out of, external circumstances that may be keeping them trapped in continuous fear-activation.

[84] DNA-protein complexes at the ends of chromosomes.
[85] Tyrka et al. (2010).

Chapter 10

Fear in the therapy room

How we notice the three main fear responses in ourselves as we work

Having looked at what happens in the body and the mind when the fear-system is activated, I now want to look at how we notice this activation in the therapy room. When we work with any level of trauma, we are working with fear, and most of the people we work with have some history of trauma whether or not this is clear from the outset. Our clients' autonomic nervous systems are often highly attuned to threat and prone to alarm, anger, withdrawal or collapse.

An important part of our work as therapists is to regulate these fear-responses as they emerge in the room and derail our work (I will look at this in more detail in Chapter 13). However, the task of therapy is not just about regulating our *client's* fear-system. There are always at least two sources of fear in the therapy room, the client's fear-system and our own. However calm and settled we might be feeling in our personal lives, our client's active fear-system will always trigger our own fear responses. As I said in the introduction, because we are highly social creatures, when we are with our clients, we are like two stringed instruments that resonate with each other. Before any conscious processing has happened, our body can react to our client's posture, tone of voice and micro-movements of the facial muscles, and trigger in us a fear-system response to the perceived threat of another person's dysregulation.

But it can get even more complicated than this. Before our client has arrived, we bring to the room the fear responses that may have been activated by the present stresses and worries in our own lives. If we are not in a calm state before we start the work, we are liable to be more deeply affected by our client's fear signals. On top of this, most of us carry our own unconscious trauma memories and hard-wired defensive reactions from the past. These are embodied in chronic tension or chronic states of hyper-arousal, immobilisation or disconnection and have shaped the way we hold our body and the way we move and speak. These may be so habitual that they do not enter our awareness, but they may render us more vulnerable to being triggered by our client's behaviour and by the material they are presenting, however well we may think we have processed our past history in our own personal therapy.

All of this just comes with the job, however, and in fact, our resonance with our client's feelings is essential to our empathic understanding, and to our ability to be of help.[86] As Wilfred Bion put it: '…in every consulting-room, there ought to be two rather frightened people…'.[87]

We need to help our clients to regulate their fear-systems in order to facilitate therapeutic change, but this is not possible until we have managed to regulate our own fear responses. It's similar to the safety instructions in a plane, where in the event of an emergency affecting our ability to breathe, we are told to fit

[86] Herman (1998) refers to the therapist experiencing 'to a lesser degree, the same terror, rage, and despair as the patient' as 'vicarious traumatisation'. I would not use the word 'traumatisation' in this context as for me this implies that such fear responses are stuck which is not necessarily the case with our 'mirroring' responses.

[87] Bion (1990), p.13.

our own oxygen mask first before trying to help anyone else with theirs. However, we can't start regulating our fear responses until we *notice* them and recognise how they are affecting our body. Let's now look at how we notice each of the different fear responses in the therapy room.

Fear-alert

Because we are in the presence of fear at all times in the work of therapy, fear-alert is the most common state we might find ourselves in, and each new subject matter, or shift and turn of the work, can re-trigger this state. The two main ways I notice this in myself is by monitoring my tension – observing my stiff, raised shoulders – and catching myself holding my breath. I might also notice a flow of anxious thoughts getting in the way of my ability to give the client my full attention, such as worrying that I can't remember some of the things the client has previously told me, or thinking I don't know what I'm doing, and worrying that my client might be getting frustrated or angry.

An important thing to consider here is that fear-alert is a *preparatory* stage of the fear response, involving no major changes in the body, but simply preparing it for sudden powerful action, should that be needed, or enabling a quick return to a calm state. That's a key point for therapists, because if we can catch the sensations of fear-alert in ourselves, and in those we are working with, we can quickly get back to a calm state and avoid going into fear-arousal, which could take the best part of an hour to recover from. All we might need is a slight movement of the body, letting the shoulders drop and taking a big deep sigh to break the tension, and we can then step back from fear-alert.

When we looked at the biology of fear-alert, we noted a higher startle response created by an increased signal to the nerves controlling the muscles of the arms and legs, and the withdrawal of signal in the ventral vagus nerve that puts a brake on our heart rate. It means our metabolism is now a bit like a car where we are revving the engine and have also taken off the handbrake, so that we can pull away suddenly.

This results in a highly volatile state, and in this state, any of the twists and turns of therapy can be liable to send us and our client into fear-arousal, or fear-collapse, which closes down any therapeutic work for some time. If we can constantly keep an eye on our bodily state and keep bringing ourselves out of fear-alert, we can stay in an exploratory mode for longer periods of time and get more effective work done.

Una McCluskey has developed a way of working in groups[88] in which the facilitator constantly monitors themselves and the group for signs of fear-activation and regularly brings this to the group's attention with brief statements such as 'tension down', or 'keep breathing' which invite all the members of the group to notice the fear-alert state and regulate themselves to a calmer place. This frequent attention to the fear-system creates a strong sense of safety in the group which enables a lot of deep work to be done far more quickly than would be expected in conventional groups.

Fear-arousal

Fear-arousal displays both in a highly active state (fight-or-flight) and in a locked and tense state ('freeze', culminating in 'fright'). As our work is mainly sedentary, fighting and running away are not typically available to us in the therapy room,[89] so I noticed my own fear-arousal here mostly as 'freeze'. The most obvious sign of this for me was tension, which can be difficult to distinguish from fear-alert, but in fear-arousal that tension is more intense, muscles are more rigid, and other signs such as raised heartbeat,

[88] Heard, Lake and McCluskey (2012).

[89] Though running out may be necessary in the face of violence from a client (which I have been lucky not to have experienced in 30 years of work).

sweating, dry mouth and nausea can accompany the tension.

While in fear-alert we might notice a level of mild anxiety in our thinking, in 'freeze' we are closer to severe anxiety, which may at times border on panic with our thoughts scrambling and our mind starting to go blank.

Few things are more liable to trigger a 'freeze' response in a therapist than a client talking about considering suicide. This is a complicated issue as the therapist's fears are powerfully amplified by a culture of fear in society generally and in the institutions that are involved in the aftermath of a suicide, so I will consider this issue separately in Chapter 21.

Even though we may not be running or fighting, we see aspects of 'fight' when we find ourselves getting angry with a client, or trying to control them in some way, and it can be easy to get into verbal 'fights' with clients if we lose our therapeutic balance. We might also notice a variant of 'flight' if we find ourselves avoiding engaging with a subject our client is trying to explore and diverting their attention to what is more familiar ground for ourselves. I wonder also whether overworking and intervening too actively or frequently in an attempt to 'fix' things, might be a form of fear-arousal.

Clients who behave in a dominant or bullying way can pose a huge challenge to the therapist, especially highly articulate clients who can use their intellect as a means of attack. In such cases it can be a huge struggle to regulate our fear-arousal response, and perhaps at times some of the energy of our own anger ('fight') response may need to be harnessed to meet the client with an equal energy in order to lay down clear boundaries of acceptable behaviour. I have sometimes found it really helpful to remind myself that, when I am working with a person in an aggressive or dominant state, I am sitting opposite a frightened person who has managed to survive by constructing a very imposing defensive shield.

When we looked at the biology of fear-arousal in the last

chapter, we noted that the amygdala inhibited the activity of the cortex, shutting down all activity not related to fighting or escaping a threat. This has a major impact on our ability to think and to be sociable, both of which have their control systems in the cortex. As far as thinking is concerned, reflective thought, including taking in and processing new ideas, is shut down. We can go into a flight-or-fight type of thinking, either avoiding anything that might be disturbing, or batting off anything new, becoming argumentative, and wanting our client to accept our viewpoint.

We might be more liable to go into a 'freeze', where often our mind will go blank, and as a therapist it is a scary experience to lose the ability to think in the middle of a session. At this stage, the only thing to do may be to let go of the content of the session and take time to attend to our own regulation. The most effective intervention may be to point out the fear dynamics in the room and invite the client to join with us in regulating themselves. We will talk about this more in Part 2 of the book, but I found that I was really helped in such circumstances if I had included some psycho-education on the fear-system at an early stage of our work.

Our client in fear-arousal will be similarly affected and may be incapable of taking in anything we might be saying, however objectively helpful we think this might be. New ideas will be perceived as a threat and effectively blocked, and any attempt by us to argue our point is simply a waste of time. Nothing useful can happen in working towards change until fear-arousal has been calmed.

I had an experience of this several years ago in a group setting in which I was a member, not the facilitator. I had made a clumsy intervention which had triggered another member's anger. Shortly afterwards a different group member questioned my intervention, which I then interpreted as a challenge. At the time I had a clear image of a solid band of steel round my forehead and the challenging words were hitting it and just pinging off. Nothing got inside and my focus was on fighting off the challenge and justifying my previous intervention.

In that moment I was in fear-arousal, (someone pointed out to me afterwards that I had suddenly flushed on hearing the question). I did, however, have a clear memory of what had been said to me, and a couple of hours later, when I was in a calm state, I was able to reflect on the question and admit that it had been a useful challenge and go on to explore it further in the group. The important issue from the therapeutic point of view is that no useful work was possible until I had physically calmed down and was no longer in fear-arousal.

The other impact of the amygdala inhibiting the cortex is that it compromises our ability to be sociable. When we go into fear-arousal as a therapist, we will start to see the client as a danger, someone who might attack or undermine us, threatening our sense of ourselves and our competence as a therapist. You might notice how hard it becomes to make eye contact with a client when we are in this state.

We also need to consider that whenever our client goes into fear-arousal we, the therapist, become the threat, and as long as their fear-system is too highly aroused, they will relate to us as a threat, and will be unable to feel any sense of connection to us. We might have been trained to think that our task as a therapist is to 'call our client into relationship', but when our client is in fear-arousal this can often have the opposite effect, particularly if we try to make direct eye contact. Eye contact can be a tricky thing to get right. In a state of calm, unbroken eye contact is a mark of intimacy and can be deeply satisfying, but in fear-arousal it will usually be interpreted as a challenge or an attack. We all know the danger of getting attacked if we inadvertently stare at a stranger in a pub for too long!

In regard to working with clients in a high state of fear-arousal, we could perhaps learn a lot from skilled animal charity workers who are trying to help terrified wild animals but can do nothing until they are sufficiently calm. They need to work patiently and slowly, not approaching or looking at the animal directly, but somehow gradually conveying a sense of being alongside as a predictable and non-threatening presence, without being intrusive in any way. I am not implying any difference between ourselves and our clients here. Each of us in a state of terror shares the same fear responses as other mammals.

Fear-collapse

When fear-collapse is present in the therapy room, the first thing I notice is my eyelids becoming really heavy, just as they do when I have been driving for too long and start worrying about falling asleep at the wheel. This is indeed very often followed by a fear of nodding off or conveying to the client that I'm tired of listening to them, as I struggle to stifle my yawns. The more profound the client's fear-collapse, the more tired we feel, and it can be experienced at times as a huge fatigue.

Alongside this fatigue, it becomes harder and harder to think. Our thoughts fog and slow down, and we lose all sense of the work we might have been doing. What thinking capacity we have left tends to hopeless thoughts, such as that we are getting nowhere, and that we are useless as a therapist. This often goes alongside increasingly anxious thinking that we have no idea what we are doing – we have lost our competence, and that the client will soon notice this and abandon the work or make a complaint. We may be further distracted as we sense the fear-collapse at a gut level, with feelings of nausea or discomfort and irritation in the stomach and bowels, and weakness in our legs.

We need to hold in mind that fear-collapse may be internally generated – for example, if there is major disturbance in our personal lives, or if the client is touching on matters that relate to a past disturbance of ours. More commonly, we might need to examine our own level of tiredness, especially if we are sleeping badly or overworking. Sometimes I realised that I *was* very tired, and I would respond honestly to a client who was very sensitive to such matters and questioned me on this. However, on many more occasions I would notice that it was just in sessions with a particular client that I would feel such overwhelming fatigue, and that in the sessions before, I had felt completely awake and on the ball. In those cases, I would conclude that my client was experiencing fear-collapse, and I would stop trying to work in an exploratory manner and turn my focus to regulating both myself and the client.

Fear-collapse in a client can be noticed in slight postural collapse, a flat tone of voice and an unmoving expressionless face. One clear sign that a client has gone into profound fear-collapse is that their face might suddenly go white (or a shade of grey, depending on skin tone). Another, which is even more shocking to witness, is that the client's face suddenly looks 10 or 20 years older. At this point, everything has to stop, and the focus needs to switch to trying to reverse the collapse.

We saw that the biology of fear-arousal severely inhibited our ability to function as a therapist, and our client's ability to work therapeutically, but the impact of fear-collapse is even more profound as it effectively paralyses the whole therapeutic process, disabling our ability to think and to socialise.

In fear-collapse there is a metabolic shutdown – a collapse of energy production throughout the body, and, as well as the physical sensations noted above, the brain cells in the cortex are de-energised, shutting down our capacity to think and our ability to relate socially. Additionally, powerful opiate painkillers are released into the bloodstream causing drowsiness and a numbing of feeling.

This means that, as the therapist, we lose the ability to connect empathically with the client as our feelings are numbed, and we become incapable of thinking. We lose the ability to pick up non-verbal social cues, so we lose our sense of connection to the client. We also find it hard to hear what they are saying as our eardrums lose the tension required to focus on the human voice.[90] What we do manage to hear we can no longer process mentally or remember.

> The first time I experienced this with any understanding of what was happening was in the same group as the one I mentioned previously, in which I made a clumsy intervention that prompted an angry response from another group member. I reacted to this response with a sense of shame, which I see as a fear-collapse response to being suddenly thrown out of connection to others. I certainly felt a collapse of energy, a downwards drop in posture and a slightly sick feeling in my stomach.
>
> What interested me most in the aftermath was the impact on my thinking. While registering that the group member was angry with me, I lost the ability to properly hear what was being said or to process anything I did hear. In contrast to the challenge that had triggered fear-arousal, where I clearly remembered the words and could reflect on them afterwards, in this case I was left with no recollection of what had been said, and no reflection on them was possible at a later period.

[90] Porges (2011).

Our clients will be similarly affected by a shutdown in their ability to hear, think and recall. I can remember so many occasions in my earlier years as a therapist, before I came to understand this, when I would get frustrated with clients who had absolutely no recollection of what I had said in a previous session, however deep and wise I thought it had been. I now realise that they had simply not been capable of mental processing at the time, and I had carried on blithely trying to help them to explore, oblivious to the fact that they had shut down and could no longer engage with the work.

I can also remember so many times when I struggled with exhaustion in a therapy session and didn't understand what was going on. One bit of psychoanalytic theory from my training proved useful to me (though I didn't properly understand it at the time). That was the idea that when (as the therapist) you felt profound exhaustion, there was 'anger in the room'. This actually makes sense from a fear-system perspective as a fear-collapse is usually preceded by a sudden fear-arousal, sometimes experienced as anger, even though this can at times be fleeting and go unnoticed. Also, as we saw in Chapter 2 (when the collapsed antelope noticed a window of opportunity to escape), fear-collapse can often be followed by a powerful fight-or-flight response, so a client can sometimes recover from a collapse in the therapy room with an outburst of anger or rage.

Conclusion

There are two key gifts that, as therapists, we are able to offer our clients. These are empathic connection and help with cognitive processing. The activation of the fear-system disables both of these, effectively shutting us down as a therapist. The most important skill we can learn is to notice this disabling process whenever it occurs in the therapy room (and it happens with great frequency) and to regulate our fear-system responses so that there is once again an effective therapist in the room.

Chapter 11

The prevalence of complex trauma in our society

Proposing the idea that complex trauma is ubiquitous as a normal condition of our 'traumatised species'

Viewing complex trauma from the perspective of the fear-system that becomes unable to goal-correct (to reset when it is not currently required) gives us a deep understanding of its nature and points towards a variety of ways in which it might be alleviated. It also raises the idea that complex trauma may be far more prevalent in our society than we had imagined.

We have seen that, when the fear-system cannot reset after a threat has passed, it creates an ongoing state of autonomic nervous system volatility which can involve a constant switching between fear-arousal and fear-collapse. We have seen that this is frequently expressed as anxiety and depression. We know that these conditions are very commonly diagnosed, affecting many millions of people, and this may just be the tip of the iceberg, with most of those affected not presenting themselves for a diagnosis, so I believe that very few of us are immune from some level of anxiety and depression in our lives.

There are many other manifestations of complex trauma which affect a significant proportion of the population. There are many whose fear-systems are stuck in a chronic fight mode. Some develop bullying, aggressive or even violent patterns of behaviour. Of these, those with fewer financial resources or social advantages form a significant part of the prison population. Some in chronic fight-mode are submissive in contexts where they feel powerless, such as the workplace, but then behave in a dominant and controlling manner in the home. Those who start life with more advantages can often manage to get themselves into positions of power and wealth through dominant and aggressive behaviour towards others, which our society mistakenly views as a sign of strength.

There are many whose fear-systems are stuck in patterns of flight or of fear-collapse, who either avoid getting close to anyone, or habitually submit to more dominant partners and never manage to fulfil their potential in life. There are huge numbers who try to dampen the emotional turbulence and misery of fear-system responses through a whole variety of addictions ranging from highly dangerous drugs to spending hours on social media or watching TV.

There are many millions whose unregulated fear-systems make the task of forming supportive relationships with others highly problematic. This can vary from domestic violence at one extreme, through a whole range of personality disorders and difficulties, to the day-to-day misery of bickering and unsupportive partnerships.

I would suggest therefore, that complex trauma is far more common than we think. We tend to associate the term with debilitating symptoms that shut down day-to-day functioning, but I would describe such symptoms as 'severe complex trauma' or 'complex-PTSD'.[91] In its less severe forms, I think complex trauma is ubiquitous – perhaps the most common state of modern-day humanity, and the result of countless generations of violent, brutal, oppressive, neglectful and shaming fear-driven behaviour. This may not entirely shut down our functioning,

[91] See Appendix 1.

but it certainly prevents us from living fully and fulfilling our potential, and it leaves us vulnerable to anxiety, depression and a multitude of relational, emotional and physical health problems.

Another way of looking at this, is to see humanity as a traumatised species, whose evolution as social beings is still far from complete.

Part 2

Working with the body

Chapter 12

Why we need to work with the body

The stuck fear-system is an embodied condition

Trauma arises from the automatic responses of the body to sensed danger. These responses, which I describe as the fear-system, are primarily physiological changes to the body, either acute reactions to threat, or chronic bodily states established over time. If we want to reduce the distress our clients experience when their fear responses activate, we have to help them to become aware of these responses, find ways of making changes to them, and find new ways of relating or reacting to them. One of the key things we learn from looking at the biology of trauma is that we need to work with the body.

This is necessary for a number of reasons. A key one is that states of hyperarousal or collapse paralyse emotional awareness, social connection and cognitive functioning, which are the very processes that make therapeutic work and therapeutic change possible. When our client's fear-system activates in the therapy room, effective therapy stops,[92] and we need to regulate fear responses before work can commence again.

[92] I am oversimplifying here for the sake of clarity. In the course of therapy, once an ability to regulate fear responses has been established, it can become possible for fear responses to activate and be sufficiently regulated to allow them to be reflected on in the moment.

When a client comes to see us in a state of fear-arousal, presenting with anxiety, panic or rage, other feelings may be numbed, and their thinking and social engagement systems are inhibited. The client is attuned to seeing us as a potential threat and cannot at this stage take in or process much of what we might say to them. The first thing we need to do is to help our client *down-regulate* their metabolism, slowing down breathing and speed of talking, reducing tension and helping them to bring their heart rate down.

When a client comes to see us in a state of fear-collapse, with the body in shutdown, and presenting with low mood, depression, dissociation or physical lethargy, their cortex is shutting down, they are losing the ability to hear and process information, and also the desire and ability to connect socially. In this case, we need to help them to *up-regulate* their metabolism, trying to enliven them, get them moving and raise their heart rate.

This regulating function was what Dan Siegel was addressing in his book *The Developing Mind*,[93] with his idea of the 'window of tolerance' (Figure 11). This refers to a metabolic state when our body is sufficiently calm for our social engagement system[94] and our thinking faculty to be fully functional.[95] The model of the 'window of tolerance' matches the diagrammatic way of representing fear-system activation which I have used

[93] Siegel (2012).

[94] Porges (2011). This is the biological system involved in sending and receiving signals of safety which enable us to engage with each other without activating defensive responses. The social engagement system allows us to give and receive care, share interests, work co-operatively, and establish and maintain affectionate relationships.

[95] Once again, an oversimplification. The window of tolerance varies from individual to individual. Some traumatised people have very narrow windows of tolerance, while those with strong ventral vagal regulation may have very wide windows of tolerance which enable them to experience certain levels of fear-arousal and collapse while still retaining an ability to relate socially and think reflectively. The expansion of the window of tolerance is an important goal of therapy.

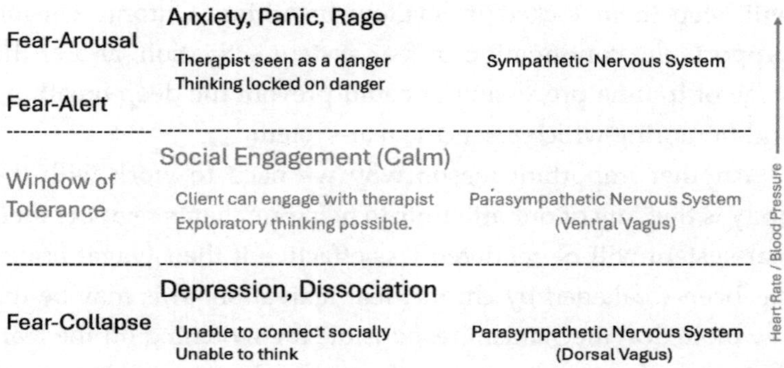

Figure 11: The window of tolerance

in Part 1. Within this window, we can connect with another person, and we can take in new information, reflect on it and integrate it. When a client comes to see us in this state, therapy is possible and the exploratory process that brings about real change can be active.

So, we have two very different tasks to undertake as therapists. First, if our client is not in the window of tolerance, our only task is to help them to regulate their body until they have calmed or re-energised sufficiently to allow them to enter this window. Once they are there, or if they start from that place, our task is to help them in their exploration. However, whenever that exploration triggers fear and throws them once again out of their window of tolerance (as will happen repeatedly in trauma therapy), we switch back to regulation until exploration becomes possible again.

A further reason we might need to work with the body is that many people with complex trauma suffer from chronic tension. In the early stages of the work this may undermine any of our efforts to regulate our client's fear responses in the therapy session – for instance, it may be impossible for them to slow or deepen their breathing as a chronically tense diaphragm will keep them locked in shallow breathing. Chronic tension supports the continuation of fear-system activation, and at the stage of trauma processing, it could prevent the deep breathing and tremoring which resets the fear-system.

Another important reason why we need to work with the body is that any of our attempts to help our clients regulate their fear-system will be rendered less effective if their 'vagal brake' has been weakened by chronic fear activation. This may be the key biological mechanism responsible for switching off the fear-system, so if we are to work with complex trauma, we may need to make use of the variety of ways in which the signal on the ventral vagus nerve can be strengthened.

Finally, when we work directly with a client's trauma, we often find that, in order for the fear-system to reset, the body may need to complete the initial defensive responses activated at the time of the trauma but then interrupted by fear-collapse. These are *physical* responses, such as the need to shout, run, hit, ward-off or tense the limbs against a blow. If we work just at the level of thinking and talking, and do not encourage an active engagement with the body, we can miss out on a crucial element of our client's recovery.

In conclusion, we need to regulate the body out of hyperarousal or metabolic collapse in order to make it possible for our clients to make use of therapy. I will look at how we go about this in more detail in Chapter 13. We may also need to encourage the reduction of chronic physical tension, which can prevent fear-system deactivation and block therapeutic progress. This will be examined in Chapter 14. Chapter 15 will consider ways of strengthening the signal on the ventral vagus in order to improve emotional regulation. Finally in Chapter 16 we will look at different ways to help the body to complete the physical impulses of defence as part of deactivating the fear responses. I will include brief case examples to illustrate these points.

Chapter 13

Regulating fear responses

Therapeutic progress is dependent on fear regulation

When I talk about regulating the body in order to help the client to recover the capacity to think reflectively and to engage socially, so that the work of therapy is possible, this is actually the essence of the first stage (establishing safety) of Judith Herman's three-stage trauma therapy model[96] (see Chapter 18). As I mentioned above, it has two aspects. If the client is in a state of fear-arousal, we need to *down-regulate*, to slow down metabolic activity. If they are in a state of Fear-Collapse, we need to *up-regulate*, to speed up the metabolism and enliven them.[97] I am going to look at a number of ways we can provide that regulation.

Posture

This may sound strange, but for me the starting point of regulation is the type of chair provided for both therapist and client. I began my career as a therapist using comfortable chairs

[96] Herman (1998). Stage 1, stabilisation (learning emotional regulation). Stage 2, processing the trauma to the point where it no longer activates the fear-system. Stage 3, reintegration – helping the client to reconnect to the world in a different way post-trauma.

[97] Preferably returning them to fear-arousal, as the only effective way of recovering from collapse.

with a slightly reclining posture and continued this when I set up my private practice, but once I discovered the importance of regulating the body, I switched to straight-backed chairs where it is possible to sit upright with a straight spine and find a point of balance where the weight of the head can be held without muscular tension in either the stomach or the back.

This is the posture I return to time and time again, whenever I need to regulate myself. It makes it possible to take deep breaths right down into the abdomen, so at any point in the work when I am noticing fear-activation in myself or my client, I will pause, recover my posture, take a deep breath and just notice the sensations of my body for a moment, and I will invite my client to do this along with me wherever this seems appropriate.

Getting grounded or centred

Some clients (in my own experience, particularly those with a severe trauma history), can react against any attempt to regulate them in this way, and this has to be accepted as necessary self-protection, and worked with patiently. However, particularly in the latter part of my career, I found it hugely helpful to start each client session with a period of regulation, allowing the body to settle and lasting up to three or four minutes. This can be very useful in helping the client to get straight on with the important issues for exploration rather than wasting a good deal of the session in summaries of events, lists of difficulties or long rants that can be hard to interrupt, that come from a mind in a state of fear-arousal rather than reflection. A description of such a 'grounding exercise' can be found in Appendix 5.

Psycho-education

I see psycho-education as an important part of 'working with the body'. If we want to use a grounding exercise at the start of sessions to help bring our clients to a place where they can be reflective and exploratory, and if we are constantly attending to our own fear-responses and inviting our clients to do the same, it's very important that we educate our clients in the operation of the fear-system, and simple practices of regulation right from the start of the therapy.

The physical responses of the body to trauma triggers can be deeply disturbing, but if we can explain them as biological processes, and go through the various sensations these can trigger, we can greatly reduce the disturbance they can cause.

> A client of mine with a history of childhood sexual abuse was terrified whenever her trauma was triggered, and her legs failed to support her. She thought she was going crazy, that she could not trust her body, and was afraid of leaving the house. She was hugely relieved when I explained fear-collapse to her as a biological mechanism with which her body was trying to protect her. She could then begin to tolerate these episodes so that they no longer created a vicious circle of triggering further fear activation.[98]

Even where I have been tentative in my thinking about what is happening, I have found it really beneficial to share my ideas on how my client's experiences might be related to the biology of fear.

> Another client had been deeply frightened by a diagnosis of cancer. After surgery she had been treated with intensive radiotherapy which had completely wiped her

[98] Levine (2010), p.58, notes that when you separate fear and other strong negative emotions from the biological immobility response, it 'breaks the feedback loop which rekindles the trauma response'.

out for weeks. Shortly after the end of the radiotherapy, she came to a session in great distress. She had exploded with her partner who had shown her great care during her treatment, losing herself with an intensity of rage she had never experienced before, and shrieking things about her partner that he found deeply hurtful. The experience shook both of them to the core. My client thought she was going mad and turning into an evil person.

At first I couldn't understand this at all, but when I started to think about it in the context of the fear-system, I wondered whether my client's outburst was the equivalent of a 'disorganised fight-flight' response following fear-collapse. Levine[99] notes that the greater the fear on going into fear-collapse, the more powerful and disorganised the fight-flight response is on coming out of collapse with a very limited sense of safety. This is perhaps the same mechanism that enabled the antelope to escape from the hyena (Chapter 2). I hesitantly shared this thought with my client, and she was greatly relieved and calmed very quickly.

A few months later, I came across the same reaction from another client who had had major surgery for cancer followed by chemotherapy. She too had been wiped out for a time but then, having finished chemotherapy, she lost her temper with her husband, attacking him physically. She had never behaved in this way before and was completely distraught in the aftermath of the attack. I shared the same idea with her, pointing out that this was a fear response she shared with the whole of humanity, and once again, this simple explanation of something that had made no sense produced great relief and calming.

[99] Levine (2010).

Chapter 13

Breathwork

One of the most effective ways of fear-system regulation is through attention to breathing. There is a close connection between breathing and heart rate, and breathwork activates the ventral vagus nerve which is so important to fear regulation.

It's always good to start in the simplest way with breathing, and nothing is simpler than to just breathe as it comes naturally to you without trying to make any changes, and then, for a few moments, just observe the sensations of your body as you breathe.[100] You can focus on the cool air entering your nostrils as you breathe in, and the warm air as you breathe out, and what that feels like in your nostrils and on your upper lip. This can have a very calming effect on the body.

When we notice the slight tension, holding the breath and slight rise in heart rate which indicate fear-alert in a session, all we might have to do apart from re-establishing our good posture, is to take a deep breath in and out – a big sigh. This acts as a 'kick on the vagal brake' and can bring us back into the window of tolerance. When we are working with trauma, we will be constantly tipped into fear-alert along with our client and may have to regulate in this way many times during a session.

As I noted in Chapter 8, each in-breath we take prompts the sympathetic nervous system to raise our heart rate, and each out-breath prompts the parasympathetic nervous system (via the ventral vagus) to lower the heart rate. This means that we can use our breathing as a means of regulating autonomic nervous system responses, such as fear-activation.

When we are in fear-collapse, we can up-regulate the metabolism with a series of long in-breaths followed by short out-breaths. This raises the heart rate and inflates the body out of collapse, helping to re-establish a good posture. For fear-arousal, when we need to down-regulate our metabolism, I use

[100] As in Anapana meditation.

slow equal breaths, or a pattern of shorter in-breaths and longer out-breaths, to slow down the heart rate. De Couck and others[101] note that both of these types of breathing increase the strength of signal in the ventral vagus nerve, as measured by increased heart rate variability.

The short in-breaths and long out-breaths that slow our metabolism down are the same patterns used in singing, which is why it can improve our sense of wellbeing, particularly when we sing in the context of a companionable choir.

It can be confusing at first trying to remember which way round these breaths go, especially as the activation of the fear-system will be interfering with our ability to think this through. I find it helpful just working in pictures, thinking of the lungs as a balloon which is deflated when our body posture is collapsed, therefore needing inflation (long in-breaths). With fear-arousal, where we can be over-breathing, I think of the balloon as being over-inflated and needing deflation (long out-breaths). However, when first working with a client with a severe trauma history, where they might not be able to take in much information, I found that the simplest and most effective approach was to keep in- and out-breaths at the same length, but to gradually increase the time taken with each breath. There is an example of working with this in Chapter 15.

Movement

Movement forms an important part of regulating our fear responses. In fear-alert, a slight movement that breaks the tension and re-establishes a good, relaxed posture, combined with a deep sigh, can be enough to restore the vagal brake and move away from a volatile state. In a less severe onset of fear-collapse, such as low mood or a mild depressive episode, inviting a client

[101] De Couck et al. (2019).

to get up and move about can be sufficient to raise their heart rate and blood pressure, which can help to reverse the start of a shutdown.

The most effective use of movement for regulation is rhythm. We have this built into our genes, and a young child in distress without the regulation of a caregiver will instinctively rock backwards and forwards to self-soothe. One of the regulation exercises I found most effective was a slow side-to-side rhythmic tapping of the knees with the palms of the hands which therapist and client can do together, keeping in time with each other. This combines soothing rhythm with bilateral stimulation[102] and can be used by itself to calm or can accompany the recall or the processing of traumatic events.

A very similar method is to use a juggling ball, thrown rhythmically from hand to hand. Andrew Austin has produced a very useful video[103] of this as an aid to working on anxiety, but it can be used as part of trauma processing in the same way as the knee tapping. Another rhythmic exercise that client and therapist can do together is a 'butterfly tap'. You cross your hands over your chest with the tips of your fingers touching the collar bone on each side, and then tap the collar bone rhythmically, alternating side to side. Several of my clients reported that this also helped them to get off to sleep at night.

Regulating ourselves

As we work to regulate our clients so that they can access the exploratory reflective thinking that is possible in the window of tolerance, it is just as important that we also work to regulate ourselves. It is a simple fact of human relationships that our bodily states are altered by the bodily states of those we are with.

[102] This also provides a useful variant to eye-movements in EMDR (Shapiro, 1995).
[103] See Appendix 5 for video link and information on obtaining the right sort of juggling balls.

Aroused clients will arouse our metabolism and collapsed clients will collapse our metabolism. Additionally, however advanced we might be on our therapeutic journey, there are few of us that do not have a number of triggers to our own past trauma that can be activated by our clients' stories or behaviours.

We will all be well acquainted with feeling tense and holding our breath when a client pushes us out of our comfort zone. We will all also have experienced times when it feels as if things are spinning out of control. This can happen if our client is angry with us or emotionally overwhelmed and we're not sure what to do or say next. We will all probably have experienced the sudden and surprising exhaustion that can come on us when we are with a collapsed or dissociated client, where our eyelids are drooping, and we are scared we might fall asleep. These are the moments where our fear-collapse response has been activated.

These are times when *we* are thrown out of our own window of tolerance and start to lose our capacity for reflective and exploratory thought and our ability to relate socially. In therapy, and particularly when we work with complex trauma, our first priority should be to regulate ourselves. Then, we can turn our attention to regulating our clients.

Coming from a psychodynamic training, where we simply sat and talked with our clients, and were not supposed to move or suggest exercises, I found it a huge adjustment to start working with the body, and it took me many years to work in this way with confidence. Strangely, it was the knee-tapping, which I picked up from one of my clinical supervisors, that I found hardest to put into practice. I think I was afraid of looking like a prat, but a lot of clients really took to it, and I regretted my delay in introducing it into my practice.

In the final years of my practice, I did a lot of my own regulation by working alongside my clients and mirroring all the activities I was asking them to do. It certainly helped to reduce my clients' sense of embarrassment if I was accompanying them in exercises such as breathing or tapping.

In Appendix 5, you will find further details of practical ways of regulating both yourself and your clients in the therapy session that I have picked up over the course of my career, used regularly in my work, and found to be extremely helpful.

One final point to consider when thinking about regulating our clients' fear responses, is the use of medication. This falls outside of our remit as psychological therapists, but there are many instances where anxiety is so acute, or depression seems immovable, and none of our attempts to regulate are making any difference, when we may need to recommend that our client consults their GP. If a suitable medication can be found without significant side-effects, this may be able to provide temporary regulation which restores the capacity to think reflectively and to socialise and thus makes the work of therapy possible.

Chapter 14

Reducing chronic bodily tension

Fear-system deactivation may require the release of chronic tension

Apart from physical regulation aimed at helping a client to stay within the window of tolerance, we may need further work with the body to help the fear-system reset in cases where chronic physical tension is blocking the body's ability to relax and thus contributing to the continuance of fear activation.

It has often been reported that deep tissue, or medium pressure, massage can, at times, have the effect of suddenly releasing emotions related to past disturbing events, or triggering lost memories from the past,[104] which can be related to the part of the body that is being massaged. This would indicate that emotional release and the recollection of past memory are obstructed by chronic tension in the body, and massage is a direct physical means of releasing this tension.

There are methods of working with the body which can be effective in releasing chronic tension without any physical contact being required. Let me give an example of this:

[104] See Tozzi (2014), who introduces a number of interesting theories about how this process might work.

A young woman who came to see me with anxiety and depression had become a premature caregiver to her depressed father and complaining mother in childhood. At the age of 12 years, she had had an accident where she was hit by a car. At the roadside, she was attended by the driver of the car who was furious with her, and by a highly distressed teacher who had told her it had been safe to cross the road. Later in hospital, she felt she had to convince her parents she was fine so that they would not be too upset. So, in the aftermath of the accident, there was no place of safety for her either by the roadside or in the hospital afterwards.

She was not long married when she came to see me, as thoughts about possibly having a baby terrified her and made her feel miserable. Thinking directly about her fears of having a baby got us nowhere, so we used a focusing-oriented approach.[105] This gives very slow and focused attention to sensations in the body. I helped her to alternate between noticing these sensations for protracted periods of time and then describing[106] them with no attempt to theorise or explain them.

My client noticed tension in her calf muscle in the leg injured in the car accident, and we paid attention to this for almost 10 minutes. Then, this tension dissipated and was replaced by a sensation of tension around her right shoulder blade. I encouraged her to focus on this sensation, once again, sitting with it and just noticing it and then trying to describe it. Suddenly there was an audible

[105] Gendlin (1996).
[106] Here I found the teaching, in Lawley and Tompkins (2000), on asking 'clean questions', which keep the focus on the client's experience rather than the therapist's assumptions, was extremely helpful.

'crack'[107] (which surprised both of us), and she reported the tension had gone from her shoulder.

From that point on, her level of general anxiety dropped significantly. Her mood improved and, over the next few weeks, she reported becoming able to state her own needs and establish boundaries with her parents. Shortly afterwards, she became pregnant, and we finished our work just before the baby was due, with her feeling more grounded and more mentally prepared for becoming a mother.

Up to this point, my client had been unable to relax and deactivate her fear-system even in the safe context of the therapy room because her body was chronically tense. However, when her muscles were able to fully relax following the focusing work, her fear-system deactivated, and her anxiety and depression dropped away. It is likely that chronic physical tension blocks the deep breathing and tremoring, which are the mechanisms by which the body naturally recovers from fear activation once the immediate environment is safe.

This raises the point that, in working with the body to overcome trauma, we have to acknowledge that important areas of this work are outside of the scope of talking therapies. We should be outward looking and encourage our clients to use a

[107] The 'crack' phenomenon was described by my client as being exactly the same as the crack she was familiar with when being manipulated by an osteopath. Osteopaths understand this as carbon dioxide and nitrogen being released from fluid in the joints (Protopapas, 2002). It would appear that the focusing technique can result in a similar release of muscular tension. In my practice, the audible crack has only happened twice (once in face-to-face work and once online), but, even without this audible indication, the experience of tension release after focusing work was common. As far as the nitrogen element is concerned, I wonder whether this is related in any way to the function of nitric oxide, an unstable molecule involved in the dilation of blood vessels, which is the key mechanism activating fear-collapse.

much wider range of resources. Complementary therapies such as massage (as indicated above), acupuncture or osteopathy may be necessary for some clients to give their body a chance of relaxing, and these can serve as a very useful adjunct to the work of psychotherapy.

Another helpful method to release chronic tension associated with trauma is TRE[108] (tension and trauma release exercises). These exercises are designed to activate the natural tremoring of the body as the fear-system 'resets' in the aftermath of trauma (as noted in Chapters 2 and 6). One of the exercises involves lying on your back on the floor with feet drawn up, soles of the feet held together, and the knees dropped out to the sides in a butterfly position. When you very slowly bring your knees towards an upright position, your thighs will start tremoring, affecting your whole body core. There is a global association of TRE practitioners[109] who provide support and training to emergency services first-responders, who are frequently working in highly distressing or dangerous situations. They also offer individual work which can contribute to the release of chronic tension.

Once you have been taught this method, it can be used thereafter as a regular daily exercise to reduce the impact of chronic tension on the body. I regret the fact that I came across this method after I had retired as a psychotherapist, as I would otherwise have been interested in training in it and experimenting with integrating it into my therapeutic practice.[110]

[108] Herold (2015) gives a simple account of David Berceli's development of TRE as a means of helping people to recover from trauma and gives a brief description of the exercises. PDF available at:
https://periodicals.karazin.ua/psychotherapy/article/view/5018/4656

[109] There is an introductory talk explaining TRE on
https://www.treaustralia.com/product/start-shaking-to-stop-ptsd-burnout/. The UK TRE website is https://www.treassociation.co.uk/what-is-tre/

[110] There is an introductory three-session online course at
https://www.trecourse.com/ as a taster to see if you'd like to take this further. This offers a three-tier price dependent on your income.

Chapter 15

Strengthening the ventral vagus

Simple ways to increase the regulating power of the ventral vagus nerve

I now want to look at the important role of the ventral vagus nerve and our need to strengthen its signal when we work with complex trauma. We noted in Chapter 3 how this nerve regulates our heart rate by sending a signal to the heart's pacemaker, which calms our metabolism. However, in fear activation this signal is withdrawn (or 'switched off'). Kolacz and Porges[111] note that where there are long periods of fear activation, this signal to the heart's pacemaker becomes weakened.[112]

Once this signal is chronically weakened, the autonomic nervous system becomes more volatile and the task of deactivating the fear-system becomes harder. This can seriously undermine therapeutic approaches relying on reason, narrative and building a therapeutic relationship, unless these are underpinned by a focus on reducing fear activation. We may therefore have to find ways of strengthening the signal in the ventral vagus nerve in order to regulate the fear-system.

I have already touched on the use of breathing exercises (see

[111] Kolacz and Porges (2018).
[112] I think of this as equivalent to the way in which a muscle will become weakened if it is not used for long periods of time.

pages 99–100) when talking about fear-system regulation. This is a powerful tool for the therapist, because slower patterns of breathing strengthen the signal in the ventral vagus nerve,[113] and increase the ability of the autonomic nervous system to regulate fear-system responses. Let me give an example of this from my practice:

> A young man who had recently left the army, presented with uncontrolled anger towards his children. This resulted in his wife telling him to leave home, though he was still of necessity involved in a certain amount of childcare. He had experienced three 'layers' of trauma – being held down to be anaesthetised in hospital aged 4 years, suffering physical violence from his father during his primary school years, including when he wet himself, and more recently, surviving a bomb blast when his armoured car hit a roadside device in Afghanistan. One of the main triggers for the rage that got him thrown out of the family home was when his 8-year-old son wet himself.
>
> I started by inviting him to work on his breathing as part of the stabilisation phase of trauma work. My client's breathing was shallow, with in and out breaths taking about one second each. We practised lengthening the time of each breath until we could slow his breathing down to 4 seconds for each inhalation and each exhalation. Then, I proposed he went about this like a military training and did not just practise once or twice a day, but 20, or 30 times a day, getting in a few minutes practice in every possible gap.
>
> At first, he only managed the breathing exercises a couple of times a day. However, after a week of this, he found he

[113] De Couck et al. (2019).

was able to notice the rise in his heart rate before his anger exploded, and he was able to get himself out of the room before taking it out on the children. He had previously told me that he had absolutely no warning of a temper outburst. This encouraged him to take the breathing seriously, doing the exercises even more frequently than I had suggested.

It was three weeks before he could see me next, and when he did, he was beside himself with delight. His 8-year-old son had wet himself, previously a key trigger for his rage, and he experienced no anger response whatsoever. He just said, 'Oh dear, let's get you cleaned up'. He described his son just looking at him in disbelief and saying, 'Aren't you going to shout at me, Dad?' Needless to say, I was delighted at the change, but a bit shocked and disbelieving, wondering how long it would last. With his immediate aims achieved, my client finished counselling at this stage, but his wife contacted me six months later and told me that his anger was still well under control, and she could completely trust him to look after the children.[114]

A caveat here – regulating breathing is not a magic bullet that immediately gives us control over our emotions. My client, in this case, was only able to deactivate his fear response triggered by his son's bedwetting because his intensive practice of slower breathing changed his *habitual* breathing patterns, thus re-establishing a degree of ventral vagal control over emotional volatility.[115]

[114] Contact several years later showed that the reconnection with his children which our work had enabled had been maintained and strengthened.

[115] I do not believe that this brief intervention alleviated the legacy of a long history of trauma; it did not preclude the need to seek help for other aspects of trauma in later years.

Furthermore, there is a key rule of thumb which is 'do not go against the body'. If the body is convinced that hyperarousal is required and we try to force our breathing to be slower, we'll find our heart rate will shoot up even further as our body tries to override our efforts. This is why breathing exercises need to be practised repeatedly *while we are in a relatively calm state*, in order to change the capacity of our autonomic nervous system to regulate volatility, and not just be used as a one-off when we are feeling panicky.

Regular practices that support changes in breathing, such as yoga and meditation, are known to strengthen the signal in the ventral vagus and thus calm the metabolism.[116] Singing, too, with its pattern of short in-breaths and long out-breaths has a calming effect and, over time, can help with emotional regulation, particularly when this takes place in the sociable context of a choir.

Moderate pressure massage, which we looked at in the last chapter, has also been shown to increase ventral vagal activity (and decrease cortisol).[117] It is also generally known that regular physical exercise is beneficial in reducing the symptoms of depression.[118] It would appear that regularly stimulating the sympathetic nervous system by physical exercise in a non-fear context increases the signal in the ventral vagus nerve[119] and thus exercise plays an important part in regulating fear-system responses.

Once again, this raises the point that much that is needed in the task of changing the default settings of our autonomic nervous system, in order to heal the impact of trauma, has to be found outside of the therapy room. Part of our task may be

[116] Gerritsen and Band (2018).

[117] Field (2014).

[118] Josefsson, Lindwall and Archer (2014).

[119] Measured as increased heart rate variability: Goldsmith et al. (1992); De Meersman (1993).

to educate our clients about the workings of the body and to encourage practices that regulate their fear responses. However, we share the responsibility for helping our clients to recover from the impact of trauma with practitioners from many other disciplines, whether these be yoga, meditation or TRE[120] teachers or masseurs, chiropractors and osteopaths, personal trainers or sports coaches. As psychological therapists we cannot do all of the work in healing trauma, though we might be the only ones in our clients' lives with something approaching an overview of this area, which can act as a map for their journey out of fear.

The issue of intensity

The remarkable outcome of my client's intensive breathing exercises in the above example got me thinking that, in working with ways to strengthen the regulating power of the ventral vagus nerve, I hadn't taken the issue of *intensity* of practice seriously enough. As a result, I encouraged my clients to practise such exercises more intensively, but the only client who got anywhere near to the striking outcome I've described, was another veteran well versed in military drill. It became apparent that, apart from those who had gone through rigorous training regimes such as the military, most people needed significant support to be able to sustain the amount of practice that would have such powerful results.

I was reminded of this after my retirement when I attended a 10-day vipassana meditation course.[121]

> This involved a rigorous and physically demanding regime carried out in 'noble silence' (no speech and no non-verbal

[120] See Chapter 14.
[121] https://www.dhamma.org/en

communication), with no contact with the outside world, no mobile phones, and no reading or writing materials. Each day started at 4.00 am and involved over 10 hours of meditation. I found the first few days gruelling but by the end, there was a marked difference – I had slowed down, was far more physically relaxed, lived more in the moment, worried less and was considerably more productive in the following months. These courses book up very quickly as changes in the participants are often very clear to their family and friends who then want to try it out for themselves.

In the same way as with my client, the course reminded me that intensive practice could have a relatively swift and significant impact on our autonomic nervous system, our chronic tension and habitual patterns of breathing. However, the intensity of the meditation course was only possible in the context of the all-encompassing support of its structure, the presence of the other meditators, and the volunteer 'servers' who provided our meals, so there was absolutely nothing to do but meditate. A major question for the client, the therapist, health services and society generally is: 'How might we be able to provide the level of support needed for intensive practice that can contribute to the fundamental physiological change that can help to release us from trauma?'

Chapter 16

Completing the body's defensive responses

Resetting the fear-system by reactivating trauma-related defensive responses

There is a further reason we need to work with the body with clients who have experienced complex trauma. When the body's automatic defensive responses to threat have been interrupted by fear-collapse, *completing the physical actions* of this defence can play an important role in switching off the fear-system. We saw in Chapter 2 that, when a prey animal has been caught and gone into fear-collapse, but a window of opportunity for escape has presented itself, the way out of immobility is through the reactivated fight-or-flight response.

Where a physical escape is not needed after an immobility collapse, there is still an impulse in the limbs to complete their defensive response. This can be seen in Peter Levine's[122] account of the aftermath of being hit by a car, in which he noticed the impulses in his arms to push out and protect himself from the impact. In one of his videos, Levine shows a National Geographic film of a polar bear being chased by a helicopter before being shot with a tranquiliser gun as part of a conservation monitoring scheme. As the polar bear comes out of the subsequent immobility

[122] Levine (2010).

state its shuddering takes the form of the running movements it was engaged in before being tranquilised.[123]

Levine uses such recovered defensive impulses in his somatic experiencing therapy. He sometimes gets a client to directly act out these actions – for example, by pounding on a cushion with their feet to replicate running. At other times he gets clients to notice the actions they want to make and then repeat these actions but slowing them right down.

However, it is not always necessary to physically replicate defensive impulses. Because there is an overlap in the brain between the neural systems controlling both imagined and actual movement, replaying these movements in the imagination can have the same effect as physical movement as far as switching off the fear-system is concerned.[124]

Several years before I came to understand this aspect of the fear-system, I was taught a method to alleviate depression by Yvonne Agazarian.[125] The method involved a detailed examination of the events leading up to a drop in mood, and very frequently it was possible to discover some event that had been experienced as a threat or a 'blow to the self' which had elicited an angry response, which Agazarian described as the 'retaliatory impulse'. In the moment, this response was often so fleeting as not to be noticed, but it would be followed immediately by a drop in mood.

The method involved inviting the client to notice and re-experience this retaliatory impulse, to give it a voice and act it out in the imagination. This would often result in the depression dissipating and a rise in mood. I now understand this method from the context of the fear-system. The retaliatory impulse

[123] Levine (2015), YouTube. Nature's Lessons in Healing Trauma: An Introduction to Somatic Experiencing® (SE™): https://www.youtube.com/watch?v=nmJDkzDMllcandt=858s The polar bear episode is between 10.58 and 14.10.

[124] Guillot et al. (2012).

[125] Agazarian (2004).

is a brief fight response that can quickly peak, triggering fear-collapse, experienced as depression.

The reason that this fight response may be so fleeting is usually to be found in the relational dynamics of childhood. Expressions of rage in infancy (so common around the age of 2-3 years) are often met by parental rage and punishment (or sometimes by parental anxiety or distress), so the infant becomes terrified of their own rage because it triggers such a frightening response. Subsequently, bodily sensations of rising anger can evoke body memories of the parental response, triggering a swift fear-collapse. Over time this can become the 'default' response to the arousal of anger.

The onset of this depressive collapse can be so rapid that the preceding sensations of rising anger or rage are not usually noticed. Where these can be noticed again and given space in the safer environment of the therapy room, the retaliatory impulse (the physical actions the body wants to make in response to the perceived threat) can be given expression in the imagination.[126] Thus, the fear response reaches completion, is able to reset, and the depression is resolved.[127]

Let me give an example of working with this retaliatory response:

> A young woman with an early history of emotional neglect, who had been driven from her job by a bully and abandoned by her husband, was forced to move to a different area and accept a job at a lower grade. She wanted to get a job at her original grade, but whenever she applied for a new job, she failed the interview as she went

[126] Or indeed expressed physically, such as by punching a cushion.

[127] This illustrates the necessity for us to go through fear-arousal in order to escape from the paralysis of fear-collapse.

into fear-collapse. Her body would feel small and weak, and her mind would go blank, leaving her unable to think. Another bully dominated her present team at work, and she felt powerless to voice her opinions.

I helped her to get in touch with her retaliatory impulses – what her body wanted to do in response to those who had mistreated her in the past. Shortly afterwards, frustrated by the workplace bully's dominating behaviour in a team meeting, she imagined herself slamming this person's head into the ground repeatedly with real force. The next moment, she found herself speaking out – she challenged the bully, survived the counterattack, and ended up with most of the team supporting her viewpoint.

Further work on the retaliatory impulse helped her to focus on tension in her arms – she wanted to really shake the first bully who had driven her out of her better-paid job, and I encouraged her to imagine herself doing this. Afterwards she reported she was much calmer and mentioned 'shuddering' in bed before falling asleep at night. Soon after, she managed two interviews without collapse and got a job at her original grade.

So, this is an example of a fear-arousal response that had been interrupted by collapse in the past, but when it was revived and the original physical impulses of defence were completed, it was instrumental in deactivating the fear-system. The shuddering in bed afterwards was the body's natural response of neurogenic tremoring,[128] restoring her to normal vitality after a long period of depressive immobility.

This principle of completing the physical actions of the

[128] Similar to the antelope's tremoring in Chapter 2.

original defensive response underpins the effectiveness of many other ways of working in therapy that encourage the expression of anger in a safe context.

Important note about the retaliatory impulse

It is very common for people to be scared by the violence, power and brutality of our retaliatory responses, and many people will not admit to such imaginings, even to their therapist, incorrectly seeing them as evidence that they are a bad or a 'sick' person. As therapists, it is important that we treat our own retaliatory impulses as morally neutral, neither good nor bad, just useful information arising from our fear-system over which we have no control. We exercise control in not *acting out* these impulses on others, but if we can accept the imaginings they generate without fear, these can become a pathway to recovery from depressive collapse. We can then educate our clients and help them to be less scared and ashamed of their retaliatory impulses and be able to use them in our work to deactivate chronic fear responses.

Part 3

Working with complexity

Chapter 17

The problem of complexity

Working with the tangle of problems created by complex trauma

We saw in Part 1 that when the fear-system cannot reset and remains continually active over time, this disrupts many other systems and areas of life, triggering a whole series of difficulties which can include emotional turmoil, chronic illness and disability, personality, behavioural and relational problems, social disadvantage and poverty. Problems in each area continuously compound the difficulties in other areas, creating a tangle of dysfunctionality which becomes progressively harder to alleviate over time.

This was illustrated by the example I used in Chapter 4, which I will repeat here:

> Laura's biological father left before she was born, and her mother was self-absorbed and neglectful. Laura felt there was no point trying to seek care, so she became self-reliant at a very young age. Dyslexic and emotionally troubled, she was dismissed by her schools as a failure despite being highly intelligent. Her stepfather sexually abused her, resulting in a traumatic abortion in her teens.

In adult life her partners were dominant and violent, and she found herself as a single mother of four children struggling to make ends meet. She suffered flashbacks that could leave her physically collapsed for hours, anxiety, panic attacks, depression, agoraphobia, chronic back pain and low energy. Many of the people she thought of as friends disappointed her. They relied on her support, but when she needed help, they weren't there for her, leading to friendship rifts.

For years she was unable to work because of the level of her anxiety, so she was trapped in a hostile benefits system that intermittently pulled the rug out from under her. She found herself having to live in substandard housing with bullying neighbours, which caused her great distress. She was very easily triggered by disappointment and would reject those who were in a position to help her at the first sign that they might let her down, leading to fallouts with police, advocates, support workers and doctors.

Laura worked with me for over 10 years. Progress was very slow, sometimes just focused on getting by day to day as her external environment threw up so many disturbances for her.

By the end of the therapy, Laura had a good understanding of her body's defensive reactions and she was no longer scared of them. She had a stronger sense of self, and was in a long-term affectionate relationship, but she still faced many of her old difficulties, and while much better at regulating her fear responses, she still had to deal with much emotional turbulence day to day.

Chapter 17

Trying to help clients like Laura who struggle with so many difficulties is complex work, which is very hard to undertake. I think, however, that there will be few therapists who have not experienced working with clients with similar difficulties. We work with biological reactions, volatile emotional states and problematic thinking processes, patterns of behaviour, relationship dynamics and social and environmental difficulties. These aspects cannot be worked with in isolation as they are constantly interacting, with problems in one system often undermining progress in another.

What I have learned over a number of years working with this level of complexity is that:

- Judith Herman's three-stage framework is helpful in navigating the complexity of complex trauma
- we have to work at the speed of organic change and there are limits to the changes that can be made
- we work with constant setbacks, and have to navigate the emotional impact of this on ourselves and on our clients
- we need to be well supported in the stress this creates and particularly when working with suicidal clients
- we need to work on many fronts to match the complexity of complex trauma
- we have to work within our own competence and try to avoid becoming discouraged.

I will look at each of these points in the following chapters.

Chapter 18

The three stages of trauma work

Judith Herman's trauma framework

Judith Herman[129] provides us with a useful three-stage framework for working with trauma. The first stage is concerned with the establishment of safety, the second with 'remembrance and mourning' (I would describe this as the 'trauma processing' stage), and the third stage is focused on 'reconnection with ordinary life'. She points out that the work must be appropriate to the client's state of recovery, and that ways of working from one stage may be unhelpful or even harmful when the client is in another stage.

Stage 1 – Establishing safety

If a person does not feel safe, their fear-system will not deactivate. If we work with them in ways that reconnect them to a trauma (for example, asking them to describe it to us) while they are feeling unsafe, there will be no trauma processing or healing, only a repeat of the unbearable feelings that will make things worse. That is why Stage 1 is essential – a client needs to feel 'safe enough' before we can work directly with their traumatic

[129] Herman (1998). A brief and very clear article that gives an excellent overview of the whole process of trauma work.

experiences. This includes their own body and mind feeling safe enough, and the environment in which they are living and working feeling safe enough.

Stage 1 includes all the work on regulation I have touched on in this book (and summarised in Appendix 5) which can be used by the therapist to calm fear responses (and re-vitalise after a collapse), making the body feel safer. These can then be used by the client for self-regulation. It also includes paying attention to the client's environment and, at times, it may be necessary to work with the client to help them to formulate and carry out decisions, such as trying to make changes – for example, in controlling or abusive relationships or toxic workplaces – or, where changes can't be made, leaving them and finding a refuge, a new home or a new workplace.

Some clients have such a tangle of difficulties, and so few resources to call on, that major changes that might reduce fear in their lives seem almost impossible, and as Herman points out, in such cases Stage 1 work can last from months to years.

Herman notes that this stage needs to start with a thorough initial assessment. This will give a sense of the scale of the work, the magnitude of internal and external threats, the different levels of trauma from different life stages, and it will help us to evaluate whether we have the required skills and knowledge for the task. There is no shame in deciding we are not the right therapist for a client and helping to signpost them to someone who is better suited to working with them.

Stage 2 – Trauma processing

Herman's second stage, of remembrance and mourning, mainly reflects a narrative approach to trauma processing – the client telling their story in some detail, allowing for reflection and re-evaluation. The reflection invariably touches on how much of a client's life and life opportunities were lost as a result of trauma, and time is required to mourn this loss. In the years since Herman formulated her three stages, there has been a huge growth of body-based ways of working with trauma, and I am a great enthusiast for these approaches, but we should not throw the baby out with the bath water in our excitement over new ways of working. From time immemorial, human beings have wanted to tell their stories, and it remains an important way to process trauma once safety has been established.

There are now many other ways of working directly with trauma in Stage 2, and I will touch on a few that I have found most helpful in Chapter 22. I used these in my work interwoven with a narrative approach depending on what felt most appropriate for each client.

Stage 3 – Reconnection

Stage 3 is perhaps the least examined of the stages, but it is hugely important in preventing a relapse back into being trapped in our fear responses. Shifting out of a chronically active fear-system into a less fearful and more socially engaged state is an enormous adjustment. The fear-system has been the water we have been swimming in and suddenly we are a fish out of water – we need to find a new sea to swim in. Whether we can maintain this adjustment and continue to live with less fear will depend a great deal on the context of our lives.

Our old social networks and relationships may have played a part in keeping us in a chronic state of fear activation, and we may need to make connections that help to sustain our new state of being. We may need to re-evaluate our social networks and relationships, considering where we might be able to influence others to change, or where we might need to draw back and find new means of support. The more we need to break away from relationships and groups that keep us trapped in fear, the greater the need we have for the support of other fellow travellers who are also making the transition from fear to a more socially connected life.

For this reason, I think that group work might be a more useful approach than individual therapy at this stage of the work, provided that all the group members have worked sufficiently on the first two stages. For us as therapists, a supportive group of colleagues who can meet and share at a personal rather than just an intellectual level, can make a huge contribution to our own journey out of fear.[130]

When we emerge from the grip of chronic fear, our thinking about ourselves, and our assumptions about our place in the world and how we find meaning in our lives changes radically, and we need help to create a new framework of meaning and connection.[131]

The 'interweave' of the stages

There can be a danger that Herman's stages are seen in a purely linear way, which would imply that the entire task of establishing safety has to be completed before trauma is directly addressed. Herman does note that a reasonable level of stabilisation should be reached before Stage 2 work is attempted, but from this point the work enters a sort of backwards and forwards 'weave' of the stages. We manage a 'good enough' attempt at each stage and move between the stages in attunement with our clients' needs. When the newness of change triggers fear responses, we go back to Stage 1 until if feels safe enough to move forward again. This will be illustrated in Chapter 20.

[130] This is discussed further in Chapter 32.
[131] Dolinsky (2020).

Chapter 19

Working at the speed of organic change

Understanding and working with organic changes in the body

Each bodily sensation we have, each feeling, behaviour or thought, arises from neurons (brain cells) firing in a particular pattern of connection. In the case of complex trauma, our fear reactions reflect patterns of strong 'hard-wired' connections that are not easy to change.

This means that working with complex trauma is a bit like trying to change the direction of a river which has been flowing in its bed for hundreds of years. Physiological reactions, feelings, thoughts and behaviours become engrained over the years when there has been no place of safety following threats. When we work in therapy, we are starting to calm our clients' bodily reactions and to help them to explore new ways of thinking, feeling and behaving. It's as if, working from the 'old river', we are together digging out an alternative channel for the water to flow along, but the new channel is not very deep and not much water will flow that way at first.

If we keep on with this work, repeating our efforts to calm the fear-system, helping our clients to manage their feelings, to do different things and to think differently, the channel deepens a bit more, and more water flows in the new direction. Over time, the channel widens and deepens further, and more water flows this way.

So, in the brain, as we work in therapy, new pathways are created between neurons, and these connections are strengthened with repetition and these new ways of thinking and feeling and doing gradually become slightly easier. However, the old riverbed is still there, and a lot of water still flows in the old direction.

How change works in the brain

My understanding of the way change works in the brain as we process traumatic memories is as follows:

- Trauma memories are held in the brain in networks of brain cells (neurons) which 'fire' between each other in a particular pattern of connection when they are activated.[132]
- It is possible to make changes to these trauma networks, but they can only be changed when this pattern of connections between the neurons is activated, and the memory is 'unlocked'.[133] This can happen when the memories are triggered by external cues, or when there is a deliberate attempt to recall them.
- When activated and unlocked, new experiences which contradict or disconfirm the survival-based learnings of the original trauma(s) can change these trauma networks. For example, the experiences within therapy of feeling safe[134] or having competence affirmed, or gaining a new perspective on the initial trauma, can

[132] Lewis, Amini and Lannon (2000).
[133] Nader, Schafe and LeDoux (2000).
[134] Rothschild (2000), p.82. 'Attention to the therapeutic relationship will, with some clients, help to transform negative implicit memories by creating a new encoding of a positive experience of attachment.'

be 'added' to these networks as an extension to the memories, gradually changing them.

- Networks remain active for about five hours then deactivate and cannot change until activated again.[135]
- Over time, when repeated activations are processed in safe contexts, traumatic memories are 'softened' with the addition of more benign associations.
- These changes to the trauma networks dampen their emotional charge and, at a certain point the activation of these networks, will no longer trigger a fear-system response that cannot be regulated. Once the fear-system can regulate, trauma symptoms disappear.[136]

I have tried to put this into a diagram which might make it more digestible. Figure 12 is a crude, and massively oversimplified, attempt to picture the development in therapy of the neural networks[137] (the patterns of firing between different neurons) in which the traumatic experience was encoded.

It starts with a representation of the pattern of the original trauma which is then deactivated as a stored memory. When reactivated in a safe context in therapy, this safe experience and any resultant changes become part of the original network, which then deactivates after a few hours. The repeating of this process over time changes the trauma memory and lessens the impact of its reactivation. However, we are biological organisms, and we must work at the pace of organic change. We may well see sudden change when a trauma network is altered to the extent that it no longer triggers a fear-system response which cannot be regulated, but with complex trauma it can sometimes take a long time to get to that point.

[135] Ecker, Ticic and Hulley (2012).
[136] On this point I disagree with Ecker, Ticic and Hulley, (2012) – see Appendix 6.
[137] The actual neural networks involved are vastly more complex.

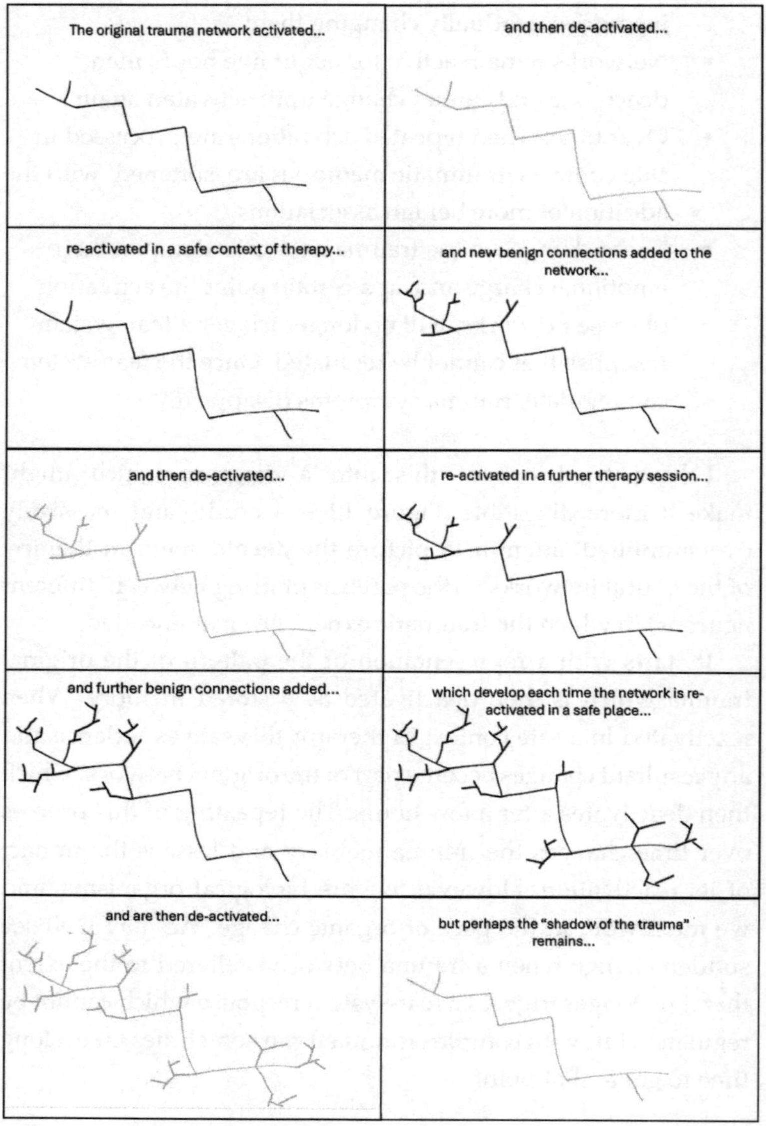

Figure 12: Changes to trauma networks during therapy (a pictorial representation)

Chapter 19

Limits to the changes that can be made

However much we manage to change traumatic memories, 'coating' them in more benign associations, diminishing their power to the extent that they are no longer able to keep the fear-system on permanent alert, there are limits to the changes that can be made because, at the core of that altered memory is the original memory, the original pattern of neural firing.

A client of mine had seen a spiritualist before coming to work with me; the spiritualist told her that a malevolent spirit had been persuaded to leave her, but that it had left a space, which would continue to resonate throughout her life. My client had found this a useful metaphor and had called this space (the ongoing impact on her of her deeply envious and destructive mother) the 'shadow' of the spirit.

The concept of the shadow came back to my mind as I played with my drawings, trying to describe the process of change during trauma therapy. It seemed to me the perfect word for describing that original memory pattern at the centre of the altered memory – the shadow of the trauma.

This then started to make sense of an idea that had been growing on me, based on my experience of working with many clients, and on my experience of my own long (and still incomplete) journey out of unnecessary fear. I suspect that once we have had a traumatic experience and, for a time, our fear-system has been unable to deactivate, when we do manage to reach a place in our life where our fear-system can reset, this may be a temporary victory. I think that once our fear-system has failed to deactivate properly for a time, we may tend to get stuck again in chronically active fear mode when we encounter serious threats and blows to the self in the future.

I now think about this tendency as 'the shadow of the trauma' and suggest this idea to balance what I see as over-optimism in

Ecker, Ticic and Hulley's[138] theory of the permanent erasure of trauma memories. (I have noted my disagreement with their theory in Appendix 6.) As I see it, there is never a complete cure. However, there is the possibility that over time the impact of past trauma will diminish, and we will become able to live our lives more and more fully.

[138] Ecker, Ticic and Hulley (2012).

Chapter 20

Working with constant setbacks

Sustaining the therapist and client through the setbacks of trauma work

We looked previously at the metaphor of an old river to try to understand organic change, but in our work with complex trauma we are working with a number of these old 'river systems', not just one. We are working to change bodily and emotional responses, defensive patterns of behaving and relating to others, old ways of thinking about ourselves and others, and to encourage changes in our clients' external environments.

Each part of each aspect of these patterns is like a separate 'old river' requiring persistent work to change the direction of flow, but with complex trauma, progress in one area can so easily be derailed by problems in another.

My work with the client I spoke of in Chapter 17 is an example of this.

We encountered many setbacks in our work together. Over a number of years, Laura made impressive progress in being able to regulate her fear responses, but time and again adverse events from many areas of her life triggered old defensive responses of rage or collapse, making it feel for a time as if all progress was wiped out.

For example, on several occasions in the time I worked with her she got a letter out of the blue telling her she was no longer entitled to the benefits she relied on. On each occasion she appealed, and she won all her appeals, but the cost in stress and emotional exhaustion was huge.

Other setbacks were triggered by a bullying neighbour trying to turn her whole street against her, her son falling out with her and refusing to let her see her grandchildren, and the Crown Prosecution Service suddenly deciding to drop the case against her stepfather (she got it reinstated on appeal). The greatest source of setbacks in our work was the constant mishandling of her case by the police, with long periods of bureaucratic inaction interspersed with demands for more evidence and further statements which seriously retraumatised her.

What I have described here are only the *external* setbacks – the adverse life events which can be multiplied by the effects of complex trauma. In addition to these setbacks are those created by *internal* defences against intolerable experiences built up over the years. Our fear-systems are finely tuned from past experiences to react to threats in the present as if we were still in the context of the past. Any therapeutic change will upset the balance of these defences, opening up vulnerabilities which can then trigger old fear-system reactions. Where these reactions are powerful, as they are with complex trauma, this creates a 'pendulum effect' in trauma work as any significant progress triggers old fears.

This is illustrated in Figure 13. We start with our client's old

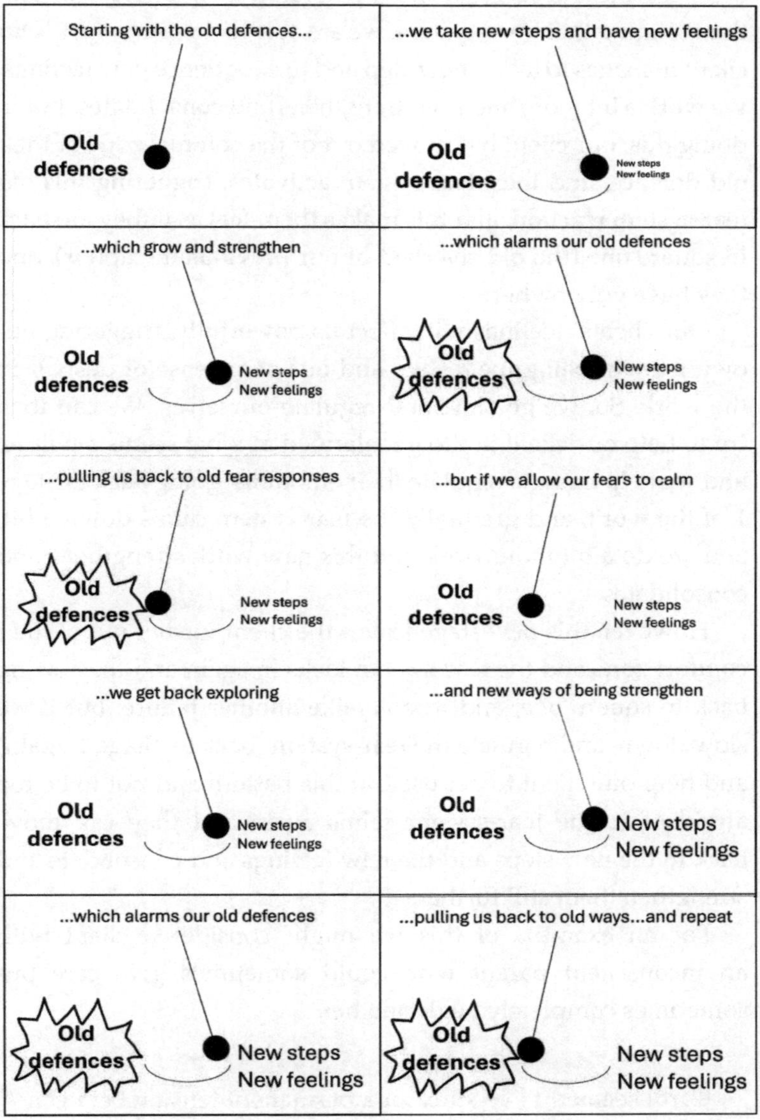

Figure 13: The pendulum of complex trauma work

defences and old feelings and, by helping them to feel safe and thus calming their fear-system, we are able to do some work. Our client manages to take a new step and to experience new feelings. We work a bit more and this strengthens and consolidates. But in doing this, our client has moved out of the comfort zone of their old defence, and their fear-system activates, triggering this old fear-system reaction, and this makes them feel as if they are back to square one (the old riverbed of our previous metaphor), and they have got nowhere.

Our clients' feelings will affect us powerfully, triggering our own fears of being ineffective and our own sense of despair in the work. So, we go slow and regulate ourselves. We can then try to help our client not to get alarmed at what seems a failure, and we help them to regulate their emotions, going back to Stage 1 of the work, and gradually the fear-system calms down a bit, and we do a bit more work and this new work strengthens and consolidates.

However, this new stage leaves the client further out of their comfort zone and the fear-system kicks in again and they swing back to square one, and it looks like another failure, but if we slow down, and regulate the fear-system (back to Stage 1 again) and help our client to get used to this pattern and not to be too afraid of it, the fear-system calms again and they can move back to the new steps and the new feelings and consolidate and strengthen them still further.

For an example of this we might consider a client with an inconsistent parent who could sometimes give care but sometimes completely neglected her.

> Carol seemed to be stuck in a permanent tension between really needing the care of others and yet being really scared of receiving care and she had a history of pushing potential

friends and partners away, leaving her isolated and depressed. She loved the session we had when I explained the biology of the fear-system which made sense to her of so much of the emotional turbulence she experienced.

She found the breathing exercise at the beginning of the next session really calming and began to reminisce about times she had felt her mother had really given her care and attention, and how hurtful it had been when she had got a new partner, and Carol had felt pushed aside and ignored. We started to think about how helpless she had been then with no one else to turn to for care and then to think what was different about her current situation as an adult with her present resources, and how she might be able to get her needs met. She was very cheerful and energised at the end of the session and thanked me for my help.

I was really looking forward to picking up this work next session, but a couple of days before the session I got a brief email from her cancelling the appointment, saying she had put a cheque in the post for it, but that she felt quite disturbed after the last session and thought it better to stop counselling for the moment.

I emailed her back and reminded her of a previous conversation I had had with her in which I told her that when we made real progress it might be followed by a negative reaction. I acknowledged her cancellation but said I would be available for our next planned appointment and would be delighted to see her if she felt able to come.

Carol did come to the next session and described what had happened after the previous one. She had been feeling really pleased with her work and started thinking how she liked coming to see me and how good it was finding someone who could really listen to her. Then one of the voices in her head started up – 'Stupid idiot! You know he's only doing it for the money – he doesn't give a shit about you!' Suddenly Carol felt embarrassed and ashamed for having trusted me and then felt really flat for days and hadn't been able to face coming to the next session.

Sometimes when we make progress with getting in touch with previously disallowed feelings, this touches on very powerful old defensive reactions.

I worked for a time with Mark who came to me feeling flat and energy-less and frustrated at being constantly criticised by his wife for all the things he did wrong. I wondered what happened to his anger, as there was no sign of it in any of his interactions with others. I explored what he felt when his wife criticised him and, at first, he couldn't really say – it just seemed like a blank.

Eventually he admitted to a bit of irritation, and we worked on this for a while, wondering what he wished he'd been able to say at the time. After some weeks working on this, Mark got to the point where he could get properly annoyed at being told off and was able to raise a forceful objection and tell his wife to stop it because it made him feel like shit. His wife was really surprised and said she wanted him to stand up for himself – she'd been really frustrated that he was always so passive. Mark was really pleased with the work and the improvement in his relationship with his wife. He liked it that he could get annoyed. However, a couple of weeks later his boss at work made a dismissive comment about him in a meeting. Mark felt a surge of anger, then went into panic, and his legs felt weak. The next day he couldn't go into work, and he was signed off with depression.

It was hard getting back into the counselling as Mark was at first too depressed to continue. However, he responded well to the antidepressants his GP prescribed and a few weeks later got in touch again and came back to see me. We spent some time considering why his boss's comment had had such a powerful effect on him.

Eventually he recounted a story his mother had told him, that when he was a 2-year-old he'd had an enormous temper tantrum in a shop when out with his father. His father had been furious, called him a stupid baby and took him home and gave him a real beating. We worked out that the sensations of a surge of anger towards his boss might have triggered body memories of his early angry outburst and the beating that had followed. This made sense of him going straight from anger into panic followed by collapse, which is how in the past he'd got stuck in passive responses and lost the ability to get angry.

The progress he'd made getting in touch with his anger in the safer context of his relationship with his wife had pushed him out of his default defence, but being in touch with his anger with his boss who had real power over him had strongly triggered this old fear-collapse defence. With this understanding, we were able to do some work on expressing what he really wanted to say to his boss in a progressively louder voice and track and complete the impulses of his arms as he wanted to hit out in rage.

After a couple of months Mark was not only able to return to work, but he felt more assertive and more sure of himself than he had been previously.

When we make real progress in our work with clients, we are helping them to override defences that have protected them for many years, but they are stepping into new territory, and it takes some time to establish new defences. This sense of vulnerability means that any threat can powerfully activate the old defence, and this appears to wipe out all the new work. However, despite such apparent setbacks, the new neural wiring from the therapeutic work remains in place and can be returned to and consolidated once the fear reaction has been calmed.

When we think of the metaphor of the river, the back and forward pendulum of trauma work, the slow organic process of neurological change and the limitations that there might be to the work because of the 'shadow of the trauma' (Chapter 19), it is really important for us to prepare our clients for the journey they are undertaking and explain all of this to them.

This will make it less likely that they abandon the work because of quite normal setbacks, and once they have completed a piece of work, they may be more alert to the impact of negative life events which could throw them back into chronic fear-system activation. This will make it more likely that they will take steps to self-care, to seek care from others, and perhaps to periodically return to a familiar therapist for further help in regulating their fear-system.

Chapter 21

Fear and the suicidal client

Surviving the stress of working with the risk of suicide

Progress towards change in complex trauma is fraught with difficulty and stress, and one of the most troubling areas is working with risk. In many different contexts, from working in the health service to private practice, we may find ourselves working with self-harm, eating disorders, drug taking, reckless behaviour and safeguarding issues. Few things, however in my experience, throw the therapist more powerfully into fear than working with a client who may be considering the possibility of suicide. It is unlikely that any therapist will avoid this experience, and for some it may be a regular part of their work.

We live in the context of a society that is prone to look for someone to blame when things go wrong. This means that the distress of a therapist, who has been trying their best to help a client who kills themselves, is compounded by being subjected to a blaming attack, and possibly having to undergo stressful and time-consuming enquires. The health service and many agencies are terrified of suicide and as a result therapists are often not adequately supported in the aftermath. This level of fear can also be highly detrimental to clients – I have heard accounts of clients being discharged at the first mention of suicidal thoughts without a careful enquiry to establish just how serious the risk might be, and without services available to take on their care.

While some of my clients expressed suicidal ideation, I have been lucky that none actually took their own lives while working with me, though one young man did so a year after finishing a brief piece of work. I had a long talk with his father who contacted me to give me the news, and we tried together to make sense of what had happened, with limited success. What follows are my reflections on what I learnt over my time in practice, which I have divided up into what we may be able to avoid, what can't be avoided and the need to seek care, concluding with some brief reflections on suicide viewed from the perspective of the fear-system.

What we may be able to avoid

What we may be able to avoid, particularly if we work in private practice or in organisations that take our codes of ethics seriously,[139] is working with levels of risk for which we are not trained or not fully supported. Therapists are often approached by potential clients who have very poor emotional regulation and a history of serious self-harm and suicide attempts. While it may be possible to offer therapy in a health service context which has the back-up of crisis or community mental health support, it could be unwise for a therapist in private practice to take on such work.

Counselling and psychotherapy, particularly in private practice, should always assume a certain level of client self-regulation. Such therapy can be effective when a client can cope reasonably well between weekly sessions without unscheduled

[139] Unfortunately this category does not appear to include the NHS. I have been informed by colleagues that clinicians in the NHS are often asked to hold more risk than is safe to hold and may not be able to avoid this without facing coercion from managers. There is an example of this in Chapter 31.

support from the therapist and can keep themselves safe during this time. Where this is not the case, what may be required is mental health nursing; in other words, clients need someone who can respond to them in crisis, sometimes visiting them at home, with the back-up of psychiatric support if necessary. The reality that this is not always available in the present underfunded NHS does not take away from the fact that psychological therapists are not always trained, equipped or adequately supported for offering hands-on crisis care, and offering it could be harmful to both client and therapist.

To avoid offering therapy where this is unsuitable, it is important that we undertake an assessment with every person seeking our help. Some counselling trainings do not cover an assessment model, which is regrettable. I think that it is essential for anyone in private practice to assess those who approach them for help. In an assessment we are simply trying to find out whether we can provide what the potential client really needs, and whether they can make use of what we have to offer.

Issues of risk can be introduced with a general question, such as: 'What have you been like when you've felt at your worst?'. If a potential client's answer to this question contains veiled hints of suicidal thoughts, I think it's really important that we don't ignore these hints, and fail to confront the seriousness of the issue, but invite the client to be specific.

If there was evidence of suicidal thinking, I would ask whether the client had ever attempted suicide in the past or made any plans for suicide, and how recently this was. Both making plans, and a history of previous attempts, indicate a higher suicide risk, and although people can threaten to attempt suicide as a way of signalling their need for help rather than as expressing a determined decision, there can be a risk of accidental death from such attempts. In private practice and without the back-up of support services, therapists need to carefully evaluate their own knowledge, experience, capability and support in the face of such risks, and not take on such clients if they feel in any way out of their depth.

One crucial thing to avoid when considering the risk of suicide is being trapped with carrying responsibility on our own for our client's safety. It is really important to establish some sort of confidentiality agreement right from the outset to the effect that, if the client gives us information that convinces us that they are at serious risk of harm (such as telling us about an intention to attempt suicide), we may have to break confidentiality and inform those who might be able take action to ensure their safety, such as their GP. In reality, informing a client's GP may not actually lead to action that keeps a client safe, but that is out of our control. What we do control is not letting ourselves be trapped holding a responsibility alone that does not belong to us, because this will leave us with crippling levels of fear and stress.

Another thing to avoid is any attempt by a client to hand over to us the responsibility for ensuring their safety. If a client told me they were contemplating suicide and I had a sense either that they were trying to manipulate my care, or rely on me to keep them safe, I would be very clear with them that their safety lay in their own hands and, if they had an intention to kill themselves, there was nothing I could do to stop them. Therapists who became habitual caregivers at a very early age as a means of getting affirmation they didn't receive from their parents, may be particularly vulnerable to such manipulation as they may be less confident in laying down clear boundaries concerning the care that can be given.

What cannot be avoided

What we can't avoid is the fact that we simply don't know if someone is going to kill themselves. In a culture that quickly looks to some care provider to blame for a suicide, this might be the most important thing to hang onto. Those who are most determined to take their own lives often keep quiet about it and ensure that no one can prevent them.

We also can't avoid the difficulty of the balancing act that's required of us in this work. We have to guard against a numbing or an emotional disconnect from the suicidal client (particularly if we work frequently with such risk), and try to stay connected and engaged, while also not being overwhelmed by the disturbance which the work creates. This balance is, of course, inherent in all therapeutic work, but may be particularly difficult to maintain when working with the risk of suicide.

We also can't avoid the blow to the self that is delivered if a client is successful in a suicide attempt. Suicide is often seen as an angry attack on the self, but it can also be an angry attack on those closest to the person who has killed themselves, and I know just how hard it can be to work with those left behind as they struggle with what feels like a huge body blow, and the tangle of their own retaliatory anger with feelings of guilt. A therapist affected in this way will need huge support, may have to pay particular attention to self-care, and may well need to take time off work.

The need to seek care

The impact of working with the risk of suicide depends so much on the support that is available to us, but at any stage the overriding message is 'seek care'. Nothing is worse than sitting with the anxiety of suicide risk and trying to cope on your own. Where there is a significant gap between this issue arising and your next scheduled supervision, contact your supervisor and see if you can arrange a much earlier consultation. If this can't be arranged that day, see whether there is a colleague you can turn to for 'supervisory first-aid', and either failing that, or in addition, seek the support of good friends to process the impact on you even where no clinical details can be shared.

As with other aspects of complex trauma, it is likely that the stress of working with suicide risk may owe less to the impact of our client's disturbance on us and more to the support available to us and whether we work in a fearful and blaming culture. Finding oneself unsupported in such an event might be a wake-up call that prompts us to a change in working environment.

For therapists who feel in need of more support in thinking about how to work with suicidal risk, I would recommend the BACP resource videos provided by Dr Andrew Reeves.[140]

Reflections on suicide and the fear-system

It has been accepted wisdom for many years that there is a particular risk of suicide in the early stages of recovery from depression. This view is often linked to the theory that as we recover from depression, we regain the energy which then makes a suicide attempt possible. A review of available data by Mittal and others[141] could not find evidence to support this view and concluded that this was a 'plausible clinical hunch that remains unproven'. However, as the data examined appeared to offer no clear definition of what constituted 'recovery', I would consider that this accepted wisdom has not yet been disproved.

I do think we should not be too hasty in dismissing the reflections of generations of previous clinicians, and what we know of the functioning of the fear-system may offer another perspective on their observations. I have long wondered whether some successful suicides might reflect a sudden emergence from chronic fear-collapse into a 'disorganised fight-flight' reaction, such as that of a prey animal sensing a window of opportunity to escape an unsafe environment.

In Chapter 13, I described two examples where such powerful

[140] https://www.bacp.co.uk/cpd/exploring-suicidal-risk-with-clients-gpiael2/
[141] Mittal et al. (2009).

reactions to emerging from fear-collapse involved an angry attack on partners. I wonder whether this same mechanism activating in people more prone to turn anger into self-attack may underly some suicide attempts seemingly coming out of the blue. This perspective appears to be compatible with the reflections of Schweizer and others[142] who hypothesised that suicide attempts might be more related to mood swings than to a resurgence of energy, and may help us to better support our clients in safety-planning for this shift from fear-collapse into disorganised fight-or-flight.

[142] Schweizer et al. (1988), quoted by Mittal et al. (2009), though this theory is only based on two observed cases.

Chapter 22

Working on many fronts

The range of different approaches and interventions we may need to consider

For me, one of the big implications of a clearer understanding of complex trauma is the need to consider a number of different approaches to working with clients.

So many things are disrupted by complex trauma – we need to work with physiological responses, chronic conditions, paranoid or hopeless thinking, self-sabotaging behaviours, relational problems and social and environmental issues.

We need to first establish a sense of safety in the body and the mind and do what we can to help with lack of safety in relationships, workplaces and social networks. When there is a sufficient sense of safety, we need to work directly with the frightening, painful and difficult experiences that lie at the root of the chronically activated fear-system. When enough work has been done here, we need to help our clients to find a new place in the world and reconnect with others in a way that will sustain them and prevent relapse.

The stage of safety and stabilisation requires us to have a number of approaches to regulating fear responses, as each client is different and forms of regulation that one person enjoys, another may hate, and some may even make some people more anxious.

We may need to examine how ways of thinking are creating a feedback loop which is intensifying the body's fear response, and a CBT approach may be helpful here in breaking this loop.

We may need to engage in problem-solving work with our clients on many aspects of their lives that are keeping them locked in a cycle of fear responses. We may also need to help clients relax physical tensions and take up practices which reverse a chronic weakening of the signal on the ventral vagus nerve.

Alongside all of this we can do much to establish a sense of safety through psychoeducation – taking our clients through the science behind their fear responses and letting them know what is involved in the work, and the setbacks they might encounter. While still in this stabilisation stage, we may also need to work with addictions. Where there is severe difficulty, the work is usually beyond the scope of therapists in private practice with issues of chemical dependency, the dangers of detox and a requirement for high levels of support, such as periods in rehab. Where addictions are less serious we may require further training or support to work effectively and may have to consider referring clients for specialist work if we don't have expertise in this area,[143] or encourage them to use support groups particularly, if we work in private practice disconnected from other services.

We may have to help our clients negotiate difficult relationships and consider whether couple work or family work may be helpful, referring on again if this is not part of our training, but perhaps leaving open the invitation to return for individual work.

When we reach the stage of directly working with trauma, there are a number of really useful methods that work with the body-based core of the problem, such as EMDR,[144] somatic experiencing,[145] sensorimotor psychotherapy[146] and focusing-

[143] I would regularly refer clients with drug or alcohol addiction to colleagues with a specialist training.
[144] Shapiro (1995).

oriented therapy.[147] There are also approaches which engage with the internal world to integrate parts of the self which were fragmented by trauma, as in the work of Janina Fisher[148] or Richard Schwartz's Internal Family Systems.[149]

I have long thought that our dreaming mind is the ultimate trauma processor and have worked with dreams at every stage in my career whenever clients brought them to my attention. This is a fascinating area of work (one that drew me into therapy in the first place), so I have included some reflections on the nature of dreaming and working with dreams therapeutically in Appendix 7.

In different ways, each of these approaches has given me real insight into working with trauma, and I have integrated aspects of all of them in my own individual approach, but my two preferred ways of working directly with traumatic experiences were EMDR and focusing-oriented therapy.

This might all seem a bit much to digest for someone just emerging from a therapy training, but I actually started out slowly, working in a fairly purist psychodynamic manner for six years before starting to branch out. From then on I really just followed my interests and investigated ways of working that others had found effective and tried to make sense of what worked and why. The fact that complex trauma presents so many fronts that require attention meant that I always felt challenged to go beyond what I knew and find new ways of understanding and working with distress. Nothing, however, can replace the healing power of someone in distress being met as a person, treated respectfully, listened to carefully, and responded to with feeling. This lies in the gift of trainee counsellors just as much as experienced therapists and stays as the core of the work whatever new skills are acquired.

145 Levine (2010).
146 Ogden, Minton and Pain (2006).
147 Gendlin (1996).
148 Fisher (2017).
149 Schwarz (1995).

Chapter 23

Working within our own competence

Understanding competence and knowing when we are out of our depth

Working with complex trauma can be overwhelming and, if we do not work within our own competence, we can block our clients' progress and risk physical and mental burnout and a collapse of confidence in ourselves and our training. It is not always easy to know what our competence is, as it's not something forever fixed, but more akin to a sense of balance which can be there one moment and lost the next.

Our competence is a sense that we are equipped to work with and be of real help to any particular client and the difficulties they would like to resolve. This is based on having sufficient personal experience of the matter involved, sufficient knowledge and understanding of how to help with such issues, and sufficient experience and skill in a way of working that can help. It also includes being well enough and rested enough to give our full attention to our client, and our ability to adequately regulate our fear-system so that our mind can be reflective, and we can stay socially connected and help our client maintain a sense of safety.

Our competence is almost like a felt-sense, a sense of when we are swimming in our depth and when we are out of our depth. If we are properly in-tune with ourselves (another key ingredient of competence), we will notice when we lose it, and our fear responses will be activated. We will lose our competence when we are physically ill, overtired, overstressed or shaken by losses or difficulties in our own life.

If we start with our experience, I find it helpful to use the metaphor of a guide who helps others to travel through uncharted territory. The territory represents the lived experience of the whole of humanity. We are potentially qualified to be guides because our life experience lies in one patch of this territory, and we become better qualified through our own personal therapy as we have hired a guide or guides who have helped us to make more sense of that part of the territory. Our life-experience and the work we have undertaken processing it are the core of our competence.

I have noticed in myself and in many other therapists a tendency to be drawn to work in the area of our own trauma and at the level of our own trauma. On the whole I think that this is a healthy thing and illustrates an instinctive knowledge of what we know and where we can be most useful to others. However, it can carry a real danger if we don't fully undertake our own therapeutic exploration. I believe that for most of us, our own emotional problems are the driving force that brings us into helping others with their emotional problems. If we do not devote a significant amount of time to addressing our own issues in the independent space of individual or group therapy, we run the risk of using our clients as guinea-pigs in our own experiment. If we do not directly address our own problems, we can end up trying to work them out through our clients, tangling them in our own issues. We can also end up blocking them by our own defensiveness as we unconsciously divert them away from disturbing matters that are unresolved for us, or fail to respond to their emotional cues.

From the competence we acquire through our life experience and our own therapeutic exploration, we can gradually expand our ability to act as a guide over a wider area of the territory. Our capacity is increased over time with each therapist, tutor, supervisor or supportive colleague we work with, and each client we learn from further increases our knowledge and competence.

To stay safe in ourselves and be safe for our clients, we need at each stage of our professional journey to be able to evaluate our competence and know which part of the territory to work in and which to leave for others. I think this task has been made much harder for some counsellors by the many training courses that have approved unsuitable placements for their students, meaning that they have not started from a sense of working within their competence. They have instead been thrown straight into working beyond their competence, which becomes normalised, thus desensitising the evaluation of competence.

I think that, however much we increase in competence, it helps to accept that in the field of complex trauma we cannot be a skilled guide in all areas. Some clients' life experiences may be profoundly different from our own, and the gap may be such that they would receive more immediate help from a therapist whose life experience was not too dissimilar. Although significant cultural differences, which can obstruct a therapist's ability to be of real help to a client, may be overcome by the therapist learning from the client over time, the client might gain more immediate help by being referred to a therapist who is either from the client's own background, or who has a better understanding of it.

It also helps (to continue the metaphor of the guide) to know that we walk with our clients for just one part of their path through life, and we are only responsible for guiding them on that part of the path. We are more likely to stay working within our competence if we can resist the pull to take too much responsibility by assuming that we are the only person who can help our clients. In reality, others may have helped them in the past and others may help them in the future. We are neither rescuers nor saviours and, if we try to be, we are at risk of overwhelm and burnout.

Part 4

The importance of safety

Chapter 24

The centrality of safety

A visceral sense of safety is essential if the fear-system is to reset

In the preceding chapters we have seen that, if there is no place of safety in the aftermath of a serious threat, the fear-system cannot reset. This is the origin of complex trauma. There are many things that can contribute to resetting our fear responses after a threat has been survived, but the essential precondition is a visceral (body-felt) sense of safety. If this is lacking, nothing else will be effective. In our work to alleviate the impact of complex trauma, nothing is more important than safety.

The centrality of safety is clear when we look at predation (one animal trying to eat another), which is the context in which our fear-system evolved. The fear-system quickly deactivates after fear-alert if the environment is assessed as being safe. Fear-arousal enables an escape to a place of safety where the heart rate can then calm and the fear-system can reset, while fear-collapse can either switch back into fear-arousal, enabling an escape to a place of safety, or reset through deep breathing and tremoring if the environment has become safe.

It is the absence of a place of safety following serious threats which traps us into a continual state of fear-alert, leaving the nervous system in a highly volatile state. In this volatile condition, any threat, deadly or minor, real or imagined, in the present or in the future, can trigger fear-arousal or fear-collapse, resulting in a continuous 'roller-coaster' of fear activation. Regardless of which fear responses are active, when it comes to regulating fear, a place and a sense of safety underpin everything.

Although our thoughts can contribute to or undermine this, our 'sense of safety' is not a cognitive process but a 'felt-sense'.[150] The safety needed to reset the fear-system is a visceral sensation – a whole body experience involving both external and internal senses (the information coming from the major organs of the body via the autonomic nervous system[151]). Our evaluation of safety includes not just what we see, hear, smell, touch or taste, but also our heart-rate and blood pressure, our patterns of breathing, temperature, hormone production, the state of our digestive system, and muscle tone throughout our body.[152]

Safety is central, because the stakes are so high, and the outcomes that depend upon it are so important. Without safety we are stuck in a continuous cycle of fear responses which, as we saw in Part 1, leads to anxiety and depression, panic, rage, low mood, chronic physical illness, pain and loss of energy, violence, self-destructive behaviours including addictions, cognitive impairment, the breakdown of relationships and a sense of disconnection and isolation. To be stuck in fear-mode is to live in misery.

In evolutionary terms, human beings and our mammalian ancestors emerged from the isolation of fear, creating safety through social cooperation. As Porges[153] puts it: '…humans as social mammals, are on an enduring lifelong quest to feel safe'.

[150] Porges (2022), referencing Gendlin.
[151] Porges (2022): '…feelings of safety emerge from internal physiological states regulated by the autonomic nervous system'.
[152] Porges (2022) refers to this evaluation as a 'neuroception' rather than a perception.
[153] Porges (2022), p.2.

When we feel safe, we are released from fear. Without the enormous energy drain of our fear responses we experience vitality, a sense of connection to others and to our environment. We can think reflectively and become creative. We can live fully and experience joy, contentment and wellbeing.

This is an issue of huge importance. The difference between a life of misery and a life of wellbeing depends on whether we are able to find places of safety and achieve a visceral sense of safety. This then places safety at the very centre of ethics. A 'morally good' or ethical action is one that can create a sense of safety which leads to human wellbeing and to lives that achieve their full potential. A 'morally bad' or unethical action is one that takes away a sense of safety, thus activating fear, which leads to human misery and to lives half-lived.

Different areas of safety

As we work with complex trauma, there are different areas of safety we may need to consider, if we are to help our clients to regulate their fear-system responses.

The first area concerns ourselves. Are we safe (or safe-enough[154]) therapists, able to regulate our own fear-responses and help clients regulate theirs through experiencing a sense of safety in our presence?

The next area, which overlaps with this to a certain extent, is what might be called 'internal safety', and it concerns both ourselves and our clients. Do we feel safe in our own body or are we frightened by the physical sensations of our fear-responses? Do we trust our bodies to be looking after us, or do we view them as somehow hostile? The same applies to our thinking processes. Do we think about ourselves in a generally supportive

[154] An allusion to Winnicott's (1973) 'good-enough mother' to remind ourselves that perfectionism is unhelpful.

way that helps us in the task of fear regulation, or are our own minds unsafe places, liable to be a source of self-criticism and attack which can throw us into anxiety, or collapse us into despondency?

The final area, external safety, covers many aspects which sit outside of the work of psychotherapy, but which may have to be explored within the therapy. We might examine the safety of our relationships, workplace, neighbourhoods and the wider society of which we are a member and examine what actions might be available to us which would lessen our fears.

I will look at these different aspects of safety in the following chapters and then examine whether popularly held ideas on the therapeutic nature of expressing emotions (catharsis) may conflict with safety. I will finish this section with a brief example of the power of a visceral sense of safety.

Chapter 25

The safe therapist

How we become 'safe enough' and enable our clients to feel safe

In order for therapy to be successful, both the therapist and the therapeutic space need to convey this sense of safety. So how do we become a safe, or an ethical therapist, one whose presence and actions lead to the creation of a sense of safety for our clients?

How we become a safe therapist

We become safe for others by being able to recognise and to regulate our own fear-system responses. However, our starting point on this journey is dependent on the random accidents of our life circumstances.

If we had parents who were reasonably good at regulating their own fear responses, gave us reasonably good nurture and taught us how to calm our own fears, and we grew up in a relatively peaceful society without belonging to a group subjected to hatred, oppression or disadvantage, and without major shocks or early loss of our caregivers, then we already have a good head-start in this process.

If our parents were unable to regulate their own fear responses, were preoccupied or neglectful, and if we grew up in a society affected by war or widespread violence, or were part of an oppressed or disadvantaged minority, or suffered major shocks or early losses, our journey towards self-regulation may be longer and more difficult. However, if we can work with and learn to regulate our fear-system, we may be able to reach clients that therapists who have faced fewer difficulties may struggle to help and to understand.

The importance of personal therapy

Regardless of where we start from, I think that undertaking one's own personal therapy plays a key role in our becoming safer therapists. I can see three reasons for this. The first is that we all have work to do on improving our fear-system regulation, and this is a key outcome of effective therapy.[155]

Despite the differences in life experience from which we approach this work, as I suggested in Chapter 11, after thousands of years of history of warfare, violence, oppression and exploitation, and the impact of this flowing through the generations, there are few of us unscarred by trauma in some shape or form. (I personally know of no one.) I believe that everyone carries a history of trauma, and my personal observations over the years that the incidence of a history of serious trauma is higher among therapists than among the general population, has some external verification.[156]

Where we have not adequately worked through our own history of trauma, disturbing past experiences will lie like potholes in the road ahead as we work with others, ready to jolt us into a disabling fear response as our body-memory of

[155] Though there are alternative pathways to fear-system regulation, such as close friendships, a regular practice of meditation or yoga, or work with a spiritual guide or director.

[156] Henderson et al. (2025), p.13: 'Mental health professionals have typically experienced more traumatic events in their own lives, compared with the general population.'

these events is triggered by our clients' accounts or by their manner of relating to us. Where trauma is unprocessed, the rigid habitual defensive patterns it develops are likely to remain unchanged, and these will undermine our attempt to provide the essential conditions (see below) for creating a sense of safety for our clients.

The second reason why I think undertaking our own personal therapy is important, is that we are setting ourselves up as guides to others to navigate the difficult territory of emotional turbulence. It is likely that we will inhabit some of the same emotional terrain as a number of our clients, but if we have not examined this terrain carefully, with the help of an experienced guide who can help us with our blind spots as well as the areas we partially understand, we will not become a safe guide for others.

The third reason for undertaking our own personal therapy is that the work of a therapist is not just a matter of intellectual learning. It requires a profound understanding of emotional distress with highly developed interpersonal skills, and the ability to function with both of these still intact in highly stressful situations. It cannot be taught as an academic discipline or as a manualised process. As with other highly skilled professions, it requires a period of apprenticeship. Good clinical supervision covers a crucial aspect of this training, but, for me, the key part of my apprenticeship as a therapist was my own personal therapy – observing minute by minute the work of a qualified practitioner, while also being able to experience internally the impact this work was having on me. I found this invaluable learning that nothing else could quite replicate.

I remember clearly the day I saw my first client – my feeling of tension and anxiety as he walked into the room and sat down opposite me. I remember the thought in my head, 'If you knew you were my very first counselling client, you would get up and run'. I also remember a strange feeling at the end of the session. As I reflected on how it had gone, I was puzzled by a surprising sense of confidence, a sense that I knew what I was doing, that I had noticed from about 10 minutes into the session. I was also aware that my sense of confidence had helped my client to settle and to get on with the work.

This baffled me at the time. I was a complete beginner and had felt panicky right at the start of the session. Where did that confidence come from? Eventually it came to me – I had already been in therapy for a number of months before I saw my first client, and in that time I had picked up a huge amount from my own therapist about how to conduct myself in the therapy room – my apprenticeship was already well established without me realising just how much I had been learning.

Self-care

Having emphasised the importance of personal therapy, I should say that this is still only one of a number of factors we might need to consider when thinking about how we improve the regulation of our fear-responses in order to become a safe therapist for others. This is a life-long task involving a 'whole of life' approach. It includes very important factors such as getting enough sleep and having a healthy diet, which many other authors are more qualified to comment on than I am, together with activities which strengthen the body's fear-regulating processes.

Among these, perhaps one of the most important is regular physical exercise, such as walking[157] for at least 30 minutes a day, plus some periods of more intensive exercise. Additionally, regular practices such as yoga, meditation and singing, and treatments such as massage, osteopathy and acupuncture, all contribute towards strengthening the body's ability to emotionally regulate. I touched on why these were helpful in Part 2: Working with the body.

One of the most powerful regulators of our fear-system responses is our connectedness to others, so the quality of our personal relationships will have a very important bearing on our ability to be a safe therapist.

If our closest relationships, either with our partner or our friends, feel equal, reciprocal, supportive and companionable, and if we have a sense that there are people we really trust to whom we can turn for help in the face of any threats or difficulties, we will manage our own fear-responses much more effectively, and we can build up a real resilience against overwhelm or burnout.

If we do not have a good level of relational support and feel there is no one we can turn to with our own distress, we may struggle to offer a sense of safety to others and are more likely to find the work of therapy disturbing and draining. In these circumstances, it may be necessary to make seeking out alternative forms of support, such as personal or group therapy, a safe professional group, or new friendships, a top priority in order to survive the emotional battering that we can experience in this work.

An important part of keeping us safe as therapists is not overworking. Working with the distress of others takes a huge

[157] Or any other form of exercise available to you that stimulates the sympathetic nervous system. My understanding of this is that the sympathetic nervous system and the ventral vagus work in constant balance, and activation of the sympathetic nervous system in non-fear states can work to strengthen the balancing signal on the ventral vagus.

amount of energy and, if we push ourselves too far, the help we can give our clients will suffer, and we risk burnout. During the period of my initial training, the recommendation from BACP was that around 20 clients a week constituted a full-time workload, (so, on average, four clients per day for a five-day working week). On a few occasions I have pushed beyond this boundary and suffered periods of stress and exhaustion, so I think this is a wise recommendation.

As I grew older and neared retirement, I became more aware of the physical demands of the work on my body, and over the years I gradually cut down on my work, reducing the number of clients I would see in a day to a maximum of four, and then cutting out evening work as I began to find this more tiring. I also gradually cut my working days down to two days a week, and increased the numbers of holidays I took, so that by the end I would work a pattern of four weeks followed by a week off in the winter months, and in the summer I would work for five-week stretches followed by two weeks off.

I gave my clients plenty of notice of these arrangements, and I think it helped my long-term clients prepare for my retirement. I also paid a good deal of attention to the balance of my workload. Having always had several clients with severe complex trauma, I made sure I worked with enough other people who took more readily to exploratory work, needed fewer sessions and with whom I was generally more energised in the therapy sessions. I took even more care over this balance as I neared retirement.

We need to be even more careful about not overworking when there are other major calls on our caring apart from our clients. Parents with young children are already committing a significant amount of time and energy to childcare, and many therapists are carers for others who are ill, disabled or elderly. Our ability to give care to others is a finite resource, as was brought home to me one day in a rather shocking manner:

While I still had a fairly full workload in my therapy practice, my mother, who lived nearby, became less able to cope with living on her own and needed much more of my time. At the end of a really hard day with a couple of particularly difficult sessions that had drained me, I was desperate to get to the end of the day and collapse in front of the television with a glass of wine and some mindless entertainment.

However, when I finished work and checked my phone I saw there was a voicemail message from my mother. Something was wrong with her cooker, and she hadn't been able to cook her dinner and needed my help. As I dragged myself round to her house I had a sudden disturbing mental picture – I imagined seeing a baby just left by the side of the road, and I imagined that as I walked past it, I just kicked it into the gutter.

This disturbing mental picture[158] jolted me into an awareness of just how depleted I had become as a caregiver. It helped me to appreciate that the energy we need for giving care to others is strictly limited, and that when we go too far beyond these limits we cease to be social, let alone compassionate, beings. The shock of this realisation was the start of my gradual reduction in workload, as I attended to the balance between my responsibilities and my available energy.

[158] I have found that many therapists and many clients have been frightened by, and ashamed of, such disturbing mental images, thinking that they represented a bad or a sick part of them, and have therefore kept them secret from others. I think it is important to understand that, just as with our retaliatory impulses (which I discussed in Chapter 16), these mental images are neither good nor bad, but simply data. When I have spoken publicly about these mental images, a number of people have told me that this brought them great relief, as they had thought they were alone in experiencing such images.

All this, of course, is much more easily achieved in private practice, and this level of flexibility may not be possible in employment. However, the responsibility for our care ultimately rests with us, and if employers are not attuned to the energy drain of the work and the need for a balanced workload, and cannot be sufficiently supportive of individuals with additional caregiving burdens, it may be time to look for a different employer. I would certainly recommend that therapists in employment give some consideration to private practice as they get on in years, as this will allow much more flexibility to adjust hours of work to available energy, and to continue in practice for a longer period than might otherwise have been possible.

Professional support

Finally, a key element of our becoming a safe therapist will depend on the quality of professional support available to us throughout our career as a therapist. This covers the support of trainers and training institutes, clinical supervisors, managers (if we are employed), and our professional friends and colleagues. This is such an important area that I will look at it separately in Part 5: Supporting the therapist.

How we convey a sense of safety

How do we convey to our clients the information that we are a safe person to be with? My first thought here is that this happens automatically, and we can't fake it. At our first meeting, and at the start of each subsequent session, and every time our clients introduce something that is triggering their own fear responses, they will be picking up our attitude towards them and our emotional responses to them from our posture and the micro-movements of the muscles of our face. They may well be picking up on our fear responses before we have become aware of them.

This is all before we have spoken a word. Once we speak, our tone of voice, rhythm of speech, emphases and pauses (which taken together are referred to as 'prosody'[159]) will convey yet more information. Our clients don't need to be consciously aware of this or have any cognitive understanding of it. They will be viscerally affected at a body level and will open up if we are sensed as safe to be with, or close down if we are not.

The essential conditions

Few people have described the essential conditions for creating a sense of safety for our clients better than Carl Rogers.[160] He spoke of three 'core conditions' that must be present in order to promote personal growth, and these are also the conditions that convey a sense of safety which is the foundation and context for that growth.

His first condition was **genuineness**, which he also described as 'realness' or 'congruence'. This relates to my comment above that we can't fake a sense of safety. Genuineness means that we present the other person with our real self, not a false mask.[161] It means that the signals given by the micro-movements of our face, our posture, gestures, tone of voice and rhythm of speech, our behaviour and the content of our words, are all conveying the same thing. If all these signals are congruent, in other words they all match, we come across as safe and trustworthy. If our words are saying one thing and our face and body are conveying a different message, then we will come across as untrustworthy, and at a visceral level we are sensed as unsafe.

[159] Porges (2022).
[160] Rogers (1980).
[161] A false mask being an unconscious 'bracing' in the physiology of the face.

I remember in the days before I trained as a therapist, thinking I was very good at hiding my feelings until a drunken leaving-do in Hull, saying goodbye to the team I had managed there, when one of my team pointed out to me (with laughing agreement from the rest) that I had a particular 'fuck-off' face that I used not infrequently at staff meetings – and I had been so certain that I had always conducted myself with politeness and had been able to hide my real feelings!

Any unprocessed trauma from our past will be manifest in habitual defensive patterns of relating to others, of which we probably have no awareness. These patterns will make it very difficult to be genuine and will be unconsciously picked up by clients as a sense that we are not safe, hence (once again) the importance of personal therapy.

Roger's second condition was **acceptance**, which he also termed 'unconditional positive regard'. Rogers described the therapist as having 'a positive acceptant attitude toward whatever the client is at that moment...'.[162] This consists of a willingness to allow a client to be just as he or she is in any given moment, without the therapist's valuation of the client being conditional on any particular behaviour or feeling state. For me, what Rogers is referring to is most powerfully captured in the idea of being 'met as a person'.[163]

I guess most of us have struggled with being met in other ways. Many of us are used to being met as a nuisance,

[162] Rogers (1980), p.116.

[163] This concept, central to Una McCluskey's approach, which I have found hugely helpful in my work, originated in Jock Sutherland's statement: 'we are born with the expectation of being met as a person'. Una quoted this at the start of her book *To Be Met as a Person* (McCluskey 2005).

or a problem, or a medical diagnosis, or as someone of no importance, someone with the wrong views, or someone who is seen as a threat. When we are habitually met in these ways, our fear-system is likely to activate.

The way we think about ourselves in relation to our clients is important in conveying a sense of safety. If we see ourselves as 'experts', and the client as a recipient of our wisdom, then we have put up a defensive shield between ourselves and our clients, because we ourselves do not feel safe, and this will be picked up by our clients. If we see ourselves as experts, we are more likely to meet our clients as 'cases', but if we see ourselves as fellow-travellers, we can meet them as persons.

When we are 'met as a person', we are met with interest and curiosity and warmth, and we are met as we are, with no judgement or prejudice. To be met this way is to be welcomed, and welcome is a place of safety where we can set aside our defences.

Rogers' third condition was **empathic understanding** – the ability to have a sense of what another person is feeling and what that means for them at that moment. It is an ability to 'put ourselves into their shoes', and then to be able to communicate this understanding to our client. We are able to do this because our body naturally resonates with another person's feelings, but in order to do this, we need to be able to listen carefully to our own body and not be afraid of its sensations.

We also need to be able to listen really carefully to the other person, sometimes reading between the lines and discerning what is clear communication, and what is a defensive shield. When this works, a client has a sense that another person 'gets it'. The experience of being understood can break through a terrible sense of isolation and offer a connectedness to others that re-attaches them to the human race. As Rogers put it, 'empathy dissolves alienation'.[164]

[164] Rogers (1980), p.151.

The following example illustrates the power of empathy to reconnect and restore a sense of safety.

A young man came to me for help with anxiety, but in his second session he was talking really fast and emphatically about something he thought I really needed to know, but to me it was completely incoherent, and I couldn't follow the logic of it. At one level it felt as if he wasn't there with me in the room at all. None of my questions about the content of what he was saying seemed to connect and the harder I tried to follow what he was saying, the more my mind just seemed to go blank.

Eventually I gave up the attempt, disconnected from the content, took some breaths and tried to calm myself. I noticed my own sensations of agitation and disconnectedness, my fear of the 'craziness' of this situation, and I asked myself 'what is he trying to say to me?'. I found myself listening to the jumble he was presenting as if it was a jumble of metaphors, and I sensed the desperate urgency with which he was talking. Then the thought came to my mind: 'He's terrified that he's going crazy', and at the same time I had a picture in my mind of an astronaut, whose connection to the spacecraft had severed, drifting off into endless black space. I wanted to check this out with him, but then I thought I might be completely wrong and make a real mess of things, and I had a moment's panic. I waited till it had subsided and then just said it: 'I'm wondering if you're terrified you're going mad?'

The young man suddenly stopped, looked me straight in the eye for the first time, took a big deep breath and said, 'Yes, that's it'. We paused for a moment, just looking at each other – there was a real sense of connection. Then we gradually started working on what lay behind his terror, both of us having recovered the capacity to think and reflect…

Creating a safe framework for the therapy

Apart from the sense of safety we might communicate, we need to consider the safety provided by the 'framework' of the therapy. A key aspect of this is our therapy room and its context. Safety will depend on such matters as whether our room feels like a 'welcoming' space, whether it feels private (conversations can't be overheard), and whether its setting is conducive for quiet reflection.

A sense of safety will be provided by the regularity and predictability of session times, so keeping changes to an absolute minimum, and giving long notice of holiday or training breaks, is very important. Boundaries, such as confidentiality and having no contact with clients outside of therapy sessions, preserve the therapeutic space as an area 'sealed off' from the impingements of daily life, and safety is enhanced when these are clearly explained from the outset and firmly adhered to.

Developing a safe way of working

It is important that safety is at the centre of the way we work, and much of this book is focused on this issue. To work safely we need to have a model, or a theoretical framework, for understanding trauma (Part 1), and we have to consider the balance needed between regulation of emotions and exploring them in order to protect our clients from being re-traumatised (Part 2). We need a good understanding of the difficulties, complications and setbacks of this work, and an appreciation of our own competence and knowledge, in order to safely guide our clients through the difficult terrain of complex trauma (Part 3); and we need to take very good care of ourselves and ensure we have trustworthy professional support (Part 5).

Chapter 26

Internal and external safety

Threats from within and without – creating a sense of safety in the internal and external worlds

There are two key areas of safety we need to consider in working with complex trauma, both for ourselves and for our clients. These are internal and external safety, and they relate to the threats that we sense from inside our own bodies and those that exist externally. Internally, powerful physical fear responses and the fearful, negative or self-attacking thoughts these can provoke, can make both the body and the mind unsafe places. Both body and mind have to start to feel safe before trauma can be healed, and this is usually seen as the core work of therapy. However, the effectiveness of this work will always be limited by a lack of safety in our external world, which will keep the fear-system active. In our personal lives and in our therapeutic work, we need to consider such things as the safety of our network of relationships, home base, neighbourhood, workplace and social and political context.

Internal safety

When we are feeling powerful sensations that make no sense to us, we become terrified of our own body – it no longer feels safe.

When this happens, it does not matter how objectively safe our surroundings are; this has no effect on calming our fear-system, and the disturbing sensations prompt increasingly anxious thinking, which then amplifies our fear.

In Chapter 5 we touched on fear-arousal experienced as 'freeze' which can leave many people terrified that they are having a heart-attack and therefore presenting at hospital A&E departments. In Chapter 13, I gave more examples of fear-responses, such as legs going weak or sudden outbursts of rage, that caused significant distress and shut down normal functioning.

These powerful responses reflect the emotional impact on us of life experiences and interactions with others. The power of this impact, and how bearable or unbearable each experience is, sometimes owes less to the experience itself, and more to what goes on inside us as we have that experience. To give an example:

> I tell a friend about something that happened to me earlier that day. I notice my friend is not really paying attention. What goes on inside me in response to this could be, 'My story is interesting, but my friend seems preoccupied – I wonder what is bothering him,' or it could be, 'My friend isn't interested in me – he must find me boring. I'm a boring person'.

The first response illustrates internal safety, a supportive 'internal environment', resulting in concerned curiosity for my friend; the second response illustrates a lack of internal safety, an unsupportive internal environment, where a relatively minor interaction can result in self-attack and loss of wellbeing.

Whether our internal environment is supportive or unsupportive depends upon the quality of caregiving we have received in the past. Our minds are shaped by all our previous relationships, particularly those with our parents or primary caregivers. If our need for care, interest and attention was met in a timely and empathic manner, we will have internalised a supportive and compassionate way of thinking about, and treating, ourselves, and we will assume that our feelings and interests are good and acceptable. If we were neglected, criticised or humiliated when we sought care and attention, we will have internalised an attacking and critical way of treating ourselves, and we will assume that there is something wrong with us, our feelings and our interests.

We notice the way our minds have been shaped by past relationships when we become aware of the 'conversations' that run through our head throughout the waking day. These are made up of a whole series of 'voices' which replay the sorts of things which people said to us in the past. Their voices have become our voices, so if they praised and encouraged us, we now do the same thing to ourselves, and if they ignored or undermined us, we replicate this internally, and our mind is no longer a safe place.

But this is not just about thoughts; when we think about internal safety, we are primarily concerned with the sensations of the body which shape the nature of our thoughts. We are concerned with our feelings, the way our bodies react to what happens around us. If our need for care and attention was met with a loving response when we were small, our bodies will calm down and relax in the company of those we are closest to in the present. If our needs were met in the past with, inattention, anxiety or attack, our bodies will tense, flinch or collapse, expecting physical or emotional pain in the company of others, and particularly those we are closest to, or on whom we rely most (such as a therapist!).

What we are talking about here is the way body and mind have been programmed by our past experiences. If our minds and our bodies feel unsafe, an environment that may look perfectly safe to others will be experienced as a place of danger, our fear-system will not deactivate, and the symptoms of complex trauma will not be alleviated.

We can work on this in our own therapy, or in the therapy we provide for others, by looking at the way we think about ourselves and the way we treat ourselves in response to our life experiences. We look at the voices in our head that are affirming and supportive or those that are negative and self-attacking. We think about who said these things to us in the past, or who reacted to us in the past in such a way that we formed these opinions of ourselves. We look at the ways we react to certain experiences in the present and try to understand the past circumstances that make sense of these reactions. Our aim is to lessen self-attack and treat ourselves more compassionately and also to physically regulate our fear responses so that our bodies do not react with such alarm or distress to perceived threats. In this way, we try to shift our internal world from unsupportive to supportive, from unsafe to safe.

External safety

However, our ability to move towards a sense of safety in body and mind can be highly dependent on the safety or lack of safety in our external environment.

> A young woman who had been estranged from her parents as a teenager had a long history of anxiety, depression and chronic fatigue which left her unable to hold down a job for long periods of time. As a result, she lived in a run-down neighbourhood, in a damp house in a state of disrepair.
>
> She was afraid of complaining about the state of the house as her last landlord had evicted her when she asked for

repairs to be done, and her current landlord employed a manager to run his properties, who terrified her. She was often in debt having had benefits removed as a sanction when she was too unwell to turn up at the job centre, and she struggled to feed herself properly even with the help of a food bank.

She was seen by a counsellor at her GP surgery on a number of occasions over the years, but for no more than six sessions in each episode. She presented each time in a high state of distress, dishevelled, and with a huge list of worries and a paranoid outlook on a world that seemed out to get her. She always had her face turned away and never looked at the counsellor. The counsellor felt overwhelmed, and their sessions were entirely taken up with trying to calm her sufficiently to help her think about some of the practical problems she was facing, and what possible resources she might be able to draw on in the local community.

After a gap of a couple of years, she was once again referred to the counsellor. It was like meeting a completely different woman. She was tidily dressed and calm, looked directly at the counsellor and smiled. She had a clear purpose in coming as she wanted time to think about her relationship with her parents and to start to get to grips with her anxious thinking.

The counsellor noted that she seemed in a very different place from her previous sessions. The reason, it turned out, was very simple. An uncle had died and left her his house and some money in his will. She now had a warm, comfortable, dry house that no one could throw her out of, and she could afford to feed herself.

With numbers of the UK population affected by food poverty and insecure accommodation now running in the millions, every therapist will be well acquainted with this sort of work, where the levels of distress are so high that the therapeutic approach may be entirely unequal to the scale of the practical help that is required. So often we treat as mental illness the natural alarm and distress caused by an inability to meet our basic survival needs for secure shelter and enough to eat. The danger is that this can pathologise our clients rather than helping them.

The safety of the external world is beyond the scope of therapy, but it hugely affects our ability to work therapeutically. We may be able to help our clients to make some changes to the safety of their external environment by examining the level of threat in various areas and exploring where there might be room for making any changes. We may be able to help clients think about abusive and controlling relationships, consider available resources and help them to contact organisations that can offer practical support and help.

We may be able to help them to evaluate fear-driven work cultures and consider whether there are any sources of support within the workplace, or whether the culture is so toxic that they need to be looking for alternative employment. It can be helpful for clients to realise that one of the impacts of trauma may be to leave them with a false sense of safety, when they confuse what is familiar (which may be abusive and controlling) with what is safe (but feels scary because unfamiliar).

Where neither of us can see ways in which the external environment can be made safer, it can still be helpful to validate the experience of lack of safety – for example, when clients work in toxic cultures or are affected by racism, misogyny or homophobia. In such situations, people may be pressured to disbelieve their own 'felt-sense' of the threat they are experiencing (in other words, they are gaslit), and if they lose the ability to trust this internal compass, this can hugely contribute to the body and the mind being felt as unsafe.

There may be ways we can help our clients to find others who struggle in the same way with lack of safety in a particular environment, and even if nothing can be done to change the external threat, there is at least solidarity and an escape from isolation in the company of others who are threatened in the same way.

One particular approach[165] which I found surprisingly powerful as a means of helping clients to start to gain a sense of agency and increase their external safety, is to focus on their immediate home environment and examine whether this is felt to be supportive or unsupportive. It is possible then to think of small changes that might be made, for example, getting rid of clutter, or introducing decorations that might give pleasure. Even just changing one room can eventually ripple out into many important changes which make the external environment feel safer and more supportive.

[165] Heard, Lake and McCluskey (2012), Chapter 10 – Working with the 'external environment'; McCluskey (2013).

Chapter 27

Safety and catharsis

The myth that expressing emotion is always therapeutic

The practice of counselling and psychotherapy has its roots in the work of Freud and the psychoanalytic tradition. A key concept within this tradition was 'catharsis', defined by Freud and Breuer as 'the process of reducing or eliminating a complex by recalling it to conscious awareness and allowing it to be expressed'.[166] If we understand a 'complex' as a set of defensive positions or reactions arising from an unresolved threat to the self, Freud and Breuer are describing a process not dissimilar to the one I outlined in Chapter 19 when looking at how traumatic experiences are processed.

However, as Freud's work came to dominate popular psychological understanding for decades afterwards, this concept appears to have morphed into a general assumption that it is 'good to emote'. Repression of feeling was thought to keep us locked in mental ill-health, while the expression of feelings could release us into wellbeing. While I don't recall seeing this expressed as crudely as this, I think I picked up this viewpoint well before my therapy training, and nothing in my early training disabused me of this idea.

[166] Freud and Breuer (2004).

One of the techniques I was taught for eliciting emotion in clients at the start of a therapy session was for the therapist to sit in silence with a relatively impassive face, waiting for the client to speak. I was taught that this was a way of encouraging the expression of the client's thoughts and feelings without too much intrusion from the therapist, but I now see this approach as chiefly eliciting anxiety, in other words activating the fear-system.

> One of my mistakes in the early years of my practice was persisting with the silent start to therapy with a client who told me it made her feel really uncomfortable. I was still too rigid in my practice and thought that this discomfort would ultimately be beneficial for her as it was putting her in touch with important feelings. Eventually she decided to end the therapy, and I was left with real regrets that I had not been more responsive to her needs.

The anxiety generated by techniques designed to elicit emotional expression can be even more powerful in a group setting. In a context where a group of people sit down together in silence, with no structure or agenda, and the so-called leader does nothing to facilitate or guide the work but occasionally comes out with enigmatic 'interpretations' of what is happening, the fear-system can activate very powerfully, resulting in attacks, alliances, dominant-submissive behaviours, tensions and silences, which can leave people frightened and confused (as will be seen in Chapter 29). Emotions are definitely elicited, but whether this is therapeutic is another matter.

This generalised assumption that eliciting emotion is of itself therapeutic has been challenged in the last few decades among those working to understand trauma,[167] but this has yet to percolate down to many counsellor training courses where groups of this nature are the model used for the 'personal development' aspect of the course. It is my experience that, as a result, many counsellors are left with an aversion to group work, which can restrict their ability to benefit from further training and development, because of traumatic experiences in such groups.

If we look at this from a fear-system perspective, knowing that fear responses shut down our ability to reflect, to explore and to socialise, I would suggest that when we think of eliciting emotions, we need to differentiate between fear-based emotions such as anxiety, rage, panic and depression, and socially-based emotions such as concern, sadness, loss, affection and gratitude.

We may need to start by turning *down* the volume on the fear-based emotions in order to create sufficient safety for our cognitive and social systems to be able to operate fully. When we can adequately regulate fear responses, we can then turn *up* the volume on any of the socially-based emotions that emerge and explore them fully.

At some stage it will be important for the fear-based emotions to be given full expression. It is necessary for our self-defence that we have access to our anger and learn to use it and control it; release from trauma after a chronic period of fear-collapse requires a reactivation of fear-arousal through anger or physical defensive reactions,[168] but we have to build a safe context first in which this can happen with a therapeutic result.

I want to give two examples of group-working that illustrate very different approaches. The first appears to be based on the principle that emotional expression is always good, regardless of what the emotions are:

[167] e.g. Rothschild (2000) on the need to 'titrate' the powerful emotional reactions of trauma-sufferers.
[168] See Chapter 16.

Richard had joined a long-standing therapeutic group and was in his second session. He shared something about his experiences in a relationship which triggered another member's distress. This member went into a meltdown, crying, interspersed with a vitriolic personal attack on him, and shouting that she didn't want him in the group. Richard was completely bemused – he had no idea what had provoked such an attack. He felt as if he had been punched in the stomach. He had no idea how to respond. He really wanted the group therapist to give him some support, but the therapist froze, as did the rest of the group. Eventually the therapist started working to try to regulate the member's outburst, but Richard was completely ignored. He left that evening, shaken and feeling really isolated.

Richard very nearly didn't go back to the group. He had a real sense of dread as the time for the next session came round, but he pushed through this and brought up in the group how he had been left feeling, and told the angry member that he thought it had been a completely unwarranted personal attack. This member replied that this was what the group was for, and if he couldn't take it he shouldn't be in the group. The therapist made no comment.

In my estimation, this was an unsafe group with its underlying belief that the expression of emotion was always helpful. It would appear, however, that this is not in any way unusual, and I am told that experiential groups provided for personal development in many therapy training courses are conducted in a similar manner.

The next example comes from the same group session I talked about in Chapter 10 (run according to the McCluskey model of group work[169]) which taught me about the different impacts on cognition of fear-arousal and fear-collapse.

As the facilitator was finishing a piece of work with one of the group members, I made a clumsy intervention, raising a question I might have asked in a therapist role – something group members are asked not to do, as, in this model the facilitator takes the role of caregiver. Our facilitator pointed this out to me in a very straightforward manner, but for some reason I can't now remember I persisted with my question. This provoked an angry attack on me from another group member – my behaviour had triggered memories of her dominant father.

The facilitator immediately intervened, cutting short the angry attack, pointing out to the angry member that the issue belonged to her to resolve, not to me, and offering her some time to explore her anger towards her father. This was agreed, but before commencing this piece of work, the facilitator turned to me, reiterated that this was not my issue, and offered me some time afterwards to process my previous intervention. In the meantime, aware that I was shaken by the angry attack, the facilitator asked another group member sitting next to me to keep an eye on me and help me to stay connected to the group.

I had been shamed by the attack, and gone into fear-collapse, so it was very hard to hear anything or take it in, and I kept drifting off into a dissociated state, but each time I felt

[169] See McCluskey and O'Toole (2020), p.68.

myself detaching from the group, I only had to look over to the member beside me, and her warm and welcoming eye-contact brought me back into a sense of connectedness which eventually pulled me out of my collapse.

In conclusion, I disagree with the assumption that it is 'good to emote'.[170] Only when emotion is elicited in a context of safety can we hope for a therapeutic outcome. While this has been an underlying principle of trauma work in the last two or three decades, I think that this understanding should be applied to the whole field of psychological therapy, particularly if one accepts the idea proposed in Chapter 11 that complex trauma underlies all of our therapeutic work.

[170] Richmond Heath, the coordinator of TRE for Australia, sees emotional catharsis as an energy-inefficient process for trauma release, believing that we only need to vent as an emotional outburst what we have been unable to release in neurogenic tremoring. (Personal conversation, September 2025.)

Chapter 28

The power of safety

The story of the twins – the biological transformation triggered by a visceral sense of safety

I want to finish this section with a story about the power of embodied safety as the antidote to fear.

> In 1995 in Massachusetts, twin girls Kyrie and Brielle Jackson were born 12 weeks premature. They were treated in intensive care in separate incubators which was the normal practice at that time. Kyrie made good progress and gained weight, but her smaller sister, Brielle, didn't thrive. She weighed just 2 pounds, was struggling with her heart rate and was blue-faced from crying. All medical interventions having failed to improve the situation, the nurse in charge, Gayle Kasparian, broke with the hospital protocol and moved Brielle into the incubator alongside Kyrie. As Kasparian reported: 'When I put Brielle in with her sister, it was amazing. She immediately calmed down. Her heart rate stabilised, and her colour changed.'[171] Kyrie wrapped an arm round her sister.

[171] Williamson (2013).

A local press reporter happened to be present and took a photo of what came to be called the 'rescue hug'. The photo and story became a media sensation throughout the world (having been over-hyped into a life and death account), but it changed hospital practices for dealing with premature twins and triplets throughout the States and is a clear example of the power of safety to transform the body's metabolism.[172]

For a premature baby, the experience of medical interventions together with isolation in an incubator can powerfully activate fear responses, and the ventral vagus, not yet fully developed in premature babies, is unable to regulate these responses, resulting in much physical distress, and in some cases, a danger of death.[173]

We spoke at the beginning of this section about safety being *visceral* – a sensation felt throughout the entire body. For Brielle, her sister's closeness, warmth, touch, breath and heartbeat, were safety viscerally sensed, and this produced a transformation that medical interventions were incapable of achieving. Embodied safety is not an abstract or intellectual idea. It is a felt-sense, and it triggers a biological system as powerful as the fear-system – one which is capable of shutting down the body's fear responses, enabling us to connect and thrive as human beings.

[172] Sylvester (2013). A CNN follow-up report on the incident includes the famous photo of the 'rescue hug'.
[173] Porges (2011).

Part 5

Supporting the therapist

Chapter 29

Training and continuing personal and professional development

Issues in training that can undermine the therapist, and reflections on my own training and personal and professional development

The more I came to understand the task of working to alleviate the distress of trauma, which is essentially the task all therapists are engaged in, the more I realised that the levels of support I needed went well beyond advice on self-care. From the start of training to retirement, we need high levels of competent and empathic professional support if we are to thrive in the work and become a 'safe enough' therapist and help our clients to flourish.

I have on the whole been very lucky in the level of professional support that has been available to me, but I know this is not always the case. In my roles as service manager and clinical supervisor, and in discussions with colleagues and therapists attending my workshops on the fear-system, I have come across many examples of failures of professional support which have sometimes had very detrimental impacts, resulting in anxiety and depression, loss of confidence, burnout and, in one case, a therapist giving up clinical work for many years.

In the first part of this chapter, I am going to note some of the problems in training that can undermine the therapist. While it may be difficult to avoid these problems, I think it is important to spell them out, as I have met many therapists who internalised such problems, thinking they happened because something was wrong with them. Based on my experience of meeting and talking in depth with a quite a number of therapists, I realised that many carried unwarranted doubts about their ability to undertake this work, based on having been undermined by failures in their training courses.

In the second part of the chapter, I will share some thoughts on my own journey through further training in different ways of working, and the difficulties and benefits that this can bring. I will then talk about my further personal development in the context of experiential group-work.

Initial training and commonly experienced difficulties

I was extremely lucky in my initial psychodynamic training with WPF North. Over the two-year diploma and a further two-year advanced diploma, we were based in well run counselling agencies, provided with clients who had been assessed as suitable for our level of practice, and supervised in-house by extremely experienced therapists.

I know from my contacts, however, that many have not been so fortunate with their training providers in more recent years. The fact that there are many problems in some therapy training courses came into very public focus just recently with an *Observer* article[174] commenting on toxic cultures in some courses, including bullying from course members and tutors which was not addressed, and inadequate complaint procedures.

The complaints I have heard from my own contacts mainly related to counselling courses at colleges and universities and

[174] Bradley (2024).

covered three key areas of dissatisfaction. The first related to feeling that courses left therapists poorly equipped to work with the needs of clients, chiefly by being limited to one or two approaches without an adequate theoretical framework for understanding trauma. As a result, many felt out of their depth in their post-training work and needed to make up the deficiency through further training before they recovered their confidence.

The second complaint related to unethical placements. Many courses left their students to find their own counselling placements, a stressful task for which most first-year trainees are completely unqualified.

> One counsellor who found her own placement with the agreement of her course, reported that the charity concerned didn't really understand about counselling and had no policies or procedures in place relating to counselling.

I have been told of training placements in bail hostels, and charities working with addiction and domestic and sexual abuse. In all these cases, trainees are thrown straight into working with severe complex trauma where they are utterly out of their depth and can be left feeling entirely inadequate to the work. This is completely unsafe for clients, and both unsafe and deeply undermining for trainee therapists.

The third complaint, which is perhaps the one I have heard most frequently, relates to 'personal development' groups, which are a standard part of most courses. Many people have told me that they had no idea what was going on or what they were supposed to do in these groups and reported that facilitators seemed to take no responsibility for what happened, allowing bullying and attacking behaviours and the dominance of the group by a few, while many were scared to speak, but would be criticised for their silence.

A colleague of mine gave me this account of her personal development group:

> 'The group was too large, consisting of all 22 of the year's cohort; those of us introverts who spoke less in the group were challenged by the tutors for not contributing enough, which felt as if we were being pathologised.
>
> The two facilitators were also our tutors who marked and assessed our skills practice and our academic assignments, so the group felt unsafe as there was always a sense that our personal development was also being assessed.
>
> The tutors tried to bring person-centred principles to bear to the running of the personal development group, so rather than setting out ground rules for us, we were asked, 'What do you want this group to be and what do you need to make this group work?' This meant that I (and possibly others) remained confused throughout the two-year training about the purpose of the group and what we were trying to achieve. It was therefore very hard to challenge when things went wrong (which they did). One group member said plaintively, 'Surely this is a place where we practise the core conditions towards each other?' after another group member slated someone else.
>
> When conflict arose, which it did with a lot of hurt being caused, the tutors did not step in and take responsibility for steering the group towards greater understanding, growth, learning etc. My memory was that they let whatever drama play out and did not check with participants afterwards how they were.'

The impression I have gained from such accounts is that courses were loosely based on a psychoanalytic model but often run by tutors without adequate training in this model, making their own adaptations. I am strongly of the opinion that every aspect of a therapy training course should reflect the individual care, understanding and support that therapists need to give to their clients, so each aspect contributes to the students becoming safe therapists. I entirely agree with the group member's comment above that, on a person-centred course, the 'core conditions' (see 'essential conditions' in Chapter 25) should have been central to the group experience.

Ongoing training

I see the initial training course, whether it is two or four years in length, as just the starting point. The work of therapy is an ongoing exploration. We may work with familiar themes, but each client is unique, and, as we get a sense of what works well and what doesn't, or what only works for some, our curiosity can lead us into new areas and attract us to different trainings.

With a good core training as a foundation, we may not need further, long, expensive trainings. The complexity of complex trauma often means that we need to learn how to work in different ways (as was examined in Part 3), but the more we gain in experience, the more we can benefit from shorter courses in other modalities and find our own ways to incorporate them into our particular way of working. This is sometimes no easy task, and learning new ways of working can feel very destabilising and take some time to be integrated into our own approach.

EMDR (eye-movement desensitising and reprocessing)[175]

I found just how difficult it could be to learn a new modality when I became interested in EMDR six years after qualifying as a psychodynamic counsellor.

> I attended a workshop on working with trauma and was fascinated by a video of a couple of EMDR sessions which appeared to be very effective in eliminating trauma symptoms following a traffic accident. This seemed like a really useful skill to acquire so I signed up for the training, which in those days took 17 hours, over three days.
>
> The first shock was that there were 90 of us on the course (all my training so far had been in small groups) and professionally it was a very mixed bunch. I also came across a very different mindset, with one participant commenting to another when we were asked to choose an event that was not too disturbing for our practice sessions with our neighbours, that 'that shouldn't be a problem – it's not as if we're like our patients'. That shook me a bit as it was a core tenet of my training that we were exactly like those we were helping.
>
> The training was fascinating, however, and when I got back from it I joined an EMDR group for further learning and supervision. The nature of the work was completely different from a psychodynamic approach. It seemed to be an 'intervention', and we didn't do interventions. There was also a lot to learn, and a number of protocols, so we used clipboards for all the paperwork, collecting brief

[175] Shapiro (1995). See brief example of this work in Chapter 4 (p.24).

descriptions of various traumatic moments, and using scoring frameworks for levels of distress.

This took a huge adjustment; it was such a different way of working. However, I had several clients with recent traumas, including a shocking attempted murder, and I got a real sense of what a powerful tool EMDR could be. The support group was helpful until the leadership of the group changed, and the new leader focused heavily on protocols and paperwork, producing a checklist 13 pages long to work from. I had become increasingly impatient with the clipboard approach, which seemed to signify an 'expert' stance and distanced me from my clients, so at this stage I left the group and focused on incorporating EMDR into a relational approach.

In all, it took me about 10 years to fully integrate EMDR into my own way of working where it could be woven seamlessly into my other approaches without any paperwork and clipboards. It was a difficult and disruptive process, and I don't regret a minute of it. Even in the early stages, when I was still chiefly working psychodynamically, the theory and practice of EMDR deepened my understanding of trauma and guided me in my work even when I was not using EMDR. Looking back, I can see that it also taught me a lot about fear-system regulation and establishing safety in working with trauma, before I came to a clearer understanding of these issues with a deeper insight into the fear-system.

CBT (cognitive behavioural therapy)

Shortly after training in EMDR, I attended an introductory course on CBT at York University. It was very well taught, and I found its structure of breaking thoughts, feelings and actions down into small, manageable parts and focusing on practical in-the-moment changes, a helpful addition to short-term counselling within GP surgeries. For me it sat fairly easily alongside the time-limited psychodynamic way of working which had been introduced in the last two years of my core training. It helped me to focus on the important task of breaking the feedback loop whereby the mind could intensify anxious thoughts, thus further strengthening the body's fear responses.

I had reservations about the way CBT either implied or stated that the client's mind was in some way wrong and needed correcting. The more I have understood the fear-system, the clearer I am that our thinking processes are secondary to our bodily reactions to threat, and that anxious thoughts are simply the mind doing its job in 'danger-mode'. When we attend to the core task of focusing on safety so as to regulate the body's responses, the mind automatically reverts back from danger mode to reflective mode.

I think that trauma work requires a whole spectrum of approaches, and CBT can form a really useful part of this spectrum. Its limitations lie in the fact that it works most effectively when the client can reflect on the differences between the content of their anxious thoughts and the reality of their present situation and accept that they are not aligned. The problem is that, once the fear-system is sufficiently aroused, reflective thinking is shut down, and CBT becomes increasingly ineffective. I think a lot of damage was done when this highly useful but partial approach to mental distress was fraudulently sold to government and thus to the NHS as the be-all-and-end-all of psychological therapies.

SCT (systems-centred therapy)

Not long after starting work with Una McCluskey as my clinical supervisor, she introduced me to systems-centred therapy, and for three years in a row I attended a week-long foundation training in this approach. SCT is an interesting blend of psychoanalytic and CBT ways of working developed by Yvonne Agazarian.[176]

The training was in the context of group work and introduced me to the idea of bringing safety into group working, with the concept of 'sub-grouping' – an approach which encouraged members to join with and support other members in their sharing so that, where differences were raised within the group, instead of there being a conflict around the differences, or the person that raised a difference feeling isolated, each person expressing a different response or outlook had the support of their own sub-group within the larger group.

What I found most useful in this approach were ways of working with anxiety and depression which fitted well with my later interest in working with the body. I have given an example of working with depression using this modality in Chapter 16 (pages 117–118).

EGCP (exploratory goal-corrected psychotherapy)

The most significant subsequent training that I undertook was with Una McCluskey in the early stages of her work developing a new model of attachment-based practice which she subsequently formulated as exploratory goal-corrected psychotherapy. This is a model based on a theory of interaction for caregiving which she developed from her research into adult psychotherapy. She also drew on others' research into early infant development in which she could see that accurate attunement to the affect of the other was related to the effective management of the fear-system in very young children.[177]

[176] Agazarian (2004).
[177] McCluskey (1997; 1999; 2001; 2005; 2013).
[178] McCluskey (2001).

The core of the model is based on Una's research[178] into empathic attunement between adult careseekers and caregivers (therapists) using video-based analysis of the physiological micro-movements involved in their interactions. These detailed observations highlighted the difference between caregivers who were able to attune to the feeling state of the careseeker, and those who were not.

Those caregivers who were able to attune in this way, helped their careseekers to regulate emotional distress and to engage in an exploratory way with their problems. In this way, the 'goal' of careseeking was reached, and the fear-system responses that prompted the careseeking were alleviated, resulting in feelings of relief and an increase in vitality.

Where caregivers were unable to empathically attune to the careseeker, the careseeking goal was not reached, and the careseeker was left with their distress unassuaged and their fear responses unregulated. The key contributor to failures to attune to the careseeker, was the activation of the caregiver's fear-system.

During a long co-operation with Dorothy Heard and Brian Lake, Una brought together their work, extending John Bowlby's attachment theory to apply to adult life, with her own research on goal-corrected empathic attunement. This created a way of engaging with a person within a structured framework of seven aspects of the self[179] which is able to provide 'an exploratory space where professional caregivers can explore the biological systems within themselves that interact to enable them to maintain as much well-being as possible'.[180]

The work keeps a focus on the moment-by-moment activation of fear responses in order to regulate them in a timely manner, thus enabling the maintenance of empathic

[179] Careseeking, caregiving, interest-sharing with others, sexuality, self-defence, our personally created external environment, and our internal environment – Heard, Lake and McCluskey (2012).
[180] McCluskey (2013), p.164.

attunement and facilitating deep exploratory work, which can lead to a transforming and strengthening of the self. Heard and Lake referred to the dynamic relationship between these seven aspects of the self as the 'restorative process' whereby progress in reducing the power of our fear responses in one aspect of the self, impacted all other areas of the self, leading to an increase in wellbeing. This way of working is applicable to individuals, couples or group therapy, and has also been successfully applied in workplace and organisational contexts.[181]

For me, this approach involved both a more responsive way of relating to the client than I had learned in my initial training, and a developing awareness of the continual activation of the fear-system, and the flow of sensation that it generated in the body.

This took a lot of adjustment, particularly as I had started my career with a highly intellectual approach which I think was my way of coping with a limited access to my own feelings (a default fear-system defence of freezing and feeling numb), and I went through patches where I felt de-skilled and a bit at sea.

I found the aspect of the training which involved taking video recordings of my work with a client particularly scary. In line with Una's research, we recorded our work sitting beside a full-length mirror, so the camera captured an image of myself and the client side by side, so we could examine the micro-movements of the face and of posture of both myself and the client, as well as picking up on tone of voice throughout the session.

This brought home to me very clearly the extent to which my fear-system was being activated in the therapeutic work and helped me to understand just how hard I needed to work to regulate my own fear responses, especially when working with a highly unregulated client. The training was very supportive and non-shaming, so I was able to survive my embarrassment

[181] Neath and McCluskey (2019).

and accept the ever-present reality of my fear responses. As I gradually became able to use this approach with my clients, I found that the majority of them responded very positively, and the central concept of the fear-system gave a real clarity and focus to my work and started a deep interest in further exploring this system which has such an impact on our lives.

Personal exploration

Over time, as I integrated the theory and practice of this approach into my own particular way of working, I became more aware of gaps in my understanding and frustration at the slow progress of my work with my clients with severe complex trauma, and this started me reading more widely on trauma, eventually coming across the work of Peter Levine. His book *In an Unspoken Voice*[182] opened my eyes to parasympathetic collapse as an aspect of the fear-system and introduced me to the work of Stephen Porges and his polyvagal theory.

I have spoken about my further journey of exploration into the fear-system that started from reading Peter Levine in Chapter 8. I was also very curious about Levine's way of working with the body, which he termed 'somatic experiencing',[183] and a related method of working with the body to release trauma developed by Pat Ogden and others, called 'sensorimotor psychotherapy'.[184]

Reading about these approaches while being much more in touch with the sensations of my body than I had been previously, I found myself linking back to working with metaphor based on bodily sensations[185] which I had been introduced to over 15 years previously but had never managed to fully integrate into my

[182] Levine (2010).
[183] https://traumahealing.org
[184] Ogden et al. (2006).
[185] Lawley and Tompkins (2000).

practice. Over a period of time this developed naturally into a way of giving slow attentive focus to bodily sensations related to trauma which owed much to all three of the above approaches. I found it could be woven seamlessly into EMDR, allowing me to help my clients work with trauma in whichever way they found safest.

Focusing-oriented therapy

At this stage I was introduced to focusing-oriented[186] work by Celia Dawson at the Complex Training Institute.[187] I have given an example of this way of working in Chapter 14 (pages 106–107) – I think of it as closely akin to vipassana meditation, which gives focused attention to the sensations in every part of the body. Focusing therapy, however, involves working with another person, and working, more slowly than in meditation, on sensations related to trauma experiences, rather than being practised individually and constantly moving through all parts of the body. It turned out that focusing-oriented work was very close to the approach I had started practising, which felt like a validation and a reconnection. Around that time I also changed clinical supervisor, finding a psychotherapist with a psychoanalytic background and an exploratory nature who was also fully trained in sensorimotor psychotherapy.

Learning new approaches – a risk or an opportunity?

I left the BACP (British Association for Counselling and Psychotherapy) and joined a different professional association a year before my retirement over my perception of a bias against new ways of working within the BACP. Over the course of a few

[186] Gendlin (1996).
[187] https://www.complextraumainstitute.org

years, I had submitted three articles to their monthly magazine *Therapy Today*, linking depression to parasympathetic collapse, and had them all declined. I then raised a complaint about an article published in *Therapy Today*[188] which dismissed both EMDR and polyvagal theory as 'therapy fads that undermine our profession'. The reply I got in response, while claiming that *Therapy Today* was a 'forum for debate', (which had not been my experience), summarised the view of the article's authors in the following terms: 'The ever-growing number of new models of therapy that are developed ultimately undermines both clinicians' and clients' confidence and faith in the efficacy of therapy, as well as pressuring practitioners into unnecessary investment into "add-ons" that may not sit with their core modality.'[189]

In contrast to this viewpoint, I have found that each of the approaches I explored gave me a different perspective into the problem of trauma and human suffering and what can be done to help alleviate it. Having a variety of perspectives helped me not to get stuck in one approach as the 'correct' way of working, trying to shoehorn different clients with very different defences into the same approach. Over my 30 years in practice, I made significant changes to the way I worked, but I valued all of my learning and took much from each approach, which gradually built up a way of working that was rooted in who I was as a person.

My advice to a therapist starting out on this journey would be to go slow and give time for integration, starting with sufficient time to become proficient in your core training model. Then follow *your* interests, not anyone else's, to find a way of working that really suits you. In essence, all that we need is a familiarity with fear-system regulation (your own as well as the client's), a way of working directly with trauma, and a way of meeting

[188] Wotton and Graham (March 2022).
[189] Personal correspondence (14 April 2022).

others as a person in order to support their own exploration. Your core training may provide all of these, but if not, there are many different ways to learn them.

A model for continuing the personal and professional development of caregivers

I have spoken of the importance of personal therapy as a key support for our work as therapists in Part 4, but in the latter part of my career I was introduced to a continuing professional development course for members of the caring professions run by Una McCluskey which focused on exploring the dynamics of attachment in adult life. This course impacted the way I practised professionally and also helped me to develop as a person. It sustained, supported and encouraged my work as a therapist up until my retirement. It involved taking part in experiential groups which explore our systems of attachment and the way these are infiltrated by our fear responses.

These 'McCluskey Groups' are run in a variety of formats, varying from once-monthly sessions over seven to nine months, to intensive courses over a number of days. They explore each of Heard and Lake's seven aspects of the self: careseeking, caregiving, interest-sharing with others, sexuality, self-defence, and also our personally created external environment, and our internal environment, both of which may be supportive or unsupportive of the self. Each session, lasting for three hours, focuses on one of these seven aspects of the self, with time left for exploring the integration of the whole. These are one-off courses but are even more beneficial if taken on a number of occasions with the same or different facilitators.[190]

The first two systems, careseeking and caregiving, are

[190] A detailed account of the purpose, workings and outcomes of these groups can be found in McCluskey and O'Toole (2020), pp.74-89.

particularly pertinent for professional caregivers such as psychological therapists. Over the years I have been a member or facilitator of a number of these groups, and a common theme emerged of the difficulties therapists have in seeking care or help in the face of difficulties. There tends to be a big imbalance between seeking care and giving care, and many stories emerged of difficulties with getting our needs met in the past, which prompted us to look after others (trying to keep parents and siblings happy) in order to retain some sense of being connected and valued.

This can mean that an early-established pattern of being a caregiver to others (which eventually leads us into work as a professional caregiver), can in fact be an indirect way of trying to get care for ourselves. As this is an ineffective way of getting care, and frequently leads to disappointment, it can leave us vulnerable to frustration, overwhelm and burnout if we rely on our clients for our sense of meaning and value in life.[191]

In the careseeking sessions of these exploratory groups, we explore how good we are in the present at turning to others for help, and if we don't do this, what is preventing us. We examine whether we have effective caregivers available to us, and whether we cause ourselves additional distress by seeking care from those who are unable to give it. We examine our history of how we were responded to in childhood when we sought care, in order to understand our present reactions and examine which patterns of relating no longer work well for us.

The aim of working on this aspect of the self is to help us to develop a well-functioning careseeking system, so that we can more readily turn to others for support in the face of stress, overwhelm or a blow to the self, whenever a caregiver is available. We also look at the indirect and ineffective ways we might be seeking care and learn to ask in a clear and straightforward way

[191] See McCluskey and O'Toole (2020), pp.84-86.

for what we need, and to carefully discriminate between those in our lives who can give us effective care and those who can't. The ability to turn to others for help is the most effective way of regulating our fear responses and it plays an important part in us becoming safe therapists for our clients.

In the sessions where we explore ourselves as caregivers, we look at who we give care to in the present and how we experience this – whether this activity energises us or drains us. We examine who asks for our care, and whether they make straightforward requests that trigger our instinctive caregiving, or whether they seek care from us in a controlling or manipulative way that leaves us feeling trapped and resentful.

Working on our caregiving self in the groups can help us to become more effective caregivers, as we become more aware of the activation of our own fear-system and become better able to regulate it. It can help us to see whether our pattern of giving care may in fact be a round-about, and perhaps ineffective, way of getting our own needs met, and prompt us to seek care in more straightforward ways. It can also help us to consider what changes we might wish to make in relationships where our care is sought in a controlling or manipulative way, and what changes we could work towards in the balance between caregiving and careseeking in our lives.[192]

After exploring our careseeking and caregiving selves, we move on, in subsequent sessions, to examine the ways in which the fear-system has impinged on our interests and creativity, our friendships and intimate relationships, our ability to stand up for ourselves, our ability to shape a supportive external environment and the way we view and treat ourselves internally.

I have found all these areas of exploration of enormous benefit, as, once we identify the ways in which the fear-system can limit our lives, we start to become clearer about the actions we can

[192] McCluskey (2013).

take to lessen its impact. However, the exploration of careseeking and caregiving has been for me the most important foundation and support in my journey to be a safe therapist for my clients, and I would highly recommend this work for all psychological therapists from whatever professional background.[193]

[193] Experiential groups run by facilitators trained in the McCluskey model can be found via the Association for Exploring the Dynamics of Adult Attachment (AEDAA) website: https://aedaa.co.uk/events/.

Chapter 30

Clinical supervision

Reflections on what we need from our clinical supervisors

Training courses should (at least in theory) provide a high level of support for counsellors, but once out of initial training, the level of professional support that is available becomes crucially important, and the first aspect to consider is our clinical supervision.

Clinical supervision is the absolute bedrock of our professional support. If we don't have a good working relationship with our supervisor, the work of therapy will take a greater toll on us, and our work with our clients will suffer.

I should clarify that when I am talking about clinical supervision, I am not talking about case management. I am describing the approach used in the relationally-based therapies, where supervision is not a management function but chiefly a supportive and exploratory one. For me, supervision was the place where I could bring anything that happened in my work with my clients, whether it was things that had gone really well, mistakes I felt I had made, or the times I felt really stuck and had lost all sense of direction.

I started learning this early in my training following the difficult session with a client I described in the Introduction where I was left with little recollection of what had happened. My sense of competence was shattered, I had a feeling of dread in my gut, and I was only able to write down three words as a record of the session:

> I attended my next supervision with the same sense of dread, and a feeling of shame that I had failed so badly as a counsellor. I apologised to my supervisor for not being able to remember anything about the session, and for only having these three words instead of my usual detailed notes.
>
> My supervisor told me that I didn't need to apologise for anything. She explained that it was normal for a client's distress to have this sort of an impact on the therapist, and she was very curious about the three words I had salvaged from what seemed like the wreckage of the session. She spent the entire session chewing over these three words with me, linking each one to the way I had been left feeling in and after the session, and to the details of the client's history contained in the initial assessment I had inherited from another therapist. As we went on I was gradually able to recall a bit more of what had happened in the session.
>
> By the end of the supervision I understood that my client had communicated her distress to me, not in clearly articulated words, but viscerally, so I was left feeling something of what she had been feeling. My supervisor pointed out to me how valuable this information was and helped me to think about how I might work with that level of distress.

So from very early on I learned that supervision could be a place of safety – somewhere I could bring anything. That didn't always make it easy to use that safety – there were many times when I would think of an intervention I'd been worried about or ashamed of, and I'd think 'I can't bring that to supervision'. However, I learned over time to recognise that, if I flinched at bringing a subject to supervision, that was the very subject that I most needed to discuss.

It takes quite an act of courage to be this transparent with another person, and this makes the choice of supervisor (where this is possible) a matter of great importance. We need to find someone trustworthy, but it may take time to establish that level of trust.

The consequences of staying with a supervisor we don't trust can be detrimental to our self-confidence, our development as a therapist and to our clients.

> A therapist (I'll call him John) whom I met at a training day, told me he had continued with his training supervisor (Gareth) for years after he qualified even though he'd never felt quite at ease with him. The supervisor had always been quite directive, which, as a student, John had found quite reassuring, but over the years this had not changed. As John gained in experience, read more widely and explored other modalities, he found his supervisor increasingly critical and undermining. However, he was afraid to leave and find someone else because he thought he would be judged and found wanting by a new supervisor.[194] Over time he stopped bringing to supervision anything he felt might be criticised.

[194] That really resonated with me. I had always found changing a clinical supervisor a scary process, thinking, 'Well, I managed to pull the wool over the eyes of the last one, but the next one's going to find me out!'

He started working with a new client, a young woman to whom he was very attracted, both physically and emotionally. He mentioned nothing of this to his supervisor over several months, during which time his attachment to this client increased, and his way of working with her started to change, including a level of self-disclosure.

One day, just before a break of a couple of weeks, matters came to a head when John's client made a seemingly casual remark near the end of the session about her imagining meeting up with him for a coffee outside of the counselling room. She looked him straight in the eyes as she said this. John experienced a huge wave of desire and a powerful impulse to invite her for a coffee there and then. He then had a wave of panic and broke into a sweat as another part of his mind imagined him being struck off the register of counsellors. He froze and was unable to say anything for several minutes, and as the session ended, only managed a clumsy response that they would pick things up after the break.

John was in a state of agitation after the session and confided in a friend who was also a therapist. His friend told him this had to be discussed in supervision but couldn't persuade John to contact his own supervisor after so many months of not talking about this client. His friend then asked him why he'd stayed with his supervisor for so long when he felt the need to hide things from him, and eventually recommended his own supervisor, but stressed that he'd have to tell her everything.

His friend's supervisor (Gill) agreed to an urgent appointment with John who told her everything that had happened. Gill commented on how powerful our feelings of attachment for clients could be, normalising his experience, and putting him more at ease, but then got him to explore what his client's needs were. Guided by her questioning, John outlined his client's distress when her father, who had been very close to her, suddenly became distant when she turned 12 years old. This was now creating problems in her marriage as she got very upset and withdrew at any sign of distancing from her husband.

Gill invited John to consider why his client's father might have suddenly withdrawn his affection. John said he had wondered whether his client had reached puberty, and this had brought her father into a clearer awareness of his sexual feelings for her which frightened him into cutting off from her. Gill then helped John to see that the father-daughter transference had powerfully activated in the therapy. She noted that if John went with one of his impulses, which was to finish working with his client, he would be repeating the trauma of her father abandoning her. She also helped him to see that if he had broken the boundaries and started a relationship outside of the therapy, he would have enacted the scenario her father had been trying to avoid when he withdrew from her.

Gill helped John to formulate a way of working which would note the attachment with the client and the imagined relationship but firmly reestablish the boundary of no relationship outside of the therapy, linking the feelings within the therapy back to his client's distress over her father's behaviour, and to the way this was causing problems in her relationship with her husband.

At the end of the session John asked Gill if he could continue to work with her. Gill agreed on condition that he promised to hide nothing from her in their sessions, and that he dropped his plan to finish his supervision work with Gareth by email, and went and ended face to face, giving the reasons why he thought their work together was no longer what he needed.

The reason supervision can be so helpful is that the powerful sensations created between the client and the therapist can shut down thinking and derail the therapy, whether these are the sensations of the fear-system (as in the first example from my own training) or the sexual system *and* the fear system (as in the example of John's difficulties with supervision).

The supervisor picks up the feelings from the vivid account the therapist is encouraged to bring, so gets a real sense of the work, but their thinking is less affected than the therapist's as the emotions are experienced at second-hand. The therapist therefore has an informed guide who can hold on to their own reflective thinking and acts as an anchor for the therapist in the middle of emotional storms.

The protection of both therapist and client from harm depends on supervision being a safe place to which any aspect of the work can be brought and explored, particularly instances where therapists think they have made mistakes, are ashamed of their interventions, or feel completely out of their depth. Anything that prevents a therapist from accessing a supervisor with whom they can feel that level of safety is therefore unethical.

This is a simpler matter in private practice where each therapist needs to take responsibility for finding a safe supervisor who can help them to grow and develop in the work. There can be limits to what we can learn from one supervisor unless we are lucky, and they are constantly learning and growing alongside us. It usually helps our learning to work with several different supervisors over the course of our career.

It is important to be aware of any power imbalance in the relationship. While it is usual in training for a supervisor to be much more experienced and knowledgeable, so there is a sense of a student-teacher relationship, as we progress in our work and gain experience, we should feel more of a sense of equality and autonomy. It is particularly important that we choose a supervisor who will support us with enthusiasm as we explore new approaches and develop our own unique way of working.

Ensuring that we have a safe supervisor can be more complicated for employed therapists who often have little or no choice of supervisor and who are sometimes allocated a clinical supervisor who is also their line manager. This particular dual-relationship can be unsafe and highly unethical,[195] as it is extremely rare for anyone to be able to make themselves as vulnerable as we need to be in supervision for the sake of our clients, and to trust as a supervisor someone who has real power over us when we work within an organisation that may well be fear-driven.

It seems to me, however, that the various professional associations on whom clinicians rely for support are either unable to protect us from the potential harm of this dual role, or do not see it as a significant problem.[196] While most recommend against this practice, and some say it would be 'useful' to separate line management and clinical supervision, they fall short of saying that separation of these roles is essential for clinician and client safety.

[195] There is a disturbing example of this in the next chapter.

[196] To give two examples: the BACP 'Ethical Framework for the Counselling Professions' recommends that 'a substantial part or preferably all of supervision needs to be independent of line management' (BACP, No date, para. 61). The British Psychological Society (BPS) recommend that supervision/consultation is kept separate from line management, but states: 'Whilst it should not be a substitute for line management, a psychologist's supervisor may also be their line manager'. (BPS Explore, No date, Chapter 1.5). In my mind, these ethical codes are inadequate for protecting therapists and their clients from harm given the number of clinicians working in fear-driven organisations such as the NHS.

While there is evidence that the absence of supervision makes it more likely that therapists will suffer from vicarious traumatisation,[197] it seems highly probable that the same will be true for those who are not able to trust their supervisors and therefore cannot be open with them.

Before leaving the subject of supervision, I just want to mention the importance of seeking the help of colleagues in the immediate aftermath of a session which has been really difficult or has shaken or disturbed us in some way. When I worked in the NHS, there was a general understanding that we could seek the help of any colleagues who might be available at the time to help process a session we had found particularly difficult. There can often be a gap of weeks between a disturbing session and our planned clinical supervision appointment and being able to debrief and download with a supportive colleague who fully understands how difficult the work can be at times, can be a really useful form of supervisory 'first-aid' which can very quickly reduce stress and restore wellbeing.

I think this is particularly important when working alone in private practice, where it can help to belong to a local network which can offer this sort of mutual support (see Chapter 32). I was greatly helped by working alongside my wife, Fran, in private practice, where we would frequently help each other to debrief after the day's work.

[197] Pearlman and MacIan (1995).

Chapter 31

The management of therapists

The support therapists need from their managers

Working in any context, therapists will face two potential sources of fear activation which can both impair their effectiveness and take a toll on the body. These are the clients' fear responses, and our own fear responses related to our personal history and to the current stresses and difficulties of our personal lives. Employed therapists may have to navigate a third source of fear activation in the workplace if this is not well managed.

For all therapists in employment, the quality of management is a key factor in their ability to stay safe and support their clients without the risk of being overwhelmed by the work and suffering burnout. Supportive management can enable us to work safely with high levels of disturbance, but fear-driven management and organisations harm both therapist and client.

An ethically-managed therapy service

I want to start with an example of an ethically-managed therapy service. When I moved into the NHS, I became part of a large Psychological Therapies department which was staffed by counsellors, psychotherapists, clinical psychologists, mental health nurses, and a psychiatrist. Its services ranged from primary-care counselling to a personality disorder group programme, and covered a full range of specialist services. I joined this department as a primary-care counsellor at a time when counselling had become well established within many GP surgeries, and I was recruited as part of a drive to provide this coverage to all local GP practices.

Each of the primary-care counsellors worked in one or more surgeries with a home base in the department. We had a great deal of professional autonomy in our work and managed our own waiting lists in consultation with the doctors. While the doctors were very busy, it was still possible to make time for consultation about patients, along with discussions and feedback to ensure that referrals were appropriate. It was accepted that counsellors were a significant support to the GPs, particularly with respect to patients with longer-term mental health troubles who had previously taken up a lot of the doctors' time.

The clinical psychologist who led the department enabled a respectful and exploratory culture. I joined the department with two other counsellors as the first group of a larger team, and we were initially allocated psychologists as clinical supervisors. They were not trained in our model of clinical supervision, and though very affirming they did not offer the in-depth evaluation we were used to, so we insisted on a change of supervision which was readily agreed.

There was a great deal of cross-fertilisation between the different professions in the department. There were regular meetings and joint training sessions, and a monthly large supervision group where we could bring difficult cases and get the benefit of very different perspectives. I learnt a great deal from the clinical psychologists about the regulation of anxiety and panic and, along with colleagues, shared my knowledge of clinical supervision, psychodynamic practice and EMDR.

The department head was a fast decision-maker, but where he made decisions I really disagreed with, he was always open to me arguing my case. On a few occasions I was able to change his mind and win my point, so I was fully accepting of the times when he listened to me but still stuck to his original decision.

One of the key factors in making the department feel like a safe place to work was that we were all clinicians whatever other roles we had. Most of us had managers from the same profession and, where this was not possible, we shared closely aligned codes of ethics. All of us worked with managers who understood the difficulty and complexity of the work.

Providing safety and support for therapists

Having flourished within the supportive culture of this department, I was delighted to then take up a management role and build on what I had learned from my years in management in Royal Mail before I trained as a therapist. As the service manager for primary-care counselling, I saw my key role as supporting the counsellors in their work with clients, removing problems, disruptions and unnecessary stresses, and ensuring a sense of connection and involvement. We regularly met to discuss our work, the way we organised ourselves, measured our success and integrated with colleagues in the GP practices.

To work effectively with their clients, therapists need managers who are approachable, generous with their time, and who understand the nature of the work, and the levels of stress it can induce, particularly at times when it coincides with difficulties in therapists' personal lives. They need to give time for group support, one-to-one support between therapists, and consultation over any changes.

It is particularly important where therapists can be severely shaken, by working with a suicidal client for example, to foster a culture where seeking help in the face of difficulties is the norm. If outcome measures are used in a service, it is the manager's job to remove the stress these may cause to individuals, understanding that the difficulty of the task varies hugely from client to client, and that such measures are highly subjective. Finally, where the work is part of a larger organisation going through turbulence, a manager should be prepared to do a certain amount of 'fighting upwards' to shield the team from unnecessary stress.

The impact of poor management

A manager of therapists who can't regulate their own fear-system and allows the turbulence of a fear-driven organisation to cascade down to therapists is useless and dangerous both to clinicians and to their clients. I am very much in agreement with researchers who claim that issues such as vicarious trauma and burnout do not chiefly flow from the difficulties of the work, and the shocking stories that we hear from our clients, but are more related to lack of safety, stability and adequate support in the workplace.[198] One study concluded: 'We may need to shift paradigms, moving our focus away from individualistic efforts at education and training and toward a more systemic approach of advocacy for healthier working conditions.'[199]

[198] Devilly et al. (2009) found that that work-related stressors best predicted therapist distress, rather than patients' traumatic material.

Chapter 31

In the last years of my time in the NHS there was a significant move away from clinicians being managed by fellow-clinicians sharing the same code of ethics, resulting in therapists being managed by those who had little understanding of their work and what constituted safe practice. What I hear from colleagues and friends indicates that working conditions for psychological therapists in the NHS have deteriorated still further. A clinical psychologist who made the decision to leave the NHS because of failures in management support, across two different NHS services, told me:

> 'In one team, on several occasions I said, "I am at capacity, and the entire team is at capacity – we are holding too many clients, and we are holding too many clients presenting with too much risk - it is not safe for me, or the clients for me to work with any more risk," and, rather than being given support, I was put into an HR capability process.
>
> 'The implication was that I was not "capable" of doing my job, purely because I was acknowledging the limits of safe practice. This process then negatively impacted my ability to potentially get hired in a different team, meaning I was then essentially trapped within this toxic workplace. The only option I was left with was to file a grievance against my supervisor and manager (who were the same person). Needless to say, this was not upheld because, as I discovered the hard way, it seems that "the house always wins" in a toxic, fear-driven system.
>
> 'Years later, in a totally different team, I found myself again feeding this same idea back to my manager (who, in this

[199] Killian (2008).

service too, was also my clinical supervisor): "We do not have enough resource in this team to safely manage the demands of the referrals coming in." I said this on many occasions, and there were no changes made to the way we were being asked to work – no new boundaries were set to better match the resources we had with the numbers and types of referrals coming in.

'When I did not back down from pointing this out, and when I began to decline to pick up new referrals, due to the already unsafe levels of caseload I was holding – I was referred to Occupational Health to assess if I was "fit or capable to do my job". Of course I was both fit and capable, but the demand was simply too much for any clinician, or any team. There was no pathway to assess whether the services and system were fit and capable to keep clinicians and patients safe.

'By this point, I felt the only way I could keep myself safe and practise with integrity as a clinician was to leave the NHS and set up my own private practice. I now provide a safe service to my clients, with an awareness of fear-system dynamics, the importance of self-care for the clinician, and safe boundaries around clinical practice, to keep both myself and the clients safe and supported.'

One of the worst examples of poor management in the NHS is the IAPT (Improving Access to Psychological Therapies) service. The introduction of this service closed down well-functioning services, such as the one I worked in, on the false promise of delivering a cheaper, more accessible and more effective provision of psychological therapies. James Davies noted that, to cover up lack of effectiveness, IAPT services routinely manipulated data to demonstrate success while creating a target-driven and highly stressful culture which had a demoralising effect on its own therapists.[200]

Quoting a 2015 British Psychological Society survey which revealed that half of the IAPT therapists reported feeling a failure in the work they do, and a significant proportion suffered from depression, stress and long-term chronic conditions, Davies commented that: 'being employed as an IAPT therapist is now far worse for your mental health than working in almost any other UK job or industry'.[201]

[200] Davies (2022), Chapter 4.
[201] Davies (2022), p.118.

Chapter 32

Creating a network of friendship for professional support

How to find supportive colleagues to sustain you for the long term

The poet William Blake,[202] at the end of the 18th century, wrote the following:

> *The bird a nest, the spider a web, man friendship*

Nowadays we would replace 'man' with 'humankind', but the message is powerful – friendship is the fundamental place where we belong, and the foundation of that visceral sense of safety that we need to reset our fear-system and to become effective caregivers to others. This applies just as much to our professional support as it does to our networks of personal friends.

The importance of friendship in a professional context

The importance of such support was brought home to me a year or so before I left the NHS during a period of great turbulence, when the NHS was being restructured and undergoing huge budget cuts.

[202] Keynes, Ed. (1966). From 'The marriage of Heaven and Hell'.

On two occasions I took a stand against what was going on. On the first occasion, when a group of counsellors employed directly by GPs had their posts cut with no notice, stopping counselling work in progress, I threatened to go public with a newspaper article unless this cut was reversed (which it was – for the time). On the second occasion, when a newly appointed senior manager started bullying some of the staff, I called it out publicly and asked to speak directly to the Chief Executive about this.

On each occasion, though I was simply doing what I thought I had to as a manager, I would get quite a few patches where my resolve crumbled and I'd start to think I'd overstepped the mark and would be humiliated or lose my job, and this would be followed by moments of panic or a huge energy slump with a sense of dread in the pit of my stomach. However, having learned much about the importance of careseeking, on each occasion this happened I would immediately contact one of three close friends on the management team, either picking up the phone or going straight round to their rooms if they were free. All were strong supporters of the actions I was taking, and it took no more than two minutes of me describing my wobble and receiving their affirmation for me to be able to calm and get on with my work. Even in the middle of all the worry, their solidarity gave me a real sense of stability and wellbeing.

My experience of supportive professional groups

I hugely benefited throughout my career from belonging to supportive groups of fellow therapists. My first such group consisted of therapists who had trained at the same institute over different years, and we used to take turns leading discussions on aspects of our work that were really interesting us at the time or sharing our learning from courses we attended or new books we read. This group introduced me to working with the sensations of the body using metaphor,[203] which greatly enhanced my practice over the years.

The next support group I joined consisted of therapists who were a great deal more experienced than I was and included ex-tutors and ex-supervisors. A number of them had come from a much larger group which they had found increasingly toxic and riven with rivalries, where presenting a paper at the meeting was often a fearful process, running the risk of shaming criticism. They wanted to find something much more nurturing and exploratory, and this was also exactly what I was looking for at that stage. In this group, our own personal interests and our work interests blended seamlessly together as we read and discussed novels and poetry, but a big difference from other groups was that the meeting centred round a meal, and we took turns at cooking and hosting the meeting.

My own contributions varied from presenting some of my earliest ideas on the fear-system to running a blind wine-tasting and reflecting on the delight of our sense of taste. Eating together is a very companionable and bonding experience and, aided by lovely food and often a glass or two of good wine, we would approach our discussions from an amiable and relaxed mindset – in other words, a totally safe place, in which my anxieties about being a 'junior' member fell away, and I felt completely at ease. This was a support group in the style of an ancient Greek 'symposium', and it nurtured me for many years.

In 2008, I joined Una McCluskey's first UK-based training group, working with the dynamics of attachment in adults,[204]

[203] Lawley and Tompkins (2000).
[204] Heard, Lake and McCluskey (2012).

and after the first two years of formal training, we continued to meet over several weekends a year. The ongoing group originally offered supervision for those who were using the model in their work but became a supportive and interest-sharing group which greatly enhanced our personal and professional development. Seventeen years later most of us were still meeting for a couple of weekends a year and deep friendships have developed. There's just about nothing I know about myself that I haven't been able to share in this group.

About eight years ago, as we started to cut back a bit on the frequency of our training group weekends, I suggested that those of us who trained together who were based in York met up on a monthly or six-weekly basis. We have lunch together for which we all bring a contribution and then meet as a group for the rest of the afternoon, sharing what has been happening in our lives, supporting each other with our difficulties and sharing our interests and enthusiasms.

Six years ago, I set up another support group to broaden this way of working to therapists who had not worked with Una McCluskey. On the basis that monthly meetings (like monthly supervision) can leave long gaps when support is often needed more quickly, this group met at our house every week on a Friday (apart from holidays), starting with a shared lunch and followed by a group session. I had noticed that regular groups could be a burden during stressful times, so the idea was that there was no obligation to attend any given week, and that you did not send apologies for absence, but just made contact to say if you *were* coming. I would make a soup so there was always something to eat, but we had lovely, varied lunches based on whatever people brought with them.

This group ran until the start of Covid, becoming a weekly online group and then a mix of online and in-person on alternate weeks as the pandemic subsided. It then reverted to in-person based round a shared lunch until I retired a couple of years ago.

Since then, other members have taken on the task of hosting and facilitating the group.

So much of what I have been able to do has been down to the support of friends. Without them I would never have started on my exploration of the nature of fear and depression. My ability to write this book has been due in no small part to a group of 16 friends and colleagues who volunteered to read my first attempts, cheer me on, and offer suggestions for improvement.

Creating safety in a support group

There is such a lot of fear in the world of therapy. As I noted in Chapter 25, mental health professionals tend to have experienced more trauma in their lives compared with the general population,[205] and many of us come into this work searching for an understanding of what is going on in our own bodies, minds and lives. Bringing us together in anything other than a safe environment is a risky business for those of us who would prefer to avoid emotional turbulence.

We notice the activation of fear responses in mental hierarchies, whether we see them from the perspective of thinking others are far more experienced and better qualified than we are, or if we look down on others as less well trained and less competent. There is, of course, a reality that some training courses are more comprehensive than others, and we all start out inexperienced, but the fear element creates a 'pecking order' and prompts us to defend our place in it. I have come across mindsets where the higher the level of disturbance worked with, the greater the level of kudos and, in some cases, the greater the level of disdain for those working with simpler problems.

As therapists, the whole of who we are is invested in our work, so it is very exposing to be in contexts where we are sharing

[205] Henderson et al. (2025).

our work and ideas. The more anxious we are in such contexts, the more we put on a mask, but it doesn't support us. We're not fooled by our own mask, knowing we feel very different behind the calm or competent façade it presents, but we're often fooled by everyone else's mask and think we are the only one in the group feeling insecure.

Before the start of my 'Fear and the Therapist' workshops, where people come early for a cup of tea in the kitchen, or if they chat in the group room before we begin, I ask everyone to avoid any discussion of their profession, ways of working, job titles, or length of training and experience. I had noticed in some of my earlier workshops how this sort of discussion at the beginning of the morning had set up hierarchies and rivalries and triggered fear responses, making it harder for the group to feel safe.

I find that a group becomes safe when we meet as persons, setting aside the ego[206] and accepting our commonality as human beings with powerful fear responses who are drawn to the task of helping others in distress. Where this can be stated at the outset, particularly when it can be a shared experience, this sets the foundation for a safe group.

> There is a moment very near the start of my workshops when I finish my introductory remarks to the group, most of whom have never met before, and say that I'd now like to hear from each person in turn about their expectations of the workshop.
>
> There is a pause, and then I ask everyone to stop, close their eyes and notice what just happened in their body when they were asked to address the group for the first time. I then ask them to open their eyes, and I list some of the

[206] I understand the ego as the self in the grip of fear.

sensations they might have felt, such as faster heartbeat, weakness in the legs, or mind going blank. As I go through the list of possible sensations, I see a flicker of a smile on peoples' faces, and then everyone notices everyone else's response. Suddenly the group relaxes – we realise that we all experience these fear responses – hierarchies disappear – we are all just human beings, and from that point on we usually have a safe group.

It is helpful if groups can find a way to notice and name the fear responses as they arise. In a facilitated group, this would be the task of the facilitator, sometimes with a very simple instruction such as 'just breathe everyone', or 'tension down'.[207] In a peer group, each person would take responsibility for noticing what was happening in themselves or the group and naming it (perhaps something like 'I'm starting to feel a bit tense; is anyone else?'), so that everyone can regulate their responses.

One important point is to work and share *alongside* other peoples' sharing, but to resist the urge to jump in and be the therapist. I have been in groups where one person's courage in sharing their distress was met by a rush of those jumping in to play the therapist. It made me think of a flock of vultures swooping down on a piece of carrion. Don't be that vulture! Approaching as a fellow sufferer is usually much more supportive and helpful and makes everyone feel safer.

Finding or building supportive professional networks

I would strongly encourage any therapist who does not already have a safe and supportive professional network to make it a

[207] Frequently used by Una McCluskey in her group work.

high priority to either search out any in their area or take responsibility for creating one. This can seem like a daunting task, so the best first step might be to find someone who will join you in the task.

A lot of people set up their first support group with therapists they have trained with and know well, but if you do not live near your training base, that may only be possible with an online group. Online groups can be very helpful, but I don't think they can replace actually being with other people.[208] If you start with an online support group, I would still recommend trying to find or build a local in-person network. Locally-based training days can be another way to meet like-minded colleagues; supervisors might be able to help you to get in touch with other therapists if you ask them for help, or you could even use notices in your professional journal to make contacts.

If there isn't an existing group to join and you want to start one, but are feeling underconfident, I have given a few simple suggestions in Appendix 8 for setting up such a group which I have found useful in the past.

Our work as a therapist has a huge impact on us, and the scale of support needed is far greater than is often assumed. Having a network of fellow therapists with whom we feel safe can be a real help in surviving difficulties with a sense of wellbeing. Finding or setting up a support network can seem daunting, but if you commit to doing it, even just mentioning it to one other person may set a ball rolling and open up doors you didn't know were there. There are many wonderful people engaged in this work and I'm so grateful for having met and shared with those I've been lucky enough to find.

[208] Platforms such as Zoom have to edit out a huge amount of data in order to be able to stream at speed, so many of the micro-movements of the face and of posture that convey emotional states and help us regulate each other are lost in the process. This is by no means all that is lost in online meetings.

Conclusion

I started this book with a claim that complex trauma was everywhere, a normal condition of our traumatised species, though we see a wide spectrum in its severity. I defined complex trauma as a condition in which our fear-system, having activated in response to a threat or threats, is chronically unable to deactivate (or reset) even when the original threat has passed, and we find ourselves in a place of safety. To put it crudely, we get stuck in 'fear-mode', and the longer we remain in fear-mode, the harder it gets to deactivate our fear responses.

At the centre of all of this is our biological fear-system – our oldest set of responses to threat in evolutionary terms. I have described its three main ways of activating as fear-alert, to assess the danger, fear-arousal, to escape from it, and fear-collapse as our last resort when there is no escape.

I have described the biology of the fear-system, breaking it down into its constituent parts and noting the range of fear responses designed for different types of threat and the varying ways we experience these responses, from hyper-arousal to collapse, and from terror to rage to an absence of any sense of fear. I have also described how the stuck fear-system creates a tangle of dysfunction affecting every aspect of our lives and how the way humans have treated each other in a state of fear throughout the whole of recorded history has affected all of us, its impact passing down from one generation to another.

I have noted that the impact of trauma is held in the body, and we need to find ways of working with the body in order to release trauma and allow our fear-system to reset. I have also examined the tangle of complexity that we face when we work with complex trauma and the stresses and setbacks of the work.

I have explained how the fear-system cannot deactivate if there is no place of safety, and that helping to create a visceral sense of safety is central to our work with trauma. I have also considered the huge amount of support we need throughout our careers as therapists and reflected on the key professional sources of that support.

I have tried for many years to understand the range of human suffering I came across in my work as a therapist, and to find different approaches to alleviating it. Ultimately the theory of our biological fear-system, which I have outlined in this book, has been my greatest source of clarity. This theory, which explains the way our fear-system works, the way it can get stuck, and what we need to do to help it reset forms, for me, the hub of a wheel into which the theory and practice of most of the different therapeutic approaches fit. Once I understood how the fear-system worked, everything else fell into place and, most importantly, I could start to better understand the whole range of impulses and feelings that made up my own experience of life.

What I have learned from this theory is the following:

The unregulated fear-system is perhaps the chief cause of human misery and understanding it offers a clearer guide to working to alleviate this misery.

*

A visceral sense of safety is central to the deactivation of fear responses, but we live in fear-driven societies in which few can feel a real sense of safety.

*

Human beings are biological organisms – we change at the pace of organic change. There are no quick fixes in complex work.

*

Anxiety and depression are the most common symptoms of the unregulated fear-system.

*

We need to stop pathologising human suffering. Our clients' responses are not 'wrong' and in need of correction.

*

We need to pay more attention to social change to alleviate the isolation, poverty, inequality and oppression that cause much of our clients' suffering.

*

Careseekers (our clients) need relatively fear-free caregivers.

*

Our job as a therapist is either to regulate fear-system responses – our own as well as our clients' – or support our clients' explorations.

*

Our own physiological state gives us insight into our clients' fear-states and guides us, moment by moment, as to whether we can explore or need to regulate.

*

Understanding our fear responses helps us to avoid becoming alarmed by them.

*

The fear responses we sense during our work are not signs of weakness but sources of information.

*

Fear responses can, however, wipe out our reflective thinking and our ability to relate to our clients.

*

Our ability to be aware of our fear responses and to regulate them is the core of our usefulness as therapists.

*

The regulation of fear responses in the therapy room starts with the therapist.

The tangled complexity of complex trauma means that our work is difficult, often deeply frustrating, many faceted, often long-term or requiring many episodes of work, rarely complete and requiring enormous learning and the development of many diverse skills. For a therapist not long out of training, this probably seems really daunting, but each of us starts from our own life experience, which is the core of our map of this territory, and our knowledge of this map is hugely enhanced by our own therapeutic journey.

Each of us also starts from a solid training base, whichever approach we begin with, and from that point the addition of a biologically-based theory of trauma can illuminate many aspects of the map which might not previously have made sense. Our therapists, supervisors, colleagues and all our clients further enhance our knowledge and skills, and we integrate the knowledge and experience of others with that of our own.

If you don't waste time comparing yourself with others, but ground yourself in what you know, stay curious, follow your interests, keep reading and take short courses, you will acquire skills in different ways of working. Take your time exploring new ways of working – it's like eating slowly and allowing plenty of time for digestion.

Make it a real priority to meet and talk with colleagues and find supportive friendships to help sustain you. Where you find people you can trust, turn to them for help with the difficulties, upsets and stresses of the job. *Never try to manage on your own.*

Avoid those who tell you that their approach is the only correct way to work and gradually integrate all you need to build your own individual approach to working with complex trauma. In this way, over time, you can become the best therapist that you have it in you to be.

Go well.

Appendices

Appendix 1

Complex post-traumatic stress disorder (CPTSD) in *ICD-11*

Introduction

Counsellors and psychotherapists do not tend to use mental health diagnoses in their work, as these belong to a medical model of working which does not always sit easily with a relationally-based approach. They tend more to try to come to an understanding (a 'formulation') of each person's difficulties which will help to clarify the most effective way to work with the presenting issues.

The concept of 'complex trauma' (Part 1 of this book), which outlines the many complicated ways a person's life can be affected by adverse and shocking events, is more of a formulation, or a framework for understanding the unique problems of each of our clients, than a diagnosis. However, many clinical psychologists use both medical and relational models in their work, and it can be useful for other therapists to have an understanding of trauma diagnoses, especially when working in health service contexts, or in roles which require liaison with medical professionals.

The diagnosis for CPTSD in the *International Classification of Diseases, 11th Revision (ICD-11)* is built on that for PTSD, so this is given first.

PTSD (post-traumatic stress disorder)

Experiences which qualify for this diagnosis: 'Post-traumatic stress disorder (PTSD) may develop following exposure to an extremely threatening or horrific event or series of events.'

Symptoms: 'It is characterised by all of the following:

1. re-experiencing the traumatic event or events in the present in the form of vivid intrusive memories, flashbacks, or nightmares… typically accompanied by strong or overwhelming emotions, particularly fear or horror, and strong physical sensations;
2. avoidance of thoughts and memories of the event or events, or avoidance of activities, situations, or people reminiscent of the event(s); and
3. persistent perceptions of heightened current threat, for example as indicated by hypervigilance or an enhanced startle reaction to stimuli such as unexpected noises.

The symptoms persist for at least several weeks and cause significant impairment in personal, family, social, educational, occupational or other important areas of functioning.'[209]

CPTSD (complex post-traumatic stress disorder)

Experiences which qualify for this diagnosis: 'Complex PTSD is a disorder that may develop following exposure to an event or series of events of an extremely threatening or horrific nature, most commonly prolonged or repetitive events from which escape is difficult or impossible (e.g. torture, slavery, genocide campaigns, prolonged domestic

[209] Full ICD-11 details: https://icd.who.int/browse/2024-01/mms/en#2070699808

violence, repeated childhood sexual or physical abuse).'

Symptoms: All PTSD symptoms plus 'severe and persistent:

1. problems in affect regulation;
2. beliefs about oneself as diminished, defeated or worthless, accompanied by feelings of shame, guilt or failure related to the traumatic event; and
3. difficulties in sustaining relationships and in feeling close to others.

These symptoms cause significant impairment in personal, family, social, educational, occupational or other important areas of functioning.'[210]

[210] Full ICD-11 details: https://icd.who.int/browse/2024-01/mms/en#585833559

Appendix 2

Thoughts on the confusion in language within the literature of trauma

Outlining the problem

In the course of trying to understand our fear-system there have been many occasions where I hit a 'roadblock' and just couldn't make sense of what I was reading. Over time, the problem resolved into two main issues.

1. I could not understand why there was such confusion over the use of the word 'freeze'. It is used with great frequency throughout the literature of threat-response, but it means different things for different writers. Some use it to describe fear-alert, (the orienting response where we evaluate a threat and our body prepares to respond to it), some use it to describe a rigid 'locked-muscle' state of hyper-arousal (fear-arousal), where the fight-flight response is active but 'put on hold',[211] while many others use it to describe the state of metabolic shutdown when death seems imminent (fear-collapse).

2. I struggled to get my head around the concept of 'tonic immobility' and whether this refers to a rigid or a weak muscle tone. 'Tonic immobility' is a phrase

[211] Kozlowska et al. (2015), p.269.

> used by scientists who study animals in their natural environment, to describe the physical collapse of prey animals when caught by a predator. Stephen Porges' polyvagal theory[212] explains the evolution of this physical collapse as a parasympathetic shutdown with weak muscle tone triggered by the dorsal vagus nerve. This appeared to conflict with many authors who describe tonic immobility as a state of sympathetic nervous system arousal characterised by rigid muscle tone.

Why does this matter?

Each of the three fear responses, fear-alert, fear-arousal and fear-collapse, is a distinct set of biological processes, so applying the same word, 'freeze', to these different responses is a recipe for confusion. Lack of clarity around 'tonic immobility' limits our ability to help our clients recognise and understand the biological processes related to trauma. This confusion cost me a lot of time as I struggled to make sense of the biology of trauma, and delayed my efforts to fully integrate it into my work with clients. A number of therapists attending my workshops reported experiencing similar difficulties.

My first struggles to understand

I first hit this confusion reading Peter Levine's book, *In an Unspoken Voice*. I found it eye-opening and exciting, but on second reading I had some problems with understanding, starting with the passage: 'When an organism perceives overwhelming mortal danger (with little or no chance for escape) the biological response is a global one of paralysis and shutdown. Ethologists[213] call this

[212] Porges (2011).
[213] Scientists who study animal behaviour in the wild.

innate response tonic immobility (TI). Humans experience this frozen state as helpless terror and panic.'[214]

This last sentence seemed to contradict my own very recent experience of an immobility collapse (see Chapter 8), and what I had been reading of Stephen Porges: 'In humans we observe a behavioural shutdown, frequently accompanied by very weak muscle tone. We also observe physiological changes: heart rate and breathing slow, and blood pressure drops.'[215]

Both my experience and Porges' observations relate to parasympathetic nervous system collapse, while Levine's description of 'tonic immobility' in humans places it clearly in sympathetic nervous system arousal, matching Le Doux's definition of 'freeze'.[216] This also seemed to contradict much of what Levine himself had written. For example, Levine gives an example of an experience of 'overwhelming mortal danger' using the explorer David Livingstone's account of being attacked by a lion which seized him by the shoulder in its jaws, and shook him like a rat: 'It caused a sort of dreaminess in which there was no sense of pain nor feeling of terror, though quite conscious of all that was happening.... The shake annihilated fear, and allowed no sense of horror in looking round at the beast'.[217]

As I examined sources to try to make sense of this confusion, it gradually dawned on me that, taken as a whole, the literature relating to our biological threat responses was a mess. Before reaching this conclusion however, I struggled with a sense that something had gone wrong with my brain, because I couldn't arrive at a coherent understanding of what I was reading.

[214] Levine (2010), pp.23-24.

[215] Porges (2011), pp.13-14.

[216] LeDoux (1998), pp.141-2, describes a rat, subjected to a fear conditioning experiment which '...stops dead in its tracks and adopts the characteristic freezing position – crouching down and remaining motionless, except for the rhythmic chest movements required for breathing. In addition, the rat's fur stands on end, its blood pressure and heart rate rise, and stress hormones are released into its bloodstream'.

[217] Levine (2010), p.50.

An overview of different frameworks

I found it helpful to draw up a chart to reflect my understanding of the terminology used by the key authors I looked at in trying to resolve this issue (Table 2).

More than a century ago Cannon[218] wrote of the 'fight-or-flight' response, which later became very well known, and dominated our understanding of fear responses until relatively recently. By the time I first came across the concept of a 'fear-system', Cannon's 'fight-or-flight' had already been supplemented by the 'freeze' response, a hyper-aroused but 'locked' rigid-muscle sympathetic nervous system response adopted when there was no obvious escape route from danger.[219]

Bracha[220] expanded Cannon's work, including the 'orienting response' (the body's preparatory response to danger at a distance) in the fear-system, but he named it 'freeze', while describing the state Le Doux had called 'freeze' as 'fright'. Bracha also described 'fright' as 'tonic immobility'. Having therefore characterised 'tonic immobility' as a rigid-muscle hyper-aroused state, he then proposed the term 'collapsed immobility' to cover the parasympathetic state of loss of muscle tone.

Levine[221] also included the 'orienting response' in the fear-system but used the term 'arrest' for this stage, instead of 'freeze'. He used the word 'freeze' for hyper-arousal (consistent with Le Doux's use of the word) and proposed the term 'fold' for parasympathetic collapse. He used the term 'tonic immobility' for both 'freeze' and 'fold' (though he often also referred to both as 'freeze').

Schauer and Elbert[222] in their 'fear-cascade' followed Bracha's terminology ('freeze') for the orienting response but described

[218] Cannon (1915).
[219] LeDoux (1998).
[220] Bracha (2004a, 2004b).
[221] Levine (2003).
[222] Schauer and Elbert (2010).

Table 2: Terminology used for fear-system responses

Function	Orienting	Mobilising				Shutdown			
ANS Branch	Sympathetic Nervous System					Parasympathetic Nervous System			
Description	Body preparing for action	Body active		Body locked	**Tipping-Point**	Mild shut-down	Moderate shutdown	Severe shut-down	Uncons cious
Cannon 1915		Flight	Fight						
LeDoux 1997		Flight	Fight	Freeze					
Bracha 2004	Freeze	Flight	Fight	Fright or Tonic Immobility		Collapsed Immobility			Faint
Levine 2003, 2010	Arrest	Flight	Fight	Freeze or Tonic Immobility		Fold or Tonic Immobility (but often described as Freeze)			
Schauer & Elbert 2010	Freeze	Flight	Fight	?	Fright or Tonic Immobility	Flag			Faint
Baldwin 2013	Freeze-alert	Flight	Fight	Freeze-Fright or Tonic Immobility		Flaccid Immobility			
Kozlowska *et al.* 2015	Arousal	Flight	Fight	Freeze	Tonic Immobility	Collapsed Immobility			
Guilding 2020	Fear-Alert	Fear-Arousal				Fear-Collapse			
		Flight	Fight	Freeze	Fright				
Symptoms	Anxiety		Anger & Rage	Panic		Low Mood	Depression & Collapse		

'fright' (which they also described as 'tonic immobility') as a tipping point into a parasympathetic collapse. They divided this collapse into 'flag' and 'faint'. Their model does not appear to cover a state which is aroused but locked, but does not necessarily tip into collapse – hence my question mark in Table 2.

Baldwin[223] named the orienting response 'freeze-alert' and called the state of locked hyper-arousal both 'freeze-fright' and 'tonic immobility'. He described parasympathetic collapse as 'flaccid immobility'.

Kozlowska and others[224] termed the orienting response 'arousal', posited a 'freeze' state which was *separate* from 'fright', and agreed with Schauer and Elbert in seeing 'fright' (which they also described as 'tonic immobility') as a tipping point into parasympathetic collapse, which, in agreement with Bracha. they termed 'collapsed immobility'.

Examining the evidence

Apart from the confusion of terminology, what I found difficult to understand in all this was why the term 'tonic immobility', taken from the sudden collapse of animals in the wild in the context of predation, was being used to refer to hyper-aroused states of 'freeze' and 'fright', and not to parasympathetic collapse (apart from in Levine's 2003 article). It seemed clear to me from the work of Porges[225] on the evolution of the dorsal vagus, that animal and human tonic immobility was a form of parasympathetic collapse.

Case illustrations in the literature, supposedly describing tonic immobility, simply reinforced this view. For example, Kozlowska and others[226] gave a couple of vignettes of tonic immobility which seemed to describe a parasympathetic collapse, not a hyper-

[223] Baldwin (2013).
[224] Kozlowska et al. (2015).
[225] Porges (2011).
[226] Kozlowska et al. (2015).

aroused state. One vignette described a 9-year-old girl suffering from dissociative states, with no evidence of rigid muscle tone presented, and including an observation that her father 'used gentle touch' to shift her out of these episodes (exactly as the female doctor did for Levine himself when he was dipping in and out of parasympathetic collapse after his car accident[227]).

Their second 'tonic immobility' vignette presented an account of a soldier, who experienced shutdown during a firefight, describing him as: 'feeling strangely detached from the situation. He was unable to lift his head, move his limbs or aim his rifle. He recalled a sensation of being drawn to the ground, a heavy sensation that he could not resist.'[228]

He recovered from this collapse only when joined by another soldier, and not until he returned to his base did he realise he had been incontinent of both urine and faeces.

This account, with the emphasis on the sensation of 'heaviness' combined with complete physical collapse and the loss of bladder and bowel control, would appear to indicate a powerful dorsal vagal response with flaccid rather than stiff muscle tone.[229]

The origin of the confusion?

As I followed sources to try to understand how 'tonic immobility' came to be associated with the (hyper-aroused) 'freeze' response, the evidence pointed back to Gordon Gallup[230] who worked on inducing states of 'tonic immobility' in animals, by restraining them (or turning them upside down). The immobility states

[227] Levine (2010).
[228] Kozlowska et al. (2015), p.272.
[229] Defaecation during flight appears to be common in the animal world, involving a co-activation of dorsal vagal and sympathetic nervous system responses, but this example described a collapse rather than a flight, with no evidence presented of high muscle tone.
[230] Gallup (1977).

could last from a few seconds to hours, and Gallup noted that the higher the level of fear immediately before the restraint, the longer the animal remained immobile. Gallup proposed the hypothesis that 'tonic immobility' might be 'the evolutionary precursor to catatonic schizophrenia in man'.

He described the chickens he experimented on in words that clearly convey his hypothetical perspective. He claimed that the restrained chicken: '...assumes an almost catatonic-like state', and also that in this state, 'the legs may be flexed or extended, (often exhibiting signs of catatonic-like waxy flexibility)'.[231]

'Waxy flexibility' refers to 'a condition in which a patient's limbs retain any position into which they are manipulated by another person, and which occurs especially in catatonic schizophrenia'.[232] In other words, there is a degree of muscular rigidity which can defy gravity.

I would suggest that doubts might be raised about the scientific objectivity of Gallup's observations. I suspect that his observations may have influenced subsequent researchers, and that this may be the chief reason that so many describe 'tonic immobility' as a state of hyper-arousal, which then gets confused with the state of 'freeze' as described by Le Doux. Indeed, this approach is now built into a psychological measurement tool for evaluating 'tonic immobility'[233] which precedes each question with 'When I freeze…', or 'After unfreezing…'. These are leading questions which will preclude experiences of fear-collapse that *don't* feel like a rigid-muscle 'freeze' state.

The inclusion of such questions as 'When I freeze I take short quick breaths', alongside 'When I freeze my muscles go limp' shows that two opposing biological states are being shoehorned into the 'tonic immobility response', which in my mind deprives

[231] Gallup (1977), pp.41-43.
[232] Merriam-Webster (No date).
www.merriam-webster.com/medical/waxy%20flexibility.
[233] Lloyd et al. (2019). The Scale for Tonic Immobility Occurring Post-Trauma.

it of any value as a scientific or clinical concept. If we are to understand our fear responses and their underlying biological processes, the language we use in describing our observations needs to be precise, the metaphors accurate. If I translate the sentence 'When I freeze my muscles go limp' into plain English, it conveys the meaning 'when my muscles go rigid, my muscles are not rigid'. I think this neatly sums up the mess we have got into with the concept of 'tonic immobility'.

For me, the key question at the centre of this confusion is whether there is tension or not in the muscles when an animal or human goes into a shutdown state when there is an imminent threat to their life.

I would invite you to refer back to Chapter 2 and the antelope rescued by baboons and view the video available on YouTube.[234] This video shows an antelope in a state of tonic immobility, having been caught by a leopard. The antelope's nose is being held in the leopard's jaws, but when the leopard is distracted and loosens its grip, the antelope's head simply flops to the ground. Its muscles appear to show no sign of 'waxy flexibility', but rather the flaccidity associated with 'collapsed immobility'.

Gallup, in describing his experimental subjects, observed 'Parkinsonian tremors of the limbs'.[235] This makes me wonder whether, in his understanding of 'tonic immobility', he is conflating an immobile collapse (without muscle tone) with the subsequent transition out of immobility (where muscle tone is recovered and tremoring often follows).

[234] YouTube (100100 channel):
https://www.youtube.com/watch?v=lAtW7nJUcRA
[235] Gallup (1977), p.41. He does appear to have a tendency to view his animal observations through the lens of human mental or neurological illness.

Conclusion

As a layperson examining this literature, I am unconvinced that 'tonic immobility' and 'collapsed immobility' are separate biological states and would suggest that the introduction of the term 'collapsed immobility' only became necessary because Gallup, in pursuing his dubious catatonia hypothesis, had hijacked the term 'tonic immobility' as belonging to a rigid-muscle state.

My own conclusion is that there is a rigid 'locked' muscle state that can be properly termed 'freeze', which indicates sympathetic nervous system hyper-arousal (fear-arousal in my terminology), and a limp muscle state which could be termed 'tonic immobility', which involves a metabolic shutdown triggered by the parasympathetic nervous system (which I call fear-collapse). Some of the confusion around this term may arise from the fact that the adjective 'tonic' indicates muscle tone without specifying whether this is stiff or flaccid. However, as ethologists have used this term for many years for the collapse of animals in the face of an extreme threat to life, I think it should be retained for human collapse in similar circumstances. I would therefore discard the term 'collapsed immobility' as being redundant.

The state of 'fright', the peak of hyper-arousal, then straddles these two opposing systems as a tipping point, as Schauer and Elbert proposed. I have found this theoretical framework works well in clinical practice, describing my clients' experiences with an accuracy that often evoked in them feelings of considerable relief.

It is easy to see how confusion arises in trying to describe fear responses, as they can shift so quickly from one state to another, and there are three types of 'stillness' (fear-alert, 'freeze' and fear-collapse) that could possibly be confused.

I understand the stillness of fear-alert as being underpinned by a *moderate* muscular tension which could switch into powerful action, but also quickly relax into rest. I see the 'freeze' state as involving a stronger, more rigid muscular tension that is holding in check the powerful energy of hyper-arousal and which *cannot* calm quickly.

As for using the term 'freeze' to describe 'tonic immobility' (fear-collapse), this makes no sense to me at all. The word 'freeze' is associated in our minds with the rigid state of water at 0° centigrade, so it is an accurate metaphor for the 'locked' or rigid-muscle state of fear-arousal (fight-flight 'put on hold'), and creates confusion if applied to fear-collapse, where the muscles are limp and without energy.

Postscript – Explaining my own terminology

The confusion of language in the threat-response literature compelled me to use my own descriptive terms – 'fear-alert', 'fear-arousal' and 'fear-collapse' – in order to reach a clear understanding of the biology of our fear-system responses.

I chose the word 'alert' (used by Baldwin and, at times, by Levine) for the orienting response, as it seemed to most accurately convey the heightened attention in this 'preparation for action' stage.

I chose 'arousal' for the fight, flight, freeze and fright responses, as this reflects the heightened metabolic state of hyper-arousal underpinning these responses.

I chose 'collapse' for the metabolic shutdown of last resort as this accurately reflects our experience of the continuum of energy loss from slight postural collapse to full physical prostration.

I then prefixed these words with 'fear-' to distinguish each response to external, social or imagined dangers from a range of other autonomic nervous system responses which use the same biological processes.

- The body's 'alert' state appears to be activated when we

give focused attention to a task, such as mental problem-solving.

- The sympathetic nervous system's 'arousal' response is activated in sports, exercise and many forms of manual work.
- The parasympathetic nervous system's 'collapse' response is used by the body as a survival strategy in the event of major fluid loss, and as an energy-conservation response to allow the body to fight viral and bacterial infection, process toxins, recover from exhaustion and also assist the process of conception.[236]

[236] Levine, (2010) who notes that the post-orgasm state of dreaminess is a dorsal vagus shutdown which increases the chances of conception.

Appendix 3

Fear-collapse: A shutdown of energy production in the body

I was greatly helped in understanding fear-collapse as a shutdown of energy production throughout the body, by Sarah Myhill's[237] explanation of the cell respiration cycle which generates energy in all of our cells. This process is illustrated in Fig. 14.[238]

She points out that, unlike a car with a single engine linked to the wheels, the body has many millions of separate 'engines' located in its cells, all provided with oxygen and fuel (glucose) via the bloodstream, from a single pump (the heart).

In every cell throughout the body there are a varying number of mitochondria (sub-structures of the cell which produce the energy that powers the cell's activities). Mitochondria release adenosine tri-phosphate (ATP) into the cell. ATP is a complex chemical compound which has a 'tail' of three phosphate molecules. Within the cell, one of these phosphate molecules breaks off creating a burst of energy (the equivalent to the explosion of petrol vapour in the car engine which drives the pistons), and this burst of energy drives all the cell's activity.

This loss of the phosphate molecule which produces the energy, converts the ATP into ADP (adenosine di-phosphate – two phosphate molecules left) which then returns to the mitochondria and reacts with oxygen and glucose from the bloodstream to

[237] Myhill (2014).
[238] Myhill (2014), for illustration and explanation.

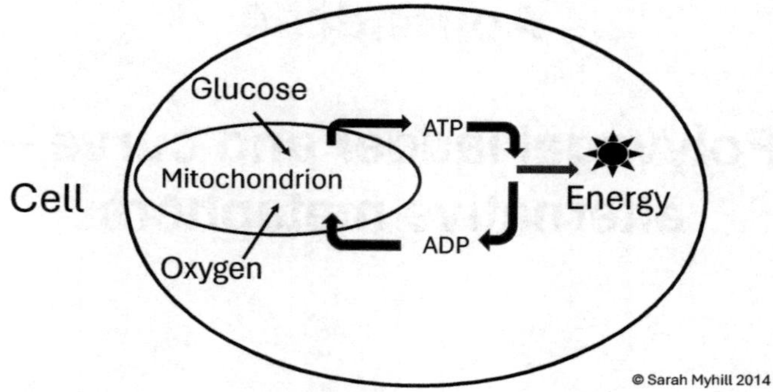

Figure 14: Energy production in body cells

regain a third phosphate molecule. The reconstituted ATP then goes back out into the cell, and so the process repeats again and again, like a little engine ticking over.

When blood pressure drops as part of fear-collapse, every cell is deprived of oxygen and glucose and these 'engines' slow down and stop working. Muscle cells can no longer contribute to movement, skin cells can no longer regulate our temperature, and brain cells can no longer support our thinking or social engagement.

Understanding the underlying biology makes it clear that symptoms related to fear-collapse, such as chronic fatigue or depression, are not just something going on 'in the head' but are intensely physical sensations experienced throughout the body.

Appendix 4

Polyvagal ladder and curve – alternative metaphors

I have been questioned by several people as to why I do not use the illustration of the polyvagal ladder[239] when my understanding of the fear-system owes so much to polyvagal theory. The polyvagal ladder (Figure 15) is a metaphor used by Deb Dana to describe the process of going into and coming out of fear activation – using the picture of climbing down a ladder and then climbing up. The state of calm which enables us to socially engage is represented at the top of the ladder, dropping down (if I use my own descriptions rather than Deb Dana's) to fear-alert and then fear-arousal when danger becomes apparent, and then dropping further to fear-collapse when the danger appears inescapable.

The process of fear deactivation is represented by climbing back up the ladder, from fear-collapse, through fear-arousal and back into the calm of social engagement. The drawback of this metaphor, as far as I am concerned, is that I find it counter-intuitive, and I like my metaphors to be intuitive and to correspond with the way my body senses things. On a superficial level, my experience of ladders is that I usually go up them and then down them, not down and then up. At a less superficial level, I experience the activation of fear responses as a powerful upwards surge of energy in the body in fear-arousal,

[239] Dana (2018).

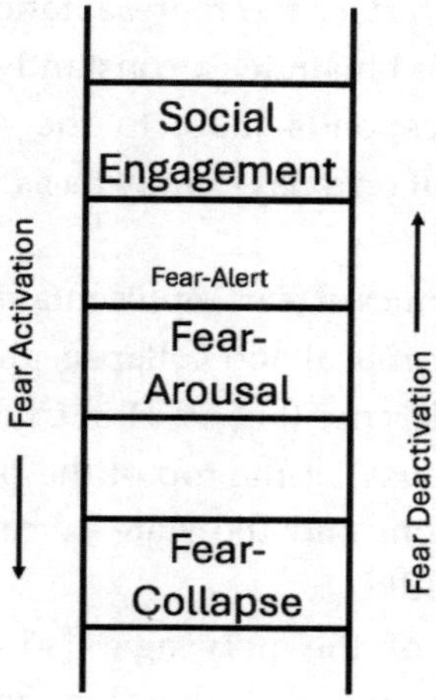

Figure 15: Polyvagal ladder

and as a correspondingly powerful downwards drop of energy in fear-collapse. For that reason, the graphs I draw to illustrate the dynamics of fear are based on my sensing the rise and fall in heart rate and blood pressure, and the graph (Figure 16) which I used in Chapter 7 (Figure 7) could possibly be called the polyvagal rollercoaster.

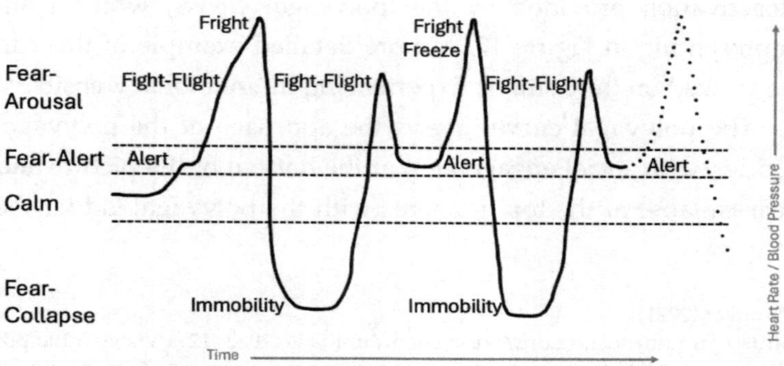

Figure 16: Polyvagal rollercoaster

Another reason I prefer the representation of fear activation in Figure 16, is that it illustrates a constantly changing dynamic process which corresponds more to the way I see our fear responses playing out on a day-to-day basis, than the more static picture of a ladder.

Finally, my 'dynamics of fear' representation (the rollercoaster) based on metabolic arousal and collapse, aligns with the model of the window of tolerance (Figure 11 in Chapter 12), which also shows metabolic arousal at the top of the page, with metabolic collapse at the bottom and the state of calm (the window of tolerance) in the middle.

The plus point of the polyvagal ladder is that it more graphically conveys the fact that we go into fear-collapse through fear-arousal and only recover from trauma involving fear-collapse by moving directly back into fear-arousal.

Because my own graphs are based on heart rate they might seem to indicate on first viewing that we go into and come out of fear-collapse through a state of calm. However, the near-vertical lines on my graph in Figure 16 do not in any way approximate to *being* in a calm state, even briefly. To be calm we need to *consistently* experience a heart rate of (very approximately) 60 beats per minute *over a period of time*.

There is an alternative metaphor for fear activation and deactivation provided by the 'polyvagal curve', which I am representing in Figure 17. A more detailed example of this can be viewed on the Somatic Experiencing International website.[240]

The polyvagal curve inverts the approach of the polyvagal ladder, with social engagement at the bottom of the picture and fear-collapse at the top. It shares with the polyvagal ladder the

[240]Walker (2021).
https://traumahealing.org/wp-content/uploads/2022/12/PVChartv10q.pdf
Despite regarding this representation as perhaps more cognitive than intuitive, I really like the way it illustrates the shift from 'I can', to 'I can't', as we move from fear-arousal to fear-collapse.

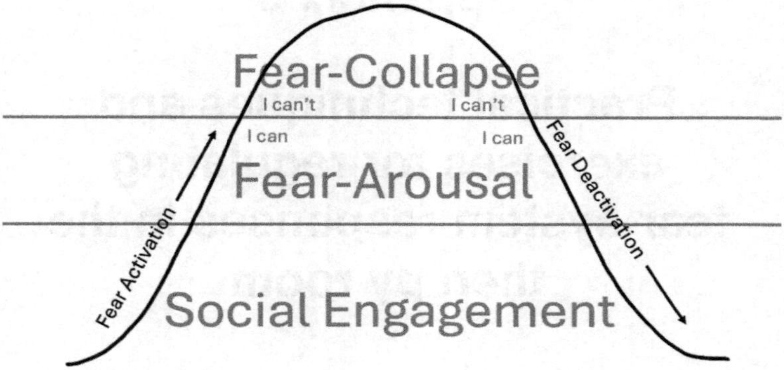

Figure 17: Polyvagal curve

ability to convey the movement of fear activation *directly* from fear-arousal to fear-collapse and back, but once again, I find it counterintuitive in terms of the ways we experience the surge and collapse of energy in our bodies.

In summary, I don't use the metaphors of the polyvagal ladder or the polyvagal curve as I don't find they match my lived experience, but they convey some aspects of the dynamics of fear more clearly than my rollercoaster graphs, and vice-versa. We all ultimately adopt the metaphors that suit us best, but I do like to be aware of a number of different metaphors, as each introduces a different perspective, and together they stop us getting too blinkered.

Appendix 5

Practical techniques and exercises for regulating fear-system responses in the therapy room

The regulation of our fear-system responses is a lifetime task involving our whole lifestyle, relationships, and many activities and practices outside of the remit of psychological therapy. However, there are many simple exercises and techniques which can be used in the therapy room to regulate both the therapist and the client. The following is a list of those I found to be most helpful and used most frequently.

Posture

Using a straight-backed chair, sit upright with feet firmly planted on the floor. Find a position where the head is held in balance with no muscular tension. I find that point of balance by sitting up straight and then swaying slightly back to front, and from side to side, to find just the right spot where the weight of my head is properly supported (do try this out but be patient - it took me about three months to get this right for myself). This allows for plenty of space in the chest, and the ability to breath deep into the abdomen.

Getting grounded or centred

The following is a series of exercises that can be used singly or consecutively to help client and therapist regulate together at the start of the session.

Notice breathing: Having established a good posture as above, close[241] your eyes, or keep them open but unfocused, and allow your breath to come naturally (whether fast or slow, shallow or deep – don't try to change anything). Focus your attention on your breath and the physical sensations it causes in your body. You can focus on the cool air entering your nostrils as you breathe in, and the warm air as you breathe out, and what that feels like in your nostrils and on your upper lip. Then move to focusing on your chest and noticing its rise and fall with each breath.

Body scan: Then give your attention to each part of your body in turn, starting with the soles of your feet, and moving up to the top of your head. Try not to miss out any part. Don't try to change anything, but in each part just notice the *sensations* (warm or cold, tense or relaxed, comfortable or painful, moving or pulsing or still – try to notice the subtle sensations that are hard to describe).

Safe place exercise: Think of a safe place where you feel completely comfortable and relaxed. It can be an imaginary or a real place, alone or with a partner, a friend or pet. Imagine yourself there. Take your time and allow your body to settle. Notice the sensations in your body (these will be the opposite of the sensations caused by your fear responses). Gradually open your eyes and come back into the room. Notice your surroundings. Make eye contact with your client. Welcome them and start the work.

Getting centred in a group (therapeutic or training): With eyes closed, or unfocused, go through posture, breathing, body scan and safe place exercise (if required) as above. At the end, invite the group to slowly open or refocus their eyes and come back into the room. Notice their surroundings

[241] For some people, closing their eyes can make them feel unsafe, so it's helpful to also suggest keeping them open but unfocused as an alternative.

in the room, then notice the group. Look at each person in turn and make eye-contact, sufficient to acknowledge their presence. (When working with an online group this is not possible, so I invite members to take time to look at each person on the screen and (wordlessly) wish them well, knowing that this is being returned.) I often remind everyone that groups are scary, and that this is normal. I invite them to notice their fear reactions during the group, and to bring them to my attention if they find them difficult to regulate. I invite them to try to stay present in the group noticing 'anxious thoughts loops' that will often kick in. I invite them to try batting these thoughts away, and to reset their posture, breathe, and then refocus on the group.

Breathing[242]

- A big deep sigh, a 'kick on vagal brake', can help us to come out of fear-alert when we've gone tense and stopped breathing.
- Simply observe your breathing without changing it (as in Anapana meditation). Notice the cool breath coming in and the warm breath going out.
- Equal breathing but slowing down the breath: Ask your client to breathe naturally and time how long each in-breath and out-breath takes. If it's 2 seconds in and 2 seconds out, just stay with that for a few breaths, breathing together with your client at the same rate, and then see if it can be slowed down to 3 seconds in and 3 seconds out. Stay with that for a longer period. Then see if it's possible to slow down to 4 seconds in and 4 seconds out. Practise this for a time then encourage the client to practise doing this at home for a few minutes at

[242] See Martin and others (2016), in the recommended books list in Appendix 9.

a time as often as is possible. This can be very effective for fear regulation if used repetitively and intensively[243] (but it also helps with falling asleep at night).

- Up-regulating the metabolism from fear-collapse: Take a long, slow breath in, if possible lasting 10+ seconds (you may have to breathe in through pursed lips to control this, though it is good to breathe in through the nose if possible). As you breathe in, your heart rate increases. Then do a quick powerful exhale from your abdomen (a 'huff'). Repeat this a number of times. This breathing 'wakes the brain'. I picture this as 'inflating the balloon'. Experiment with your client, asking them to deliberately slump. Then do a series of these breaths, feeling each one inflate their chest and gradually pull them back into a more upright posture. Try to keep your shoulders at the level they've reached on the last inhale each time you breathe out, and gradually you'll be pulled back into a good posture and feel an improvement in mood. When my eyelids feel heavy, and I use this pattern of breathing for a few minutes, I often get to the point where the sense of heaviness in the eyelids suddenly disappears and I feel 'bright-eyed'.
- Down-regulating from fear-arousal: Start with a long slow exhale, 10+ seconds if possible (again, it may work best through pursed lips). As you breathe out, your heart rate decreases. Follow this with a quick inhale – 'grabbing a breath'. Repeat this a number of times until you feel calmer (the same pattern as in singing). I see this as 'deflating the balloon'. Once again, practise this for a time and notice the changing sensations in your body.
- My favourite breath:[244] Take a quick but gentle breath in, going straight into a long breath out without being held.

[243] See section 'The issue of intensity', in Chapter 15, page 113.

Breathe until the breath is completely exhausted, then pause without breathing. Follow the impulse of the body as to when it needs to breathe next. Then a quick gentle breath in, and repeat. I noticed when tracking my heart rate during these exercises that the most marked drop in heart rate occurred during the pause after breathing out. (I am not a fan of holding the breath after an in-breath as this involves holding the body in an artificial tension which I don't find helpful.)

Movement

Shifting to re-establish a good posture can break the tension of fear-alert and help with coming back to a calm place. Re-establishing posture or standing up and moving around can stop the body slipping into a fear-collapse. **Rhythm** is very effective in regulation. It works best if therapist and client do these exercises together. It can help keep both in the 'window of tolerance'.

- Slow rhythmic side-to-side tapping of the knees, keeping in synch with the client's beat (though sometimes suggesting a slowing or speeding up as regulation requires). This slows things down, especially when the client is talking about things they find distressing, or can be enlivening in a low mood. (It is also useful as an EMDR variant.)
- Butterfly tap: With arms crossed and hands on chest with fingers on the collar bone, alternately tap in rhythm. This is soothing, and helps with sleep at night.
- Use a juggling ball thrown from hand to hand rhythmically to calm anxiety. (I also find it helpful as an EMDR variant, or as a simple accompaniment to talking which slows the pace and induces calm.)[245]

[244] From Martin et al. (2016).

Changing focus of attention

This involves switching focus from internal to external senses. During trauma work, particularly when working with sensations in the body, we have been continually focused on the internal nervous system (vagus nerve fibres from the major organs of the body sending information to the brain). During a session where a client is becoming dysregulated and needs to step back from trauma work, and at the end of a session, where a client needs to negotiate a 'return' to the world outside (particularly if they are driving or cycling from the therapy room), it is necessary to 'reset' from the work. We can do this by a deliberate shift in focus to the external nervous system (sight, hearing, touch, taste, smell). Just spend a few minutes asking simple questions such as: How many things can you see in the room? What can you see outside of the room? What can you hear inside the room? What can you hear outside? What can you smell? What can you touch? Then check that the client has made the shift from the internal to the outside world, and check whether they are feeling calmer.

Containing

Actions that connect or contain us can provide a sense of safety that regulates fear-system responses.

Anchor point: A particular stone, or an object with a satisfying feel or a particular significance which can be held onto can give a sense of 'grounding' and security. In my therapy room I kept a number of large stones with interesting markings suitable for various hand sizes. The simple act of holding them can create an 'anchor point'. I

[245] See Andrew Austin video on YouTube: https://www.youtube.com/watch?v=iOktN5fQYbE. For purchasing balls (120g weight recommended) https://www.firetoys.co.uk/firetoys-juggling-120g-thud.html

would sometimes invite clients to hold them during the session and sometimes invited them to take them home, particularly over breaks when self-regulation was still not well established. I would sometimes do the same with juggling balls (see above), which have the additional advantage of being squeezable (I did lose rather a lot of balls that way, however).

Holding self: Peter Levine's 2010 book contains many useful containing exercises.

- Self-hug: Place your right hand on your left side under the left arm, and your left hand on your right arm. Squeeze and hold for a time. Note the sensations in your body. It's surprising how effective this can be!
- Hands on forehead / chest / stomach: Place your right hand on your forehead and your left hand on your chest. Hold for a time and notice the sensations this creates. Then move your right hand to your stomach and again hold and notice your sensations.
- Hand on heart: Simply place your hand on your heart and hold for a time, noticing the sensations. This is very simple but very effective as a way of calming. You may notice that people often do this instinctively when they have had a fright.

Touch

In the immediate aftermath of shocking incidents, when a person is experiencing a parasympathetic shutdown with dissociative symptoms such as feeling detached from the body, gentle touch, such as holding the hand can often be the most effective way to reverse the collapse and bring them back into their body and back to social connectedness.

Appendix 5

The importance of touch

Levine's account of the aftermath of being hit by a car, when he had dissociated following a mis-attuned attempt to help, describes how he was regulated and reconnected to his body by the gentle hand-holding of a passing female doctor.[246] Kozlowska's Tonic Immobility vignette (Appendix 2) illustrates a young girl being brought out of dissociative states by her father's gentle hand-holding. The account of the Jackson twins (Chapter 28) clearly demonstrates the power of touch and proximity to reverse even a potentially deadly metabolic shutdown.

Apart from the fact that some psychotherapeutic modalities preclude any use of touch between client and therapist, there are important ethical issues to consider. The use of touch or its withholding can be key factors in the trauma histories of many clients, and there is a danger of sexualising the therapeutic relationship, particularly with a male therapist and female client. However, for some states of panic and dissociative or physical collapse occurring in the therapy room, where the client is beyond the reach of language, the use of gentle touch, by hand-holding, or a hand on the arm, may be the swiftest way of bringing the client back to a place of connection and safety.

It may be important for therapists such as myself, who were trained to avoid touch in all circumstances, to review this issue in the light of our relatively recent understanding of parasympathetic collapse as a fear response. It is important that a good initial assessment helps us to see what interventions might be experienced as retraumatising, but perhaps the most important preparation will be a clear explanation of human fear responses at an early stage in the therapy, prior to discussion of the possible use of touch, and a clear understanding that informed consent has been given to any use of touch.

[246] Levine (2010), pp.5-6.

Appendix 6

Can trauma memories be erased?

Ecker, Ticic and Hulley, in their book *Unlocking the Emotional Brain*,[247] refer to trauma memories being 'erased' on the grounds that the process of unlocking trauma memories, and then disconfirming them while they are active, leads to the disappearance of trauma symptoms such as panic and depression. They then contrast their own therapeutic method (coherence therapy) based on this process with 'counteractive methods', such as aversion therapy, which they claim set up separate neural networks which conflict with the original trauma networks but do not erase them.

They claim that this ability to erase trauma memories undermines the theory of the indelibility of emotional learning.[248] While I am grateful to them for introducing me to the research underpinning the notion of trauma memories being unlocked and then changed before being locked again, I am unpersuaded that this is an *erasure* of the trauma memory.

In the research into animal brains which they discuss, synaptic connections were destroyed by chemical means when memory networks were activated, which would of course produce memory erasure. However, this chemical approach is toxic to humans, and I could not understand how the therapeutic

[247] Ecker, Ticic and Hulley (2012).
[248] van der Kolk (1994).

approach they were describing would produce the same erasure.

I think that they have set up a false dichotomy between erasure and permanence of emotional (traumatic) learning. The perspective on complex trauma I have outlined provides another way of thinking about what may be happening in trauma therapy.

In my view, what leads to the cessation of trauma symptoms is not an *erasure* of the original network, but the addition to that network of more benign associations which dampens the capacity of that network to trigger the activation of the fear-system.[249] By thus allowing the fear-system to deactivate, it results in a cessation of trauma symptoms such as panic and depression, but I do not think this is the 'permanent cessation' that Ecker, Ticic and Hulley suggest, and I am not persuaded that the data at their disposal substantiates such a claim.

The metaphor of the 'shadow of the trauma' (Chapter 19) is one way of understanding the possibilities of relapse into further unregulated fear-system activation after recovery from trauma. This view matches both my own experience and the experiences of many of my clients far more closely than what I consider to be the over-optimistic conclusions of Ecker, Ticic and Hulley.

[249] Rothschild (2000), p.82. 'Attention to the therapeutic relationship will, with some clients, help to transform negative implicit memories by creating a new encoding of a positive experience of attachment.'

Appendix 7

Thoughts on dreams and dreaming

I first became fascinated by dreams as a young man at university reading C.G. Jung's *Memories, Dreams and Reflections*.[250] Nearly 20 years later, this interest was central to my decision to train as a counsellor. After my first two years of training I changed my therapist and started twice-weekly Jungian psychotherapy centred on working with my dreams. As a result, the Jungian approach forms the bedrock of my understanding of dreams and has underpinned a great deal of my work as a therapist.

What are dreams?

Dreaming is a phenomenon of the organism that each one of us is. I start with the assumption that this process has a useful purpose. I also assume that the content of our dreams has meaning – I think a lot of people have assumed this over the ages!

I see dreaming as a mental process, akin to conscious thinking, but mostly happening outside of conscious awareness, whereby we process and integrate the experiences we have each day. We know there are neurological processes where experiences are held in short-term memory and then transferred to long-term memory. In this process, 'undigested' emotional experiences are connected to linguistic processes, put into words, equated with

[250] Jung (1933).

similar experiences, and then 'filed away' so they can be used to guide us later on in similar circumstances.

I assume, when I notice one of my own dreams, that I am catching a brief glimpse of my unconscious mind undertaking exactly this sort of process. There seems to be a window of opportunity as we awake at night or start to wake up in the morning, when we are in touch with both the unconscious dreaming process and our conscious perceptions, and in those moments we can access the content of our dreaming mind.[251] I think it's likely that dreaming does its job of mental integration whether or not I notice or remember the dream, but I also think that becoming consciously aware of our dreaming process can contribute to our self-awareness and mental integration.

I think, however, that dreaming is more than just unconscious *thinking*. When we are dreaming we are not just having or connecting ideas; we are *acting* in a drama of our own creation as a means of making sense of our experience. *Acting* rather than just thinking is a key element in the dreaming process. MRI scans of the brain during REM (dreaming) sleep show that, while controlling functions of the prefrontal cortex are switched off, four areas of the brain are highly active – the visual-spatial area at the back of the brain that enables complex visual perception, the motor cortex that generates movement, the hippocampus that processes autobiographical memory, and the amygdala and surrounding areas that generate and process our emotional responses.[252] Everything is in place for experiences with a high

[251] I found that turning on the light or moving too much wiped out the memory of the dreams, so to catch as much of the dream as possible, I kept a clipboard by my bed with a pencil attached. When I awoke with a dream memory, I would lie as still as possible, reach for the clipboard in the dark, place my thumb at the top of the clipboard and start writing what I remembered, moving my thumb down so I knew where to start the next line. When I got up in the morning I'd find an untidy scrawl with some lines of writing crossing over, but I was usually able to transcribe these accurately.
[252] Walker (2018).

emotional charge to be re-enacted (and in the process, to be changed). The fact that we do not just *think*, but *act* our dreams is demonstrated by the fact that evolution has gone to the extraordinary lengths of developing a mechanism for disabling our voluntary muscles during REM-sleep so that we can act out our dreams without putting ourselves or our partners in danger.

The functions of dreaming

I think dreams fulfil a number of functions (some of which overlap).

1. Problem-solving and creativity.

When we are trying to solve a problem using conscious cognitive processes, and then go to sleep, our dreaming mind appears to take up the task and can present the conscious mind with a solution.

> As part of my university final exams I had three essays to write over three days. I looked at the question for day 3 just before I went to bed at the end of day 2. I woke the next morning with a dream in which I was planning an essay, starting with completely disagreeing with the premise of the question. I started drifting back to sleep then woke again with a jerk realising that my dream essay was exactly the one I needed to write that day. The 'dream-planned' essay was far higher quality than my consciously planned essays – my tutor called it a 'fucking showstopper'.

Experiments monitoring problem solving and creativity have demonstrated that those who sleep on a problem and dream about the problem or related themes, showed 10 times the improvement in dealing with the problem than those who had also slept but not dreamed about it.[253]

2. Clarification or insight

Dreams can really help us to get a clear picture of our situation in life, which can help us to know what we might need to do next:

> When I first went into senior management in Royal Mail, I was totally out of my depth as a quiet, reflective, cautious and polite young man among what felt like a bunch of aggressive cowboys who would steamroller over me before I had time to think. I had a dream where I was showering alongside the managing director – I was being very slow and careful and my main concern in dressing was that I kept my socks dry. He was clumsy and splashy and got all his clothes including his socks wet and couldn't care less and was ready well before me.

This dream was very useful for me as it beautifully clarified my situation. In response to it I started taking risks, acting on impulse, allowed myself to respond at times with the same aggressive rudeness I was receiving, made a pile of mistakes (got my socks wet), but survived.

3. A corrective to a conscious position

We all have internal parts, voices or impulses which have been disavowed because of the way we were brought up and responded to when we were small. The person who has disavowed anger, and therefore is not good at self-defence, may

[253] Walker (2018).

find themselves dreaming they are murdering their spouse. The dream is just trying to integrate the angry part and make sure its voice is heard.

The outcome of the dream may be to put the person in touch with anger so it can find some conscious expression in the relationship and solve the underlying problem. The murder is just a metaphor – the more a feeling is disavowed, the stronger the metaphor in the dream.

This is, of course, Jung's theory of the compensatory nature of dreams. He illustrated this with an account of a young man, who looked up to his father but was too uncritical to be able to separate and lead his own life. He dreamt his father was driving a new car clumsily and eventually collided with a wall. He shouted at his father in a rage and then realised that his father was drunk.[254] A dream, which presents a picture which is shockingly different from a conscious standpoint can give a voice to a suppressed or a newly emerging part and open up the possibility of change.

4. Trauma processing

If we accept that the brain needs to organise and integrate the myriad experiences of each day, then perhaps the processing of traumatic experience is the most important function of dreams. I am very struck by the parallels between what we know about processing trauma as therapists, and how we go about it, and what we know about the way the brain functions during REM sleep.

We know that, to access trauma in order to work with it, the neural networks that encode the trauma have to be activated, and that when activated they can be changed as present thoughts, sensations and experiences are added to that network. After a few hours, these networks close, and no new information can be added until they are reactivated.[255] It is clear from the MRI data

[254] Jung (1933).
[255] Ecker, Ticic and Hulley (2012).

on REM sleep referred to above that when we are dreaming of a specific event or theme, the memory of these events, and the related networks controlling visual perception, motor response and emotional response, are highly activated.

We know that, if traumatic memory is triggered in contexts that are not safe, the only result is re-traumatisation; in other words, we suffer all the distress of memory recall and fear-system activation, without anything being processed or resolved. Hence a great deal of trauma work consists in creating a safe place, in terms of the relationship with the therapist and the client's sense of safety, both in their internal and external worlds.

In the actual trauma work, we constantly try to keep our clients in the safe place we call the 'window of tolerance'[256] in which change is possible. We try to calm them when they are over-aroused by fear or anger and try to enliven them when they are in depressive collapse. In REM sleep, the anxiety-triggering neurotransmitter noradrenaline is shut off in the brain[257] (the only time in the 24-hour cycle this happens). Thus, while the necessary neural networks are activated, the brain itself provides a 'safe place' during dreaming to allow difficult experiences to be processed.

One of the techniques used by many trauma therapists for processing traumatic experiences is EMDR. This uses repeated side-to-side movements of the eyes, which we think helps to stimulate left-brain, right-brain connectivity. Dreaming sleep is named 'rapid eye movement' sleep as these same eye movements occur naturally.

Many trauma therapists use body-based approaches which help their clients reconnect with the physical reactions of their self-defence system connected with traumatic experiences. This is based on an understanding of trauma as the fear-system failing to 'reset' after a parasympathetic collapse. An animal which suffers this parasympathetic collapse after having been

[256] Siegel (2012).
[257] Walker (2018).

caught by a predator can recover from collapse (given a window of opportunity) by reactivating the fight-flight response.

Clients are encouraged to notice and experience the physical impulses of fight-flight in a safe context, sometimes in slow motion or using their imagination (which can be just as effective as physical action as the motor cortex is activated). In dreaming sleep the same process is taking place. The dreamer is an actor responding to and integrating their experiences – they are remembering, visually perceiving and reacting with motor neurons fully active – physically completing the defensive movements activated in the trauma so the fear-system can reset, but with voluntary muscles disabled so that this can happen safely.

5. Repair and recovery

In his book *Why We Sleep*, Matthew Walker[258] describes experiments that demonstrate that lack of REM sleep blunts our ability to accurately read expressions and emotions in the faces of others while adequate REM sleep fine-tunes this ability. This probably reflects the fact that high levels of stress or fear-system activation shut down the social engagement system in the cortex. Perhaps the elimination of noradrenaline during dreaming sleep is resetting our social engagement system?

Nightmares

It would appear that brain functions involved in dreaming are designed for trauma processing, but some experiences can overwhelm this process if they are too shocking, too persistent, and the dreamer has inadequate support in dealing with them. In such cases, the dreaming process cannot 'digest' the experience – it repeats through many dreams without resolution and the full disturbance of the experiences are activated in the dreams

[258] Walker (2018).

without diminution.

We call these dreams nightmares. It would seem that when the fear-system is too highly aroused in severe trauma, the brain cannot eliminate noradrenaline to provide a 'protected space' for experiences to be processed by the brain. PTSD sufferers have excessively high levels of noradrenaline in the brain and therefore cannot enter or maintain normal REM sleep. However, if drugs are used to lower noradrenaline levels, normal REM sleep becomes possible and repetitive nightmares cease.[259]

Ways of working with dreams

I think the most important starting point is to be really interested in another person's dream. Most people are interested in and vitalised by their dreams. If they are too out of touch with themselves to be interested, it is possible that our interest and curiosity might stimulate theirs. We might need to do no more than say 'What an interesting dream! … What are your thoughts about it?'

One useful question might be 'Why might your dreaming mind be working on these themes... Do they resonate with anything in your conscious life?' If there are parallels between a dream and conscious experience, in what way might the dream be reflecting and commenting on this experience?

Another approach is to say 'What if this dream is *your* play, and every one of the actors is a different part of yourself? What might the dream be about then?'

> One of my clients had a dream which included Donald Trump (a man she deeply hated). I wondered what part of her he might represent (bracing myself for the backlash). When she thought about this it occurred to her that Trump

[259] Walker (2018).

represented her powerful fear of being weak, and that it was this fear which was holding her back in key areas of her life.

A useful way of working with what feel like unresolved or repetitive dreams is to invite clients to complete their dreams, acting out different endings in their imagination, or writing down what they remember and then creating their own conclusion to the dream-story.

My friend Dzmitry Karpuk introduced me to a way of working with nightmares.[260] Treating them as a symptom of trauma, he avoids re-traumatisation by inviting the clients to note what aspects of the dream, or objects or people within it, seem to them to be helpful/attractive/powerful etc. He then invites them to notice what sensations are triggered in their body when they think about them. He then helps them to slowly focus on these sensations. This can help to build up a general sense of competence, solidity or wellbeing in the body. Only at this stage would he turn to the more troublesome aspects of the dream and gradually process these in the same way, allowing for a gradual integration of disturbing experiences.

Conclusion

A number of therapists I have talked to have been curious about dreams but have not felt confident enough to work with the dreams their clients have raised. This can leave the therapist frustrated and the client disappointed. It can be really helpful to set aside any thought that we ought to be expert dream-interpreters and simply support and encourage our clients' interest and curiosity in their dreams, possibly suggesting some of the simple approaches noted above, if they ask for guidance.

[260] www.complextrauma.uk/working-with-nightmares--dreams.html

Appendix 8

Simple ideas for building a supportive group

There are many ways a supportive group for therapists could be brought together and organised, but if you're thinking of establishing a group and would like some ideas to help, here are some suggestions based on what has worked for me.

- Start small, perhaps three to four people, and don't grow too big before splitting into smaller groups. A group of say six to nine people in which not everyone comes to each meeting should make for small enough groups as the norm, with the occasional larger group.
- Keep things simple. Meeting for a shared lunch is great but if it's an added obstacle, don't go there yet.
- Start every session with a good posture (see page 270) and a period of calming and regulation. There are so many ways of doing this, but if you're stuck you could use the suggestions in Appendix 5: Getting grounded or centred.
- Agree on the focus of the group at the start – do you want it to be discussion and sharing interests and new ideas, or as a place to check in and share how you are experiencing your work and your life at the moment?
- If you are sharing interests, allow a bit of time at the start for people to note anything that might be bothering them and might otherwise get in the way of them fully

participating in the meeting.

- Get a volunteer to facilitate each meeting even if it's the simplest form of facilitation, such as dividing up the time and ensuring everyone has some space without having to fight for it.
- In a slightly larger group, a long delay before someone has a chance to speak can increase anxiety and a sense of being detached from the group, so allowing everyone a maximum of one minute at the beginning to give 'headlines' of what they're going to share can help everyone to get their voice in and feel more connected to the group from the outset.
- Set up mutual agreements to support each other with first-aid supervision where regular supervision is not immediately available.
- If you're stuck for things to discuss, read a chapter of a book together. Some of the chapters from this book might be useful for kicking off your own discussions and exploration.

Appendix 9

Books and articles I have found particularly helpful

Davies, J. (2022) *Sedated. How modern capitalism created our mental health crisis*. Atlantic Books.
This is a profoundly important book, well researched and written with great clarity, which highlights the problems of our current understanding of mental health and the degree to which this pathologises the individual and diverts focus away from addressing the social problems that underly our distress. I think it is a must-read for every therapist.

Heard, D., Lake, B. and McCluskey, U. (2012) *Attachment Therapy with Adolescents and Adults*. Routledge.
This is a summary of Dorothy Heard and Brian Lake's theory of the dynamics of attachment for adults (an extension of John Bowlby and Mary Ainsworth's work on mother-infant attachment), which Una McCluskey integrated with her research on affect attunement, and an account of the new therapeutic approach which she developed from this creative fusion. The ideas here on the 'fear-system' and its impact on the dynamics of attachment were the starting point for my own interest in exploring the impact of fear-system responses and the importance of fear-regulation.

Kolacz, J. and Porges, S. (2018) Chronic Diffuse Pain and Functional Gastrointestinal Disorders after Traumatic Stress: Pathophysiology through a Polyvagal Perspective. *Front Med* 2018; 5: 145. doi: 10.3389/fmed.2018.00145

I think this is such an important article. It examines the link between the unregulated fear-system and both physical and mental ill-health. This article helped me to understand that the signal on the new (ventral) vagus was withdrawn in the fear-alert state and that it was chronically weakened in someone continually in this state.

Lawley, J. and Tompkins, P. (2000) *Metaphors in Mind: Transformation through symbolic modelling*. Developing Company Press.

I read this book early in my career and found it a wonderful introduction to using the client's own metaphors to deepen their exploration, but it also prepared me for working with the body and blended seamlessly with my later adoption of a focusing-oriented approach to body work with trauma.

Levine, P. (2010) *In an Unspoken Voice: How the Body Releases Trauma and Restores Goodness*. North Atlantic Books US.

This was the book that first introduced me to the idea of the immobility response as part of the fear-system. Despite my quibbles over Levine's use of the term 'freeze' for immobility (page 255), I found it a hugely helpful and informative book with lots of practical ideas on fear regulation. It is also very readable.

Martin, M., Seppa M., Lehtinen, P. and Toro, T. (2016) *Breathing as a Tool for Self-Regulation and Self-Reflection*. Routledge.

A very interesting and practical book by four Finnish writers who have decades of experience of the therapeutic use of breathing.

McCluskey, U. (2005) *To be Met as a Person: The dynamics of attachment in professional encounters*. Routledge.
I think this is a seminal text for therapists and other professional caregivers exploring the issue of attunement. It gave me a much deeper understanding of what was happening moment by moment between myself and my clients, and of the key role played by the activation of the therapist's fear-system in the loss of therapeutic attunement.

McCluskey, U. (2011) The Therapist as a fear-free caregiver supporting change in the dynamic organisation of the self. *AUCC Journal*.
This is an important and clearly written article on the need for the therapist to be aware of and to be able to regulate their own fear-system responses.

Myhill, S. (2014) *Diagnosis and Treatment of Chronic Fatigue Syndrome*. Hammersmith Health Books.
This is a really interesting book on chronic fatigue, and it gives a very clear account of what is happening in terms of oxygen and glucose starvation at the level of each individual cell. The first edition really helped to deepen my understanding of what was happening in our bodies during fear-collapse. It has been recently updated to cover ME and Long Covid.[261]

Porges, S. (2011) *The Polyvagal Theory: Neurophysiological Foundations of Emotions, Attachment, Communication, and Self-Regulation*. W. W. Norton & Company.
This is a collection of Stephen Porges's scientific papers over a number of years and, as a non-scientist, I found this extremely difficult to read and understand but ultimately thought it was well worth the effort. The polyvagal theory has transformed my understanding of trauma and how to work with it.

[261] Myhill and Robinson (2024).

Porges, S. (2017) *The Pocket Guide to the Polyvagal Theory: The Transformative Power of Feeling Safe*. W. W. Norton.
An approachable version of the polyvagal theory, but in the format of an interview, so I found it meandered a bit. However, if you can't face the 2011 book (and I don't blame you!) this is a must.

Sapolsky, R. M. (2004). *Why Zebras don't get Ulcers*.
I loved this highly readable book by a scientist who has the rare gift of writing clearly for the layperson. While this book was written before a wider understanding of the immobility response was generally available, it is still the best thing I have read on stress, (another way of talking about the fear-system using a slightly different lens), and its massive impact on physical and mental ill health.

References

Agazarian, Y.M. (2004) *Systems Centered Therapy for Groups*. London, UK: Karnac.

American Psychiatric Association (2000) *Diagnostic and Statistical Manual of Mental Disorders, Fourth Edition, Text Revision*. Washington, DC, USA: APA.

BACP (No date), *Ethical Framework for the Counselling Professions*, para. 61. https://www.bacp.co.uk/events-and-resources/ethics-and-standards/ethical-framework-for-the-counselling-professions/supervision/ (Accessed 6 Nov. 2025).

Baldwin, D.V. (2013) Primitive mechanisms of trauma response: An evolutionary perspective on trauma-related disorders. *Neuroscience and Biobehavioural Review* [Online] 37:1549-1566. https://doi.org/10.1016/j.neubiorev.2013.06.004

Bion, W.R. (1990) *Brazilian Lectures: 1973 São Paulo, 1974 Rio de Janeiro/São Paulo*. London, UK: Karnac.

BPS Explore (No date) https://explore.bps.org.uk/highwire_display/entity_view/node/175794/full (Accessed 7 Nov. 2025).

Bracha, H.S. (2004a) Does "Fight or Flight" need updating? *Psychosomatics* 45:5.

Bracha, H.S. (2004b) Freeze, Flight, Fight, Fright, Faint: Adaptionist perspectives on the acute stress response spectrum. *CNS Spectrums* 9(9):679-685.

Bradley, J. (2024) "Real Nastiness" therapist training courses in UK can be "toxic" and need regulating say students. *The Observer* Sunday 17 November.

Brons, L. (2015) Othering, an Analysis. *Transcience. A Journal of Global*

Studies [Online] 6(1):69-90. https://hcommons.org/deposits/item/hc:13619/

Cannon, W.B. (1915) *Bodily changes in pain, hunger, fear and rage*. New York, US and London, UK: D. Appleton. https://openlibrary.org/books/OL6576327M/Bodily_changes_in_pain_hunger_fear_and_rage

Dana, D. (2018) *The Polyvagal Theory in Therapy: Engaging the rhythm of regulation*. New York, US: WW Norton.

Davies, J. (2022) *Sedated. How modern capitalism created our mental health crisis*. London, UK: Atlantic Books.

De Couck, M., Caers, R., Musch, L., Fliegauf, J., Giangreco, A. and Gidron, Y. (2019) How Breathing Can Help You Make Better Decisions: Two Studies on the Effects of Breathing Patterns on Heart Rate Variability and Decision-Making in Business Cases. *International Journal of Psychophysiology*. 139:1-9. https://doi.org/10.1016/j.ijpsycho.2019.02.011

De Meersman, R.E. (1993) Heart rate variability and aerobic fitness. *American Heart Journal* 125(3):726-731. https://doi.org/10.1016/0002-8703(93)90164-5

Devilly, G., Wright, R. and Varker, T. (2009) Vicarious trauma, secondary traumatic stress or simply burnout? Effect of trauma therapy on mental health professionals. *Australian and New Zealand Journal of Psychiatry* 43(4). https://doi.org/10.1080/00048670902721079

Dolinsky, K. (2020) Reconstructing self and personhood when the assumptive world is shattered by trauma. *Perspectives on Trauma. The Journal of the Complex Trauma Institute* 1(1):58-62. https://www.complextraumainstitute.org/product-page/reconstructing-self-and-personhood-when-the-assumptive-by-karla-dolinsky

Ecker, B., Ticic, R. and Hulley, L. (2012) *Unlocking the Emotional Brain*. New York, US: Routledge.

Field, T. (2014) Massage therapy research review. *Complementary Therapies in Clinical Practice* 20(4):224-229. https://doi.org/10.1016/j.ctcp.2014.07.002.

Fisher, J. (2017) *Healing the fragmented selves of trauma survivors; Overcoming internal self-alienation*. London, UK: Routledge.

Freud, S. and Breuer, J. (2004) *Studies in hysteria*. London, UK: Penguin.

Gallup, G.G. (1977) Tonic Immobility: The role of Fear and Predation. *The Psychological Record* [online] 1:41-61. https://www.researchgate.net/publication/332735513

Gendlin, E.T. (1996) *Focusing-Oriented Psychotherapy. A manual of the experiential method.* New York, US: The Guilford Press.

Gerritsen, R.J.S. and Band, G.P.H. (2018) Breath of Life: The Respiratory Vagal Stimulation Model of Contemplative Activity. *Frontiers in Human Neuroscience* [online] 12:397. https://doi.org/10.3389/fnhum.2018.00397

Goldsmith, R.L., Bigger, J.T. Jr, Steinman, R.C. and Fleiss, J.L. (1992) Comparison of 24-hour parasympathetic activity in endurance-trained and untrained young men. *Journal of the American College of Cardiology* Sep;20(3):552-558. https://doi.org/10.1016/0735-1097(92)90007-a

Greenacre, A. (No date) TRE. https://www.devonpsychotherapy.com/tension-and-trauma-releasing-exercises (Accessed 5 Nov. 2025)

Guilding, M. (2020) What is Complex Trauma? *Perspectives on Trauma. The Journal of the Complex Trauma Institute* 1(1):3-18. https://www.complextraumainstitute.org/product-page/issue-1-what-is-complex-trauma-article-by-michael-guilding

Guilding, M. (2021) What is Complex Trauma? Part 2: Working with the body. *Perspectives on Trauma. The Journal of the Complex Trauma Institute* 1(2):1-11.

Guilding, M. (2022) What is Complex Trauma? Part 3: Reflections on Complexity. *Perspectives on Trauma. The Journal of the Complex Trauma Institute* 2(3):2-12.

Guilding, M. (2024) *Reflections on Fear, Anxiety and Depression*. Talk given as part of the York Festival of Ideas. https://www.youtube.com/watch?v=IWGxe1tvu-k

Guillot, A., Di Rienzo, F., MacIntyre, T., Moran, A. and Collet, C. (2012) Imagining is Not Doing but Involves Specific Motor Commands: A Review of Experimental Data Related to Motor Inhibition. *Frontiers in Human Neuroscience* 6:247. https://doi.org/10.3389/fnhum.2012.00247

Gupta, A. (2002) Unconscious amygdalar fear conditioning in a subset of chronic fatigue syndrome patients. *Medical Hypotheses* [Online] 59(6):727–735. https://doi.org/10.1016/S0306-9877(02)00321-3

Hari, J. (2018) *Lost Connections: Uncovering the real causes of depression and the unexpected solutions*. London, UK: Bloomsbury.

Hart, S. (2011) *The Impact of Attachment: Developmental Neuroaffective Psychology*. New York, US: WW Norton.

Heard, D. and Lake, B. (1997) *The Challenge of Attachment for Caregiving*. London, UK: Routledge.

Heard, D., Lake, B. and McCluskey, U. (2012) *Attachment Therapy with Adolescents and Adults. Theory and Practice Post Bowlby: Revised Edition*. London, UK: Routledge.

Henderson, A., Jewell, T., Huang, X., and Simpson, A. (2025) Personal trauma history and secondary traumatic stress in mental health professionals: A systematic review. *Journal of Psychiatric and Mental Health Nursing* 32:13–30. https://doi.org/10.1111/jpm.13082

Herman, J.L. (1998) Recovery from psychological trauma. *Psychiatry and Clinical Neurosciences* 52(S1):98-103.

Herold, A. (2015) Neurogenic tremor through TRE Tension, Stress and Trauma Releasing Exercises according to D. Berceli in the treatment of post-traumatic stress disorder PTSD. *Psychological Counseling and Psychotherapy* 2(1-2):76-84. https://periodicals.karazin.ua/psychotherapy/article/view/5018/4656

Josefsson, T., Lindwall, M. and Archer, T. (2014) Physical exercise intervention in depressive disorders: Meta-analysis and systematic review. *Scandinavian Journal of Medicine and Science in Sports* 24:259–272. https://doi.org/10.1111/sms.12050

Jung, C.G. (1933) *Modern Man in Search of a Soul*. London, UK: Kegan Paul.

Keynes, G. Ed. (1966) *The Complete Writings of William Blake*. Oxford, UK: Oxford University Press.

Killian, K.D. (2008) Helping till it hurts? A multimethod study of compassion fatigue, burnout, and self-care in clinicians working with trauma survivors. *Traumatology: An International Journal* 14(2):32–44.

Kolacz, J. and Porges, S.W. (2018) Chronic Diffuse Pain and Functional Gastrointestinal Disorders after Traumatic Stress: Pathophysiology through a Polyvagal Perspective. *Frontiers in Medicine* [Online] 5:145.
https://doi.org/10.3389/fmed.2018.00145

Kozlowska, K., Walker, P., McLean, L. and Carrive, P. (2015) Fear and the Defence Cascade: Clinical Implications and Management. *Harvard Review of Psychiatry* [Online] 23(4):263-287. https://doi.org/10.1097/HRP.0000000000000065

Lawley, J. and Tompkins, P. (2000) *Metaphors in Mind: Transformation through symbolic modelling*. London, UK: The Developing Company Press.

LeDoux, J.E. (1998) *The Emotional Brain. The mysterious underpinnings of emotional life*. New York, US: Touchstone.

LeDoux, J.E. (2014) Coming to terms with fear. *Proceedings of the National Academy of Sciences* 111(8):2871-2878. https://doi.org/10.1073/pnas.1400335111

Levine, P. (2003) Panic, Biology, and Reason: Giving the Body Its Due. *The USA Body Psychotherapy Journal* 2(2):5-13. https://ibpj.org/issues/archive/Vol2No2%20USABP%20Journal%202003.pdf#page=5

Levine, P. (2010) *In an Unspoken Voice: How the Body Releases Trauma and Restores Goodness*. Berkeley, Calif, US: North Atlantic Books.

Lewis, T., Amini, F. and Lannon, R. (2000) *A General Theory of Love*. New York, US: Random House.

Lloyd, C.S., Lanius, R.A., Brown, M.F., Neufeld, R.J., Frewen, P.A. and McKinnon, M.C. (2019) Assessing Post-Traumatic Tonic Immobility Responses: The Scale for Tonic Immobility Occurring Post-Trauma. *Chronic Stress* (Thousand Oaks) 3:1-10. https://journals.sagepub.com/doi/10.1177/2470547018822492

Martin, M., Seppa, M., Lehtinen, P. and Toro, T. (2016) *Breathing as a Tool for Self-Regulation and Self-Reflection*. London, UK: Routledge.

Maté, G. (2012) Addiction: Childhood Trauma, Stress and the Biology of Addiction. *Journal of Restorative Medicine* [Online] 1(1). https://doi.org/10.14200/jrm.2012.1.1005

McCluskey, U., Roger, D. and Nash, P. (1997) A preliminary study of the role of attunement in adult psychotherapy. *Human Relations* 50:1261-1273.

McCluskey, U., Hooper, C. and Bingley Miller, L. (1999) Goal-corrected empathic attunement, developing and rating the concept. *Psychotherapy: Theory, Research, Practice, Training* 36(1):80–90. https://doi.org/10.1037/h0087684

McCluskey, U. (2001) *A theory of interaction for caregiving in adult life, developing and measuring the concept of goal-corrected empathic attunement, PhD Thesis*. University of York Library.

McCluskey, U. (2005) *To be Met as a Person: the dynamics of attachment in professional encounters*. London, UK: Karnac.

McCluskey, U. (2011) The therapist as a fear-free caregiver supporting change in the dynamic organisation of the self. *Association of University and College Counselling Journal* May; pp.12-18.

McCluskey, U. (2013) Fear Free Exploratory Caregiving: A Challenge for Therapists in the Present Social, Political, and Cultural Environment. *Attachment: New Directions in Psychotherapy and Relational Psychoanalysis* 7 July:148–167.

McCluskey, U. and O'Toole, M. (2020) *Transference and Countertransference from an Attachment Perspective: A Guide for Professional Caregivers*. London, UK: Routledge.

Merriam-Webster (No date) *Merriam-Webster.com Medical Dictionary*. www.merriam-webster.com/medical/

Mittal, V., Brown, W.A. and Shorter, E. (2009) Are Patients With Depression at Heightened Risk of Suicide as They Begin to Recover? *Psychiatric Services* 60(3): 384–386. https://psychiatryonline.org/doi/full/10.1176/ps.2009.60.3.384

Myhill, S. (2014) *Diagnosis and Treatment of Chronic Fatigue Syndrome, 2nd ed*. London, UK: Hammersmith Health Books.

Myhill, S. and Robinson, C. (2024) *Diagnosis and Treatment of Chronic Fatigue Syndrome, Myalgic Encephalitis and Long Covid, 3rd ed*. London, UK: Hammersmith Health Books.

Nader, K., Schafe, G. and Le Doux, J. (2000) Fear memories require protein synthesis in the amygdala for reconsolidation after retrieval. *Nature* 406:722–726. https://doi.org/10.1038/35021052

Neath, N. and McCluskey, U. (2019) *To Be Met as a Person at work: the effect of early attachment experiences on work relationships*. London, UK: Routledge.

Nussbaum, M.C. (2018) *The Monarchy of Fear*. New York, US: Simon and Schuster.

Ogden, P., Minton, K. and Pain, C. (2006) *Trauma and the Body: A Sensorimotor Approach to Psychotherapy*. New York, US: WW Norton.

Pearlman, L.A. and Mac Ian, P.S. (1995) Vicarious Traumatization: An Empirical Study of the Effects of Trauma Work on Trauma Therapists. *Professional Psychology: Research and Practice* 26(6):558-

565. https://www.emdr.org.il/wp-content/uploads/2021/08/Vicarious-traumatization-An-empirical-study-of-the-effects-of-trauma-work-on-trauma-therapists..pdf

Pies, RW. (2014) The Bereavement Exclusion and DSM-5: An Update and Commentary. *Innov Clin Neurosci* 11(7-8):19-22. https://pmc.ncbi.nlm.nih.gov/articles/PMC4204469/

Porges, S. W. (2011) *The Polyvagal Theory: Neurophysiological Foundations of Emotions, Attachment, Communication, and Self-Regulation*. New York, US: WW Norton.

Porges, S. W. (2017) *The Pocket Guide to the Polyvagal Theory: The Transformative Power of Feeling Safe*. New York, US: WW Norton.

Porges, S. W. (2022) Polyvagal Theory: A science of safety. *Frontiers in Integrative Neuroscience* 16:871227. https://doi.org/10.3389/fnint.2020.871227

Protopapas, M.G. and Cymet, T.C. (2002) Joint cracking and popping: understanding noises that accompany articular release. *Journal of Osteopathic Medicine* 102(5):283-287. https://pubmed.ncbi.nlm.nih.gov/12033758/

Rizzolatti, G. and Sinigaglia, C. (2008) *Mirrors in the Brain: How our minds share actions and emotions*. Oxford, UK: Oxford University Press.

Rogers, C.R. (1980) *A Way of Being*. Boston, MA, US: Houghton Mifflin.

Rothschild, B. (2000) *The Body Remembers: The psychophysiology of trauma and trauma treatment*. New York, US: WW Norton.

Sapolsky, R.M. (2004). *Why Zebras don't get Ulcers, 3rd ed*. New York, US: Holt Paperbacks.

Schauer, M. and Elbert, T. (2010) Dissociation following Traumatic Stress: Etiology and Treatment. *Journal of Psychology* [Online] 218(2):109-127. https://doi.org/10.1027/0044-3409/a000018

Schwartz, R.C. (1995) *Internal Family Systems Therapy*. New York, US: The Guilford Press.

Schweizer, E., Dever, A. and Clary, C. (1988) Suicide upon recovery from depression: a clinical note. *Journal of Nervous and Mental Disease* 176:633–636. https://doi.org/10.1097/00005053-198810000-00009

Shapiro, F. (1995) *Eye Movement Desensitization and Reprocessing*. New York, US: The Guilford Press.

Siegel, D.J. (2012) *The Developing Mind, 2nd ed*. New York, US: The Guilford Press.

Strathearn, L., Giannotti, M., Mills, R., Kisely, S., Najman, J. and Abajobir, A. (2020) Long-term cognitive, psychological, and health outcomes associated with child abuse and neglect. *Pediatrics* 146(4):389-403. http://publications.aap.org/pediatrics/article-pdf/146/4/e20200438/1081587/peds_20200438.pdf

Sylvester, L. (2013) The hug that helped change medicine. *CNN* 21 Feb. https://edition.cnn.com/videos/health/2013/02/23/tsr-sylvester-twin-hug-miracle.cnn (Accessed: 1 Nov. 2025)

Tabor, A., Bateman, S., Scheme, E. and Schraefel, M.C. (2019) *Breathing Physiology and Guided Breathing Exercise: A Primer*. [Online] University of New Brunswick Internal Technical Report (#TR199-241), October. https://www.cs.unb.ca/tech-reports/documents/TR19-241.pdf

Tozzi, P. (2014) Does fascia hold memories? *Journal of Bodywork and Movement Therapies* 18: 259-265. https://www.bodyworkmovementtherapies.com/article/S1360-8592(13)00192-7/fulltext

Tyrka, A.R., Price, L.H., Kao, H-T., Porton, B., Marsella, S.A. and Carpenter, L.L. (2010) Childhood Maltreatment and Telomere Shortening: Preliminary Support for an Effect of Early Stress on Cellular Aging. *Biol Psychiatry* [Online] 67(6):531–534. https://doi.org/10.1016/j.biopsych.2009.08.014.

Van der Kolk, B. (1994) The body keeps the score: Memory and the evolving psychobiology of post-traumatic stress. *Harvard Review of Psychiatry* 1(5):253-265.

Van der Kolk, B. (2014) *The Body Keeps the Score*. London, UK: Allen Lane.

Walker, M. (2018) *Why We Sleep: The new science of sleep and dream*. London, UK: Penguin Books.

Walker, R.J. (2021) *Polyvagal Theory Chart of Trauma Response*. Somatic Experiencing International Website. https://traumahealing.org/wp-content/uploads/2022/12/PVChartv10q.pdf

Williamson, D. (2013) Twins still popular after all these years. *Worcester Telegram and Gazette* 17 February. https://eu.telegram.com/story/news/local/north/2013/02/17/twins-still-popular-after-all/49090494007/ [Accessed 6 Aug. 2025]

Winnicott, D.W. (1973) *The Child, the Family, and the Outside World*. London, UK: Penguin Books.

Winterson, J. (2012) *Why be happy when you could be normal?* London, UK: Vintage Books.

World Health Organization (2019-2021) *International Classification of Diseases, 11thRevision (ICD 11).* https://icd.who.int/en

Wotton, M. and Johnston, G. (2022) We need more faith that therapy works. *Therapy Today* 33(2):27-29.

Zhang, T., Chow, A., Wang, L., Dai, Y. and Xiao, Z. (2012) Role of childhood traumatic experience in personality disorders in China. *Comprehensive Psychiatry* 53:829-836. https://www.sciencedirect.com/science/article/pii/S0010440X11002008

Index

Note: *fn* refers to footnotes

Index

Note: *fn* refers to footnotes

Index

Note: *fn* refers to footnotes

Index

Note: *fn* refers to footnotes

Index

Note: *fn* refers to footnotes

About the Author

Michael worked as a counsellor and psychotherapist for 30 years including for more than a decade in the NHS, where he was Head of Primary Care Counselling within the York and Selby NHS trust. Prior to training as a therapist and following a degree in history and further postgraduate study, he joined Royal Mail as a postman, moving on to a career in senior management.

For many years he has had a deep interest in our biological fear-system responses and how these affect the way we relate to others, having been introduced to this framework of thinking by his clinical supervisor, Dr Una McCluskey of the University of York.

This book has grown out of several papers Michael wrote for the Complex Trauma Institute's journal and his 'Fear and the Therapist' workshops which help therapists to become more aware of their fear-system responses and to use this awareness in their work.

Having retired from clinical work in 2023, his focus is now on writing about the fear-system for the general public, and his 2024 York Festival of Ideas talk, 'Reflections on Fear, Anxiety and Depression' was broadcast nationally in Australia.